Simon Hoggart has been writing about politics on and off since 1973, and has worked in Northern Ireland and Washington. He also writes about wine and television for the *Spectator* and is chairman of BBC Radio 4's *The News Quiz*.

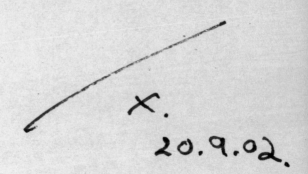

X.

20.9.02.

To Jeremy

Happy Birthday

Hope that you have a
lovely day
...

20.9.02

Playing to the Gallery

Parliamentary Sketches from Blair Year Zero

SIMON HOGGART

ATLANTIC BOOKS • LONDON

First published in 2002 by Atlantic Books, on behalf of
Guardian Newspapers Ltd. Atlantic Books is an imprint of
Grove Atlantic Ltd.

1 3 5 7 9 10 8 6 4 2

A CIP catalogue record for this book is available from the
British Library

ISBN 1 903809 66 5

Printed in Great Britain by Mackays of Chatham Ltd
Text design by Katrina ffiske

A paperback original

Atlantic Books
An imprint of Grove Atlantic Ltd
Ormond House
26–27 Boswell Street
London WC1N 3JZ

Contents

I would like to thank Toby Mundy and Alice Hunt at Atlantic Books for having the idea for this book, for carrying it through with such skill, enthusiasm and patience, and for so many lunches. I also want to thank my fellow sketch-writers, Simon Carr, Frank Johnson, Quentin Letts, Ben Macintyre and Matthew Parris, who I read with anxiety and admiration every morning and who will find many of their own jokes here, poorly disguised. But most of all, I want to express heartfelt gratitude to all MPs and peers, for their diligence in providing so much material and without whose unstinting efforts our children would go to school hungry and unshod.

To my parents, Mary and Richard Hoggart, to whom I owe much more than I have ever told them.

Introduction

In the Sherlock Holmes story, 'The Cardboard Box', Dr Watson describes a suffocatingly hot August day in London, a time when nothing is happening and nothing seems likely to. 'The morning paper was uninteresting. Parliament had risen,' he says.

This tale is set in 1889, but those two sentences make it feel as if we're reading about a far more distant era. The paper was dull because Parliament wasn't sitting? Otherwise Dr Watson would have spent happy hours ploughing through the debates, all written up in minuscule type? Some modern editors would be thrilled if there were no politics: even more room for celebrity bed-hopping, footballers' injuries and feature articles pondering whether Egyptian tombs hold the secrets of eternal life.

But it wasn't so long ago that Parliament was still regarded as the centre of our national debate. Dr Watson had no *Newsnight, World at One, Question Time* or *Kilroy*; if he wanted opinions about the crisis in South Africa or the menace of German expansionism, he had to read the parliamentary reports, as dutifully recorded in his morning paper. Even when I began reporting from the Commons, in 1973, *The Times* had a total of sixteen parliamentary correspondents, based in one vast room, whose sole job it was to provide digests of debates, statements and question times, generally spread over two full pages of the paper. (That was when *The Times* was *The Times*.

Their political editor once majestically began the paper's lead story with the word 'Notwithstanding...')

Now they have just us, the sketch-writers. (Actually, *The Times* and *Telegraph*, having abandoned straight parliamentary coverage for years, have now gone back to having a single gallery reporter each.) We are not interested in straight parliamentary coverage. We are interested in cheap jokes, unfair barbs, and a slanted version of the day's events. Some MPs hate it. Tony Benn, who took the view that newspapers best served their readers' interests by printing unchanged screeds of politicians' words, curled his lip with contempt when he told me that he never read what I wrote, though of course something had been drawn to his attention... I once told Denis MacShane that he'd be appearing the next day, and he groaned despairingly, as if he'd just put his life savings on a horse which turned out to have three legs.

However, I suspect that most MPs don't mind the sketch in my paper or others (they are *The Times*, *Telegraph*, *Independent* and *Mail*), if only because reading something displeasing about themselves once a year is a small price to pay for seeing their colleagues abused for the rest of the time. Others positively enjoy being mentioned. When the piece about Bob Marshall-Andrews (in this book, dated 21.05.01) appeared on a Monday morning, his agent rang him to warn him that there was a terrible article in the *Guardian*, it would offer great comfort to the Tories, and that he should sit down before he read it. Luckily a BBC television crew was following the candidate around, and they recorded him wiping tears of laughter from his eyes. That was gratifying, except that it was Marshall-Andrews who told me his belief that all journalists, especially sketch-writers, were playground bullies: 'You love to hear your victim's squeal. It's important that we never let you hear it,' and I'm afraid there might be more truth in that than I care to admit.

Some frequently asked questions: do they try to spin you, like they spin the proper political writers? No, or only very rarely. William Hague's team once told Giles Coren of *The Times*, who was standing in for Matthew Parris, that letters from angry *Times* readers were pouring into Central Office complaining about his attacks on the little fellow. They quickly dropped that line when Giles asked if he could see some of the letters. Once I had three Liberal Democrat aides standing round my screen saying, 'Wasn't Paddy *wonderful* at Prime Minister's Questions today!' But that wasn't spinning; why, they might even have meant it. But I can honestly say that beyond the occasional ''ullo' or, 'oh, you here' Mr Alastair Campbell has never spoken a word to me. It would be a waste of time. Like all playground bullies, we instinctively sense weakness.

Do MPs complain about what we write? Yes, sometimes. Usually they wait till you've made a factual inaccuracy, which allows them to write something like: 'normally, I would never bother to complain about your constant abuse of me. But when you allege that my constituency is called Mudville West, when its actual name is Mudville West and Cowpatting, then I feel it is my duty…' Caroline Flint, famously the most toadying of all female Labour MPs, once invited me to tea in order to find out why I kept saying this (answer: it was true). We sat in the beautiful Pugin room with its view of the sun sparkling on the river, having a stilted and embarrassing conversation, when in walked Michael Fabricant, and Michael Portillo, about whom I was halfway through writing another disobliging sketch. Now and again, MPs will send you pages ripped out of Hansard to prove you have misquoted them, though this is rare now that we're allowed tape recorders, and in any case Hansard is not a record of what MPs said, but what they were trying to say – a quite different thing.

And a very different thing indeed when you're dealing with John Prescott. I suspect that when they're supposed to record him, the Hansard stenographers simply give up, and hand the job to scientists who track his brainwaves by the latest computers, enabling them to print out what he meant, bypassing the words he actually used, which have only a marginal relationship to what he meant.

Do we get together to share out the jokes? Yes, of course. The sketch-writers' tea is a common sight in the Press Gallery cafeteria. We spend twenty minutes or half an hour, on most though not all afternoons, chewing over what happened, swapping thoughts, and even helping each other – sometimes someone has the idea of an extended metaphor, or 'conceit' as the *Telegraph*'s Frank Johnson calls them, as if we wrote metaphysical poems – and we can all chip in. Sometimes we just gossip; often MPs will say things to a sketch-writer which they would never say to a real political correspondent, because they mistakenly imagine they won't find their way into print.

Is it a job worth doing? Does the sketch have any redeeming social value? Most of the time I don't think so. If anything, we are a small *amuse-gueule* which people can polish off before tackling the main meal of real news. Sometimes, however, I allow myself to think that perhaps we do offer a small service: being rude about our politicians has been an important part of British life for centuries now and along with the cartoonists we continue that tradition. We are the jesters whispering – rather loudly – to Roman emperors, reminding them that they too are human. Or at least have very silly hair.

Year Zero

The 1997 election campaign began in early April.

Our day out with Tony Blair began at Labour's news media centre in Millbank, London. As we waited for the leader, we watched a video film of the party's rally in Kent on Monday. What a happy occasion it was, with confident, prosperous people arriving in late-model cars. Past Labour broadcasts used to show derelict factories and crumbling hospitals; now they depict an idealized, sunlit Britain, designed to force home Mr Blair's key campaign message: 'Life's better under the Conservatives. Don't let the Tories ruin it.'

Britain's favourite battling granny, the Founder and President for Life of the World Institute of Thatcherology, was out to help. When the Tories are in trouble they always call on the Baroness. But so does Labour. 'Can you imagine,' Mr Blair asked scornfully, 'Mrs Thatcher saying, "There are candidates I would very much like not to stand, but I'm sorry, there is nothing I can do about it"?' What a shame, then, that the object of his admiration holds him in such apparent contempt. So much of what he says precisely resembles what she used to say.

Yesterday he told us that the way to get a better standard of living for the poor 'is not to stop people being wealthy at the top; it is giving others hope and opportunity'. So very like Lady Thatcher's 'You can't enrich the poor by impoverishing the rich', which she had embroidered on all her flak jackets.

Mr Blair announced that Labour's policies were 'mainstream, costed, sensible', and with that battle-cry ringing in our ears we set off for the leader's cavalcade. This consists of three buses, each with a slogan on the side: 'Leading Britain', 'Into the Future,' and 'With Tony Blair'. As we sped north, we sometimes changed order, or a lorry would slide between us so that the convoy would read: 'Eddie Stobart leading Britain into the Future' or 'Daily Wet Fish Deliveries throughout the UK with Tony Blair'.

In the bus, Mr Blair was busy lowering expectations. This is his current strategy. 'All the way through I have said that we do not promise a revolution; I don't say I can wave a magic wand and put the world to rights.'

We arrived in Northampton, ready to lower a few more expectations. 'You're going to win!' one woman shouted.

'I hope so,' he said dubiously. He'll probably be saying that it's too early to predict the result if Labour takes Huntingdon.

He plunged into the crowd. 'It's that bloke off the telly, wossname?' a loutish youth yelled, but most people seemed pleased. One woman actually gave him her baby to kiss, something that politicians rarely do, since what voter wants to see her child covered with MP's slobber? A voter from hell arrived with another child in tow. She harangued him. There was no escape. 'I want to see you keep your promises!' she yelled. Clearly her expectations were very low, but he lowered them some more.

'That's why we're only making promises we can keep,' he said.

He kept tight hold of Cherie, encouraging her to wave, as if they had just spotted someone they knew in an upstairs window. This is something else politicians share with children: they too have imaginary friends. Back on the bus a spin doctor climbed on board to spin for us not just what the leader had said, but what the public had said about him. For instance, a Mrs Rowlands had reported that he seemed 'not too bad, really'. Obviously her expectations were none too high, but even so that's not exactly what she had intended to say. 'She *meant*,' said the spin doctor, 'that he was very nice and trustworthy.' In this election nothing, least of all the public, can be left to chance.

02.04.97

The wretched Conservative Party was followed by seemingly endless accusations of sleaze. At the very start of the campaign a married Tory MP called Piers Merchant was caught having an alfresco affair with a nightclub hostess.

The Conservatives held a press conference on the environment yesterday. They talked about rivers of filth, noxious vapours in the atmosphere and piles of stinking ordure. So, as you can see, they hardly spoke about the environment. Instead they were obliged by the press to talk about sleaze. Every time they tried to drag the press round to trivial matters such as 'Will our planet still support life in fifty years' time?' they were hauled back to the key issue: what was a Tory MP doing with a youthful nightclub hostess who had been recruited by his local party for envelope-stuffing only?

They tried, oh how they tried, to change the subject. Poor John Gummer and Ken Clarke can have had little idea of what was about to hit them when they bounced onto the platform. A visual aid behind them showed lush parkland, a sunlit copse and sparkling streams. 'So that's where Piers was at it,' shouted a hack at the back.

Gummer looked grim. He talked about cleaning our rivers and beaches, and cracking down on pollution. So someone asked him about Piers Merchant.

He declared that it was time to talk about cleaning up our landscape. Someone else from the back said it was time to talk about cleaning up the Conservative Party. Gummer switched to the topic of climate change, and quite right too. Something must be awry with the weather if it's so warm in March that a Tory MP can make love to a seventeen-year-old girl out of doors.

Gummer tried again. 'The word "conservation" and the word "Conservative" have the same root – that is why we are, by our nature, conservationists,' he said. (I don't know. By the same token, 'Labour' implies getting women pregnant, which doesn't seem to be the issue here.)

One kindly soul asked about the environment, but he was brushed aside by another question about Piers Merchant. Mr Clarke then made an extraordinary noise, which my notes transcribe as 'dib bid whubb whirr'. It turned out he was trying to appeal to our better natures, and so naturally couldn't get the words out.

'Most people in this room have a serious interest in politics and government!' he cried. I don't know whom he was confusing us with. We're lobby correspondents.

28.03.97

A few days later, the Tories launched their manifesto.

While we waited, we had a chance to read the manifesto. 'Abroad, the cold war has been won. At home, the rule of law has been restored,' it began. So an exaggeration and an outright lie on page one – a promising start.

'The best place in the world to live!' the document declared. Outside, angry foreign journalists from the hellish barrios of cities such as Paris and Milan were unable to test this claim; they were banished until all British hacks had been seated. No doubt Mr Major could have explained to them how the over-efficient French street-sweeping system meant that there were no cardboard boxes for beggars, forcing them to live indoors. Or how leisure time is cut in France as the Paris metro system ruthlessly delivers people to work on time.

Messrs Major, Heseltine and Mawhinney took the stage. Mr Mawhinney is the only man in British politics who can loom while sitting down. Mr Heseltine favoured the Prime Minister with his famous 'I know I've seen that bloke somewhere – was it on TV?' look. Mr Major talked about a proposal that would allow a wife to stay at home to look after the children while transferring her tax allowance to her husband. The idea lends itself so easily to misty-lensed adverts showing blissful families playing in flower-festooned gardens that it can only be days before it becomes official Labour policy.

He said that it was a 'watershed manifesto'. No one had the heart to point out that a watershed is at the top of a mountain range, so that whichever direction you turn it's downhill all the way. The only rough questioning came on taxes. Official Treasury papers showed that rises were now inevitable. Here is his reply, in its entirety:

'Tax burdens are broadly stable on rising incomes. There are environmental taxes, and an element of tax drift. The overall burden is largely the same, as you say, it actually emphasizes that unless the tax burden is to rise, we have to cut taxes. That makes the point that what we are proposing is credible, unless there a wish for increased taxes in this room, which I doubt.'

So that clears that up. On the other hand, if John Prescott had put it like that, we'd still be laughing now.

03.04.97

We were waiting for the Founder and President for Life of the World Institute of Thatcherology, who was late. Her aide briefed us about what would happen when she arrived at the garden centre in Christchurch – founded in 1742, it improbably claimed. We looked in vain for a Georgian gro-bag or a gnome in a periwig. She would be presented with a shovel. Would she shovel anything with the shovel? 'No,' said the aide, 'there is nothing to shovel with the shovel. It is a ceremonial shovel.'

The limousine arrived, and she emerged, looking more regal than ever. She has the same tilt of the head, the same gracious yet distant smile and faces the same phalanxes of children festooned with bouquets. The difference is that the Queen is said to get on with John Major. The Christchurch Tories cheered in a wonderfully old-fashioned way. 'Bravo!' 'Hooray!' they shouted, as if urging on the First XV. A colleague asked her about Neil Hamilton. 'Are *you* perfect?' she asked, as her false logic trap snapped shut.

She went inside, where she was attacked by two small dogs. Sadly, we were not allowed to witness this historic event. 'They just wanted to lick her face,' said an onlooker. One thought of all those sad right-wing fogeys who go to sleep each night dreaming of doing that very thing.

We moved to a nearby school where the reception class had been lined up to greet her. This was a sound move. Being only five, they come from the first generation that has never known her as prime minister. 'We've got *lots* of children here!' she exclaimed, and you could see everyone biting their lip so as to stop themselves saying, 'Well, it is a school.' She set out to learn all their names, with only mixed success.

'Bye-bye,' said one little boy as she left.

'You are Max,' she informed him.

'William, actually,' said his mother.

'William,' she noted. 'What's the little girl's name?'

'It's Jade,' the mum replied.

'Jade, that's a lovely name,' she said, then spoiled the effect by adding, 'You should be very careful when choosing a name, because' – her voice was lowered confidentially – 'they keep them for life!'

Fred Wood, an 89-year-old war veteran in his medals, had come to ask her about Europe. He suddenly found himself the only guest at a one-person press conference. 'I'm for Britain!' she said. 'We must recover our own parliamentary sovereignty, our own financial affairs and our own currency.' She went on in this vein for quite some time, though sadly to no purpose, since Mr Wood turned out to be completely deaf.

After lunch we visited Aldershot, which used to be Julian Critchley's seat. 'I spent 27 years making sure she never set foot in the place,' he told the BBC yesterday.

We called in at a plastics factory, which makes, among other things, the stuff that goes in flak jackets, and bomb-proof litter bins, which between them, in the absence of an armour-plated handbag, make a perfect metaphor for the Thatcher years.

10.04.97

The deaf soldier mentioned above did manage to tell her that they shared a star sign, which was a source of some pride to him. She replied that she didn't usually read the horoscopes, 'though it hasn't done me badly.' Most of us assumed that she had her own star sign: 'Thatcher. The morning would be a propitious time to start a war. In the evening, a Mr Clarke will come to your room and tell you to resign.'

One of the more curious phenomena of the 1997 election was the Referendum Party, led by the now late Sir James Goldsmith.

The Referendum Party held its mass rally at the Alexandra Palace in London yesterday. If you'd parachuted me in and told me the audience came from one of the three main parties, I'd have guessed the Liberal Democrats. Among the 7,000 or so people present was the same mixture of the earnest middle classes, wide-eyed young folk, old-fashioned working people, grim-faced dogmatists, ordinary men and women, plus the usual sprinkling of out-and-out loonies.

In most parties, the activists are bonkers and the leadership has to barter a deal between them and common sense. In the Referendum Party it's the other way round; the crazies are up on the platform. Even Andrew Roberts, the right-wing historian, whom I'd always thought fairly rational, ended: 'The politicians have debated Europe long enough. The time has come for the whole tribe to decide!' (How? By dancing round the polling station, thumping our spears on the ground?)

They have a clear list of enemies. At number three is Leon Brittan, the evil unelected Brussels bureaucrat who is selling our nation into servitude. At number two is Helmut Kohl, the evil elected dictator who is dragging our nation into servitude. But unchallenged at number one is Edward Heath, a man whose mere name brought out a sound I have never heard before: a hall full of growling like a hundred cornered pit bulls.

The mood on the platform was a blend of Churchillian rhetoric and wild paranoia. Lord McAlpine went for the first. 'We must fight on, to the last hour of the campaign, to the last minute of the campaign…and when the election is over, we must fight on and fight again!'

Robin Page, a farmer and a journalist (which means that he spends his entire life shovelling manure) wears comical yokel-type sideburns and is on the party's large paranoid wing. When the sound failed, he yelled at the technicians: 'What's the matter? Are you Brussels-minded?' The BBC, he announced, was 'the Brussels Broadcasting Corporation'. He wittily begged the party candidate John Aspinall, owner of a zoo filled with deadly exotic animals, not to breed from one endangered species. 'We don't want any progeny from Edward Heath! How would you get him into breeding condition? Show him a picture of Helmut Kohl in a bikini?' he charmingly enquired.

'I like the French, because they are French. I like the Spanish, because they are Spanish. I like my countrymen, because they are…' (I'm afraid I made that part up.) 'Tell our snivelling politicians, the BBC, ITV, the know-it-alls, that we will not have it! Slap them, straight across the face!'

Alarmingly, he then slid into Ronald Reagan mode. 'Then the rubbishing will stop, and heroes we will be. In a world of tinsel, you will have reached for the stars.'

The next loony up was Sir James himself. He knows all about the importance of nationality, having two very lovely ones of his own – French and British. His speech was well – though not perhaps rapturously – received. After all, by comparison with the speakers, the audience was flirting with sanity. I worked out halfway through the speech that it ought to have been delivered in German. He has a way of addressing his enemies that would be familiar to fans of black and white

World War II films: 'As for you, *Mr* Tony Blair…'; 'Your sense of humour seems to be contagious, *Mr* Major.' Finally, 'This government has betrayed the nation! It will, therefore, be punished on 1 May!' He exited to loud applause and, a form new to me, electronic martial music.

14.04.97

The Referendum Party did worse in the election than its leaders had hoped and won no seats at all. Mr Robin Page's programme, One Man and His Dog *was also terminated by the BBC, no doubt at the behest of the faceless bureaucrats in Brussels. Meanwhile, Mo Mowlam, recovering from a brain tumour, became the most popular politician in Britain.*

I went to the North-East to see one of the great spectacles of the campaign: the progress of Marjorie Mowlam through the streets of Redcar. She has always been popular here, but since she revealed the news of her tumour a few days ago, she has been promoted to the status of a saint.

'It was a mugging yesterday,' her agent told me. 'She had hardly set out into the High Street before the crowd came round her. She couldn't move.'

As a small boy I used to live in Redcar. It hasn't improved very much with time, though they have put some plaster penguins along the promenade. But the people remain as friendly as ever. In Mo's headquarters, where I went to wait for her, the women were fretting about me in a way familiar from my childhood. It's a general, nagging anxiety that there is a man in the room and he hasn't been fed. 'He's been here an hour and we've only given him a biscuit,' one of them whispered.

Finally she arrived, and we set off in advance, like a travelling band of faith healers preparing the way for the leader. It is an extraordinary sight. Whenever anyone recognizes her, and it sometimes takes a moment since she is plumper than she was, their face lights up. 'Ooh, Miss Mowlam, how are yer? Ooh, yer are looking good after all that, that…'

If she doesn't know them, she hugs them. If she does know them, they get the full treatment, consisting of first a hug, then a warm arm clasp, and finally the Mowlam forehead lowered onto their forehead in order to establish eye contact, almost literally.

A young woman approached with her upper lip trembling, unable to talk. 'I'm fine, I'm in very good nick,' said Mo, and the woman burst into tears. Northern people do love a good illness, and if it comes with a happy ending all the better. It would make a good Alan Bennett line: 'I'm very pleased to say that my brain tumour has turned the corner.'

In the hour I was with her, the subject of politics was raised only once, by a man who wanted to know about pensions. But this is the real politics that all politicians aspire to, when you get elected not for what you say, or which party you belong to, but for who you are. And whom you hug.

Constituents advanced en masse for their hugs, like the unemployed at a soup kitchen. 'D'you like my wig?' she asked. 'I like it this way. I'm going to keep it when my own grows back.'

'Ooh, you are looking well,' says the hundredth person in half an hour. 'You look much better than you do on telly.'

'I know. I look fatter and uglier and older on TV than I actually am.' So of course that deserved another hug.

16.04.97

I went to North Yorkshire to see a politician about a month before he rose without trace and four years before he disappeared, leaving scarcely a bubble on the surface.

It has long been my theory that William Hague, the Welsh Secretary, is a brilliant but mad scientist. As a boy he tried to invent an elixir of life that would prevent the ageing process. But he made one crucial error, and instead the secret potion made him grow old at twice the normal rate. Hence his famous speech to the 1977 Tory conference when, as a sixteen-year-old, he sounded like a middle-aged man.

If my theory were correct, the youngest member of the Cabinet would be in his 70s by now. But he clearly isn't; I'd guess he's reached no further than 58, which is 36 in human years, if you follow. What he has perhaps perfected instead is a time machine. Mr Hague is a pre-war politician who has shot forward 60 years and is visiting us.

His constituency, Richmond, Yorkshire, is a huge tract including dozens, perhaps hundreds, of villages and the only way to campaign there is to hold endless public meetings in schools and community halls. In Great Ayton, he stood at a table wearing a dark blue double-breasted suit and a Tory rosette. He is very bald indeed now, and as he speaks his hand slices the air slowly, like an elderly butcher cutting chops. You expect an old Pathé News commentator with a high-pitched voice on the soundtrack: 'The Welsh Secretary, Mr Hague, has some economical hints for housewives struggling with wartime ration books. "Try making your leek and potato pie without leeks!" he tells them.'

In fact, he offers The Ten Reasons why you should vote Conservative. The audience sat, quiet, stoical and unresponsive, in the way only Yorkshire people can. The speech did go on a bit. At '…and my sixth point is related to point five', there was the faintest imaginable stir in the hall, like a cat having a bad dream. The tenth and last Reason ('You cannot trust a Labour Party which doesn't believe anything for more than one day at a time') was met by silence, followed by perhaps three short handclaps.

At our next stop, a beautiful village called Hutton Rudby, the sense of being back in the 1930s was overwhelming. A man with a well-modulated voice enquired why there was no reference to morality in the Conservative manifesto. Another introduced his question with: 'May I venture to suggest…?'

I left for my hotel, Mr Hague no doubt for his time machine and a cup of Ovaltine as he sat in his scratchy dressing gown listening to the wireless. 'This is the Home Service of the BBC. The Prime Minister, Mr Chamberlain…'

21.04.97

'How nice to see you! How very nice to see you! It *is* nice to see you,' said Nicholas Soames.

'Actually, I'm a Liberal,' said the voter.

'But it's *still* nice to see you,' Soames replied. 'It's been delightful to see you. Lovely seeing you!'

'People are so courteous,' he said, as we toured round his new constituency of Mid-Sussex. In Crawley, his previous seat, 'They say, "Fuck off, you bastard!" Not here.'

A few moments later a man spoiled it, wobbling by on a bike and cackling, 'You're on your way out, and good riddance to the corrupt, evil bunch of you!'

Soames was unfazed. 'Put him down as "doubtful",' he roared.

We met at the Crown in Horsted Keynes, another of those idyllic, flower-infested villages of which there are more left in Britain than you might think. Some candidates grab a sandwich on the run, but not Soames. He ate five sardines, each the size of a small trout. The rest of us had roughly half a ham each, with eggs, chips and tankards of the local ale. It was like campaigning with G. K. Chesterton. Parts of the conversation were, sadly, unrepeatable. Of a gay Tory MP puzzlingly married: 'I think you'll find he's a *non-playing captain!*'

At the village school, one dad said he was a lifelong Tory, but had become disillusioned. 'I'm not voting for you. But you don't want to hear that,' he said morosely.

Soames is one of the few candidates who sees his job as cheering up the opposition. 'I'm delighted to hear that. Delighted! We have made some awful cock-ups.' Moments later the two men were chatting like old friends.

Then, to me, 'Would you like a drink? We have an icebox in the back. This is the Conservative Party, not some scruff operation. I've got a Thai girl in here too, to give me *assisted massage!*'

I'm afraid that he made the last bit up.

22.04.97

Martin Bell, the man in the white suit, stood against Neil Hamilton, the former Tory minister who was accused of taking money in brown envelopes from Mohamed al-Fayed.

'You'll notice,' said Martin Bell, 'that all Neil Hamilton's posters are on trees and hedges, never in people's houses. Unless I'm mistaken, trees and hedges do not have a vote. Nobody wants to admit that they support him.' If the posters mean anything, Bell will triumph. Last week Hamilton threatened him with several libel writs. 'I didn't know what to do. I don't even have a lawyer. I'm 58, and he's the first enemy I've ever had.'

We went to canvass in Great Budworth, a gorgeous old village, usually solid Tory territory. Apart from one blue placard on a tree, all the posters were for Bell. His reception was astonishing, quite the best I've seen for any candidate in this election apart from Mo Mowlam. A smartly dressed woman in a BMW screeched to a halt. 'We are definitely voting for you!' she said, evidently a founder member of Beamers for Bell.

The campaign has clearly been the most tremendous fun, involving several mini pub crawls between bouts of canvassing. Bell himself, his huge minder, a cameraman called Nigel Bateson, the various 'Bell belles' who include his daughter Melissa, and the substantial press entourage, spend a great deal of time pondering the campaign over refreshments. In one pub, two old geezers looked up from their pints. 'I couldn't vote for a man who drinks,' said one. (Northern humour does tend to verge on the predictable.)

'This is medicinal,' said the other.

'Then you must be very ill,' the candidate snapped, but amiably.

'I expect you'd rather be dodging bullets,' said the first man. 'Oh, I would, I would,' he replied. But it's not true. He's having the time of his life.

24.04.97

When I wrote the above article, I added a caveat that in the privacy of the polling booth, and facing the prospect of the first Labour government for 18 years, many Conservative voters might secretly plump for Hamilton and get him returned. When Martin Bell won the seat with a massive majority, I was greatly relieved that the Guardian *subs had, to save space, cut that bit out. Martin himself was so delighted that he mentioned my faith in his victory in his memoirs. Then a cruel colleague of mine told him the truth. I name no names, but Matthew Parris knows who he is. The next day I attended Alan Clark's last election campaign.*

It is a great treat to tour the Conservatives' safest seat, if not in the company of their safest candidate. Whatever happens, Alan Clark is certain to be returned for Kensington and Chelsea next week.

For one thing, this is a seriously rich constituency. Some of the voters may even be richer than Clark himself. We went into an estate agent's. This was not full of spotty young men in double-breasted suits and polyester ties. It was instead the kind of place where, if a customer asks 'Is there a chain?' they probably want to know how the drawbridge is raised. 'When I go into a pub,' Clark mused, 'I have to buy a drink. I suppose now I'm here, I ought to buy a house.' The manager perked up like mad. Coming from him, this was no idle pleasantry.

Oddly enough, Clark got the nomination here by being the most left-wing of the candidates, which gives you some idea of the rest. He had the support of Chelsea, which has always been slightly more liberal, perhaps more raffish, than Kensington. His louche reputation did him little harm among these people. He is accompanied everywhere by his wife, Jane.

'You will notice how Jane brings a uniform goodwill wherever we go, dispelling some of the cloud of suspicion that hangs over me.'

'Unaccountably,' I murmured, mendaciously.

'Err, yurrrs,' he replied.

We went into a very expensive antiques shop, suffused with the rich smell of polish, possibly made from the scrotums of rare South African bees. 'I'm afraid I'm a lost soul,' said the owner, who had written out a list of all the things he held against the Tory government. 'They do make me just a little cross.'

'You are not alone in your views,' said Clark, cheerfully. One of the curiosities of this campaign is the way that the greatest dislike of the Tories often comes from the well-to-do.

25.04.97

Clark once spoke at one of the many clubs in London that cater for foreign journalists based there. One particularly prune-faced correspondent asked him how he justified making 'unsolicited and unwanted advances to women'. He curled his lip and replied, 'How on earth do you know an advance is unwanted until you've made it?'

Michael Heseltine went canvassing in St Albans. A local resident said that there hadn't been such excitement in the town since Joanna Lumley arrived last year to make a television commercial. Clearly, what they like is blondes with attitude.

Mr Heseltine debouched from his limo and descended upon the teeming hordes at the market. He looked like a labrador attacking an ant hill. His mission? To meet the entire population within half an hour. He nearly made it. He was swathed in yards of suiting, his hair glistening, arms flailing from side to side – nobody was safe from his torrential goodwill. 'May I say how pleased I am to meet you? Thank you so very much. May I say hello?'

Voters were being processed at the rate of around fifty a minute. Now and again one would squeeze in a question. 'Scandalous lie by the Labour Party! Thank you so much, so good to meet you.' As he swept through the market like a berserk vacuum cleaner, the noise level began to rise, slowly at first, then to a series of horrible climaxes. An angry student yelled about grants, then a separate, equally vociferous row began about a local hospital. Feedback screeched from the loudspeakers. Market traders, hoarse already, had to bellow above the tumult.

As the noise level increased, the cries began to merge. 'Vote Labour, for three pairs of knickers!'; 'Remember Tory lies about lovely Coxes!'; 'David Rutley, he'll be working for St Albans, only three pahnd!'

Our Deputy Prime Minister weaved through the crush, luminous and serene, like the Hale-Bopp comet. But his tail had become a twisting maelstrom. Scuffles and fights broke out behind him. He turned to me. 'Doesn't this prove the polls are wrong? This is even better than 1992! People are coming up, to spontaneously shake my hand!'

But you couldn't miss the people who were spontaneously swerving out of the way to avoid him. In spite of everything, most British people remain very polite and dislike telling people things they don't want to hear. An elderly woman smiled at him. He advanced on her and grasped her hand. 'Very good to meet you, I hope David Rutley can count on your support!'

'No, no, no, no, no,' she said, but didn't stop smiling.

'So glad to meet you! Thank you so much!'

28.04.97

Many people say that New Labour is a party of control freaks. New Labour resents this. They particularly resent the implication that people who expect to be Cabinet ministers next week have less freedom than a crocodile of school children on an outing.

Possibly so. But to put the theory to the test I went out with Robin Cook, who is likely soon to be our Foreign Secretary. He was in Inverness, drumming up support for the Labour candidate, David Stewart, in Britain's only four-way marginal. Last time, Sir Russell Johnson, a Liberal, got only 26 per cent of the vote and still won the seat.

We drove miles out into the countryside, then turned left across open fields and wound down to the Moray Firth. Here, in the middle of nothing, is Barmac, Europe's largest maker of oil rigs. It is almost as far from Westminster as you can go while remaining on the British mainland.

We were to rise 270 feet in the air, hauled up by a gigantic crane in a 'basket'. This turned out to be a large steel tray, perhaps 5 ft by 12 ft, with fencing round it. Rather low fencing, I thought.

We were given steel-capped boots, industrial goggles, protective jackets and hard hats. Then we were strapped into harnesses, which grasped us cosily round the back and the crotch. Finally, they hooked our reins to the rails.

We began to climb, swaying gently. Mr Cook asked, reasonably I thought, if the crane driver was a Labour voter. By this time we were about 150 feet up, suspended from the top of the crane by a single hawser. 'I'd have thought it would be pretty hard to fall out of one of these,' said Mr Cook, hopefully.

'Oh, no, it would be quite easy,' said our guide, a Labour activist who works at the site. Loch Ness was to the south, Easter Ross in front of us. Seagulls cut the air far below us. Even the workers on the rig looked minute.

Mr Cook thought it would be a good idea to get closer to them, no doubt to solicit their votes. Instructions were radioed down. 'It'll be a bit rocky, I'm afraid,' said our guide. The basket began to swing from side to side, as we swerved dizzily between the struts and pipes that make up the rig. We clanged noisily into something. Fifty feet below an arc welder sent up a shower of sparks.

And at that very moment, as we stood suspended in the heavens, swaying at a height that would give a mountain goat vertigo – no, would make a condor queasy – Mr Cook's bleeper started its urgent electronic pinging and flashed this message: 'Call Millbank, as soon as possible.'

29.04.97

When we had returned to safety, Robin Cook told me that he had put a £100 charity bet on William Hague to be the next leader of the Tory Party, though he regarded the 4-1 odds as rather mean.

John Major faced his tormentors for what may well be the last time. Were we awed by the spectacle of a proud and powerful man facing humiliating defeat? Do we perhaps feel the faintest frisson of regret at the way we had dragged an essentially decent politician to the brink of the abyss?

Of course not, we're hacks. But we did appreciate two fine examples of Majorisms, maybe the last we'll hear. One came on Tuesday, when he announced, 'A soundbite never buttered a parsnip.' You almost know what he means: that fancy words cannot improve reality. Yet the metaphor leaves you spinning gently. You imagine him saying to his wife, who was also there at the press conference, 'You know, Norma, these parsnips are awfully dry, and nothing Mr Mandelson says seems to improve them.'

(This phrase once again convinced me that my theory – that Mr Major was born in Nigeria and learned his English from dusty old books in the Kano British Council library – is correct. Much of his vocabulary comes from early Agatha Christie books, with which British Council libraries were at that time stuffed.)

Earlier the Prime Minister had remarked, 'Britain is booming, in a not unreasonable way,' a perfect Major phrase, combining windy rhetoric, litotes and mendacity, in roughly equal measure. Labour, he said, was 'a coalition of interests, whose sole purpose is the pursuit of power'. In that case, what is the Conservative Party? A band of anarchists, living in a cave?

01.05.97

As it happened, Mr Major's analysis of New Labour turned out to be spot on. However, on learning the result of the election and the Labour landslide, he went off to watch a cricket match. One week after the election, the new House of Commons met for the first time. Just before they started, a confused attendant allowed the hacks in for prayers, which are normally held in private. Astonishingly, the MPs all stand with their faces to the wall and their backs to the Mace, so that the whole Chamber looks like the Gents at half-time in a football match. Almost the first thing the new government did was to announce that control of the interest rate would pass from the Chancellor to the Bank of England.

The Commons was full of bewildered bunches of people, drifting around, uncertain what to do or where to go, desperately seeking their group leader. Normally these are tourists. Yesterday they were new Labour MPs. When they finally reached the Chamber, it was full to bursting as never before. Those lucky enough to find a seat were stuffed buttock to buttock, so tightly that if anyone had wriggled, half a dozen new members would have popped up like bread from a toaster, described an arc, and landed on the Tories.

At the Speaker's chair they were jammed like a Cup Final crowd. They filled the jury boxes, usually kept for civil servants, and spilled over from the galleries. They actually looked like a landslide. It all resembled a great Frith canvas, perhaps depicting Derby Day. The 120-odd women stood out in this summer's chic shades of orange, fuchsia and lime green. Then, on closer inspection, we could see the fascinating detail. Angela and Maria Eagle, identical twins, both in black costumes with white blouses, both capable of creating massive and pleasing confusion. Anne Begg, the first MP in anyone's memory to be a wheelchair user, tucked up by the Bar of the House, tiny and sparkling with happiness. Dennis Skinner, now promoted to the Edward Heath Memorial Sulking Seat.

The Tories looked furious, with the exception of Alan Clark, who was aiming his heat-seeking eye contact at Virginia Bottomley. Surely not? He has reformed. Probably. The new Prime Minister arrived to cheers and clapping from Labour members, who didn't know that the rules forbid applause. But what do they care? They make up the rules now.

Then it was time for the election of the Speaker. Gwyneth Dunwoody, the first seconder, announced, 'This is a beautiful day. God is in his heaven, and a majority of this House are wearing the right colours.'

Next Tony Benn stood up to make the historic first attack on the new government. It was, he said, the first time he had spoken from the government backbenches since 1 August 1951.

'Then, the British government controlled the lives of millions in Asia and in Africa. Why, we even controlled the Bank of England!'

The Tories were slightly consoled by this and cheered him mightily. (So, inwardly, must a few Labour MPs have felt, on the grounds that they were not swept into office to give more power to bankers.)

Then came the moment when the re-elected Betty Boothroyd had to be dragged ceremonially and as if unwillingly to the chair. No drag queen, she. Never has anyone marched more merrily in that direction. Indeed she almost dragged her seconders along until, on reaching the Despatch Box, they retired, panting and defeated.

08.05.97

Six Tory MPs initially stood for the leadership of their party, though the field was rapidly narrowed. Any hope Michael Howard might have had ended when Ann Widdecombe, his former deputy at the Home Office, attacked him in public, saying there was 'something of the night' about him. She returned to her assault in the Chamber.

I have never seen an MP sit as still as Michael Howard did yesterday. He stared straight ahead at the new Home Secretary, but blankly, perhaps seeing nothing. Even when he wrote something on a piece of paper, the rest of him remained motionless, as if he were communicating through an ouija board. He should have been reeling from Ann Widdecombe's repeated blows, but instead he sat like a bag of sand waiting for the floods. His face was dry and white, as a dying man who knows he must face not only death but the horror of being pursued through eternity by a vengeful and indomitable Fury.

(I was put in mind of a victim in an M. R. James ghost story. 'And when we finally found his body, buried in the shingle, his mouth was set in a terrible rictus. But what was yet more horrible, his whole scalp and face were covered by thick, black, matted hair…')

Miss Widdecombe was impassioned yet cool, tumultuous yet precise. She never accused Mr Howard of lying, but of using words in their exact meanings to mislead. She began with a tribute to his successes, but it was a tribute so short it was more like an insult. At every turn she described him by his full honorific title, 'my right honourable and learned friend', which the first time sounded formulaic but went on to be edged with sarcasm, so that each repetition resembled a cut from a razor.

The most devastating passage came at the end. 'My right honourable and learned friend has made much of how he is the one to take tough decisions…' but the real tough thing would have been to come to the Commons and tell the truth. '*That* would have been tough because the opposition would have howled for a head, and they might have wanted his.'

She sat down and Mr Howard finally found the use of his limbs, flinging himself onto the Despatch Box, begging Jack Straw to publish the relevant papers.

20.05.97

Four years later, Miss Widdecombe remained unforgiven, and Mr Howard refused even to walk into a BBC studio in Blackpool because she was still present.

Meanwhile, New Labour was grabbing all the handles of power, like a demented signalman.

Business questions came yesterday, taken by Ann Taylor, the Leader of the House. The Tories have decided to use this session, normally quite bland, to mount a last defiant action. The shadow leader of the House is Alastair Goodlad, who was until recently the party's chief whip and so, by convention, unable to speak. He hasn't uttered a word in public for years.

Now, in his new job, he is having to master the art of talking. It is like watching the brave survivor of a terrible explosion regain the use of his legs. His progress is halting, but by golly he has gumption. His prose proceeds with painful slowness, as if on crutches. 'The Leader of the. House. Told us. That it might be. Possible to give. Us two weeks business in. Advance... Could we. Have more time to. Debate the Referendum. Bills?' You could almost see the nurses lining the corridor to the hospital exit, cheering him on his way.

But then that film (valiant Vietnam vet isn't gonna let some lousy VC bomb wreck his life) faded away, and instead we were in the one-and-nines watching a British film from the 1950s. The setting is Stalag Luft Blair, the impregnable PoW camp from which no prisoner has ever escaped. Major Goodlad is the British commanding officer, in charge of the 164 survivors of the defeated Conservative Regiment. Their brave six-week rearguard action bought invaluable time for the Allies, until they were swept away by the massively superior forces of the Neue Labour Wehrmacht.

Unusually, the Kamp Kommandant is a woman, played by that well-loved character actress, Ann Taylor. 'Vell,' she says, running her eyes over Major Goodlad's lithe form (this might be something of an exaggeration). 'Ve may be enemies,

Briddische major, but zat is no reason vy ve should not be able to…co-operate.'

He knows exactly what she means, but there is a certain someone back in Godalming, a lady whose picture he keeps in his breast pocket. The idea of filthy Neue Labour lips touching his makes him shudder.

'Neither I nor my men will ever co-operate with Neue Labour!' he shouts. 'All those on the other side of the House have come here as lobby fodder!' (That's the bit I didn't make up.)

The Neue Labour forces behind their Kommandant cackle with feigned laughter. 'Perhaps you do not know, but for you, ziss war is finished!' says one.

Another steps forward, wielding a whip, but she waves him back. 'I like ziss man. He has spirit!'

Major Goodlad knows the rules of the Whitehall convention. 'The massive increase in political appointments is causing rising concern about the politicization of the civil service,' he barks.

The enemy officers shriek more defiance, and the spurned Kommandant blazes with fury. 'I must congratulate you on making your complaint on the politicization of the civil service with a straight face!' she says. 'It voss about to crack at ze end!' (I only made up the accent in that bit.)

Cheered on by his men, including Ken 'Nobby' Clarke and Patrick 'Cormacky' Cormack, the Major demands that the other side be taught the rules of order. Kommandant Taylor sneers: 'Perhaps you are complainink viz your chief whip's hat on, because *you* haven't got any lobby fodder!' By now she is irked beyond reason. Just as she is about to slap him across the face, she notices the soil in his trouser turn-ups…

23.05.97

One of the new Prime Minister's first visitors was President Bill Clinton. He had recently suffered a knee injury.

The President arrived in Downing Street, hobbled out of the car and started smiling. Mrs Clinton smiled too. So did Tony and Cherie Blair. They didn't stop smiling. After a while it must have been quite painful. In any event, they looked like the participants in a mass Moonie wedding.

Mr Clinton said he was very glad to be among us. No wonder. It meant a full twenty-four hours without anyone mentioning Paula Jones. So it was unkind of a photographer to shout, 'Can you get down on one knee, please?' The other photographers burst out laughing, but the Clintons and Blairs just went on smiling serenely. The President had a walking stick, calling to mind the old American joke: how does a Razorback (Arkansan) count to 21? He drops his pants. Now Mr Clinton can count to 22.

They went inside Number 10. I checked out the limo. Just an ordinary armour-plated Cadillac Fleetwood Brougham runabout. In the back was a folder, marked 'For the President: Information', which if it's anything like other American guidebooks to London may be very misleading. 'Prime Minister Blair hates informality. Address him as "Your sublime excellency" '; 'Passengers on the tube will love to see pictures of your grandchildren…'

Inside the house Mr Blair was saying, 'We are absolutely delighted to have you here. It is a very great day for us.' Evidently this went down well, because he immediately said it again.

The President addressed Mo Mowlam. 'I saw you on TV, being optimistic about Northern Ireland, which is an article of faith in my life and my household.'

Really? Is Chelsea taught to be optimistic about Northern

Ireland over the cornflakes and pop tarts? And if she is, what other pious nonsense are her parents feeding her?

He made a little joke, about wishing he could have a 179-seat majority. The Cabinet laughed sycophantically, and when he had finished they thumped the table. A colleague who was present described it as 'a dignified banging', which is something the President knows all about.

The wives then headed off for the Globe Theatre to see part of *Henry V*. This (almost) includes the line, 'once more into the breeches, dear friends', also an important article of faith in the Clinton household. The men went to the White Room, where Mr Clinton said he had read the Labour manifesto. 'The future, not the past. For the many, not the few. Leadership, not drift.' He was getting the message: verbs lose elections.

Next they turned up in the Rose Garden. Bees buzzed, sirens whined. Mr Blair took the opportunity to coin some exciting new clichés. 'We prefer reason to doctrine. We are strong on idealism, we resist ideology.' They are intolerant of intolerance, respectful of respect. 'New times, new challenges, a new political generation...'

Good grief, we could have another ten years of this.

30.05.97

We thought we had seen the last of John Major. We were wrong.

There was a happy moment in the Commons yesterday when we heard what may be the last Majorism of them all. The present and former prime ministers fell out over Scottish and Welsh devolution. (No, wait! Please! Keep reading. You can watch *Kilroy* any day!)

Three weeks ago, Tony Blair promised that the bill to set up the assemblies would be published before the two referendums. Yesterday he said that there would not be a bill, but a White Paper instead. To the average Highland fisherman or Rangers fan, that might be an academic matter. Not to the Commons. Mr Major asked no fewer than five questions on the topic, getting angrier and angrier. At the climactic moment, he declared to Mr Blair, 'You have been caught with your fingers in the till, oratorically!'

It was a fine moment. As with all the best Majorisms, you could work out more or less what he meant, but could not figure out why he'd put it that way. Within an hour he had followed up with a letter to Mr Blair. It finished like this, and I have appended notes, rather like a Shakespeare concordance:

'If I remember my childhood days correctly (1), it was Humpty Dumpty who said, "Words mean what I say they mean, nothing more, nothing less" (2). That of course was before the fall! (3) Surely he should not be your role model (4). Yours, John M. (5).'

(1) A big if. Mr Major has always had trouble remembering his childhood days correctly, and some of his adult ones too. Remember the business about the O levels? And the older woman, who used to call him 'Rover'?

(2) Er, not quite. What Humpty Dumpty said was: 'When I use a word it means just what I choose it to mean – neither more nor less.' Not a bad stab from memory, but surely the leader of the opposition's speech-writers can run to a book of quotations?

(3) It ill behoves, as we political hacks say when feeling especially pompous, Mr Major to talk about anyone falling.

(4) A nice Majorish touch. Mr Blair's actual role model is, I suspect, the Bosun in *The Hunting of the Snark*: 'What I tell you three times is true.'

(5) I love the 'John M.' It's like those postcards people send from the seaside to people they don't know awfully well. ('Weather fine. Terry and Sue F.') One imagines Mr Blair saying, 'Oh, *that* John.'

05.06.97

In the wake of their terrible election defeat, the Tories held a leadership contest. It was during the night of the long receptions that I first heard an insult to William Hague, which somehow stuck.

All five leadership candidates held parties for Tory MPs last night. For an indecisive alcoholic, it must have been four hours of bliss. A lot of effort was being expended in pursuit of a job that will confer on the winner, for five years at least, roughly as much raw power as the Hon. Sec. of a crown green bowling club.

The air crackled with malice. John Redwood started with tea and Pimms in a private room at the Commons. One of his supporters marked our card: 'Michael Howard has been economical with the *actualité*, as usual. He's claiming at least two people who we know are committed to John…Ken Clarke's giving a beer and crisps party. Don't you hate that carapace of affected ordinariness?…Hague? Oh dear, the human embryo…'

The press hung round outside while the members arrived with their wives. People kept reminding us that this was the most sophisticated electorate on the planet. They looked more like Ladies' Night at Hartlepool Freemasons. The wives tend to a fashionable plumpness, like Sophie Dahl only with clothes on. They all had that glossy air of people who know exactly where their next meal is coming from.

Like many other MPs, Peter and Virginia Bottomley went to all five bashes. 'Michael Howard had the best champagne, Peter Lilley had the nicest garden, and John Redwood served some squidgy passion-fruit thing,' observed Mr Bottomley.

Outside the Lilley party three young men, not yet shaving I would guess, appeared with placards marked 'Portillo 4 El Presidente'. They were dressed as Mexican peasants and were swigging from a bottle marked 'tequila' but which looked suspiciously like cold tea. They spoke to the MP for North Essex: 'Meester Jenkin, what about Miguel, 'e is our 'ero. Why you no vote for Miguel? In our country you would be shot.'

They turned out to be Young Conservatives from Streatham, which leaves another mystery: where do you find four Young Conservatives in Streatham?

William Hague arrived at the Carlton Club with his fiancée, Ffion Jenkins. She did not look happy. His expression was relaxed, cool and confident. Her expression seemed to say, 'If you don't leave *now*, I shall call security!'

Ken Clarke had the biggest turnout of former Cabinet ministers, including Willie Whitelaw, now very old and frail. There was a surrealist moment when we were briefed by Peter Luff on the food: 'There were those little Indian oniony balls, bhajis is it? And some hammy, cheesy things, and those vol-au-vent thingies, and stuffed cherry tomatoes.' This was the real cutting edge of political reporting. Walter Bagehot, thou shouldst be living.'

10.06.97

William Hague could be leader of the Conservative Party by tonight, making him the first person to get the job as part of a work experience programme. Last month, seven Cabinet ministers lost their seats; another retired; John Major is off and away; and we can assume that Ken Clarke and Michael Heseltine are, like Virginia Bottomley and John Gummer, heading for the backbenches. The MP for a farming constituency will not want to trust the former agriculture minister, Douglas Hogg, with anything more sensitive than mowing the lawn, so that leaves just five survivors.

Clearly Youth will have to take the helm. The shadow Cabinet will be like one of those awful young persons' parliaments we had to endure at school.

The industry spokesman: I think we should have more jobs, so that people can earn money, and buy things they need!

The shadow health secretary: I think we ought to spend more on having hospitals and doctors, which can cure people, and less on weapons which are only any good for killing people.

The leader of the opposition: Jolly, jolly good. Well done, everybody. You've all had your say, and now it's time for biscuits and alcopops!

All: Yippee!

In the Chamber it was defence questions. The rump of the Tory Party is divided into the old Guards, such as Alan Clark and Michael Mates, and the Clowns, the kind of chinless wonders who probably think Bosnia Herzegovina is that bra model.

The Clowns asked various silly questions. Then a Guard, Nicholas Soames, appeared to sub for the unavoidably absent Michael Portillo. His question concerned 'roll-on, roll-off' facilities. I sat up with a start. Was Mr Soames discussing his own celebrated love-making techniques? (*The Pillow Book of*

Nicholas Soames: – Erotic Secrets of the Mysterious Occident.) It turned out that he mean ro-ro ferries for our rapid deployment forces.

Next they discussed a paper which – according to James Arbuthnot – threatened £3 billion cuts in defence spending. The Defence Secretary, George Robertson, said this must have been left over from the last administration. At this Mr Soames roared with laughter, pitching, yawing and heaving as his face went first red, then puce, then finally a rich, deep purple. He jabbed Mr Arbuthnot merrily with his elbow. Mr Arbuthnot did not respond, but sat with a thin, weak smile, like winter sunshine upon a coffin lid.

This may have been a mistake. Mr Soames will surely have a key role in the Youth Forum for Tomorrow's World, or 'shadow Cabinet' as we still call it.

17.06.97

In this, as in so many things, I was wrong.

The crowds parted and Lady Thatcher, shimmering in blue, was among us. Her mission? To explain how Tory MPs could still vote for her, through her medium on earth. She spoke, as ever, in typographical extremities.

'*Principles* don't change, circumstances do, but you STILL apply the same *principles* to changing circumstances. That is the way we built *up* Britain to the Strongest. Economy. In Europe.

'I am supporting *William Hague*. Have you got – the – name? WILLIAM HAGUE. Vote. For. *William Hague*. For the same kind of government *I* led. And vote for him on Thursday. GOT the MESSAGE?'

And she was gone, possibly because her fiery chariot was double-parked.

Earlier *William Hague* had held a presss conference in a Westminster restaurant. He swept down the curved stairway to the podium. All the scene lacked was Dame Edna and a bunch of gladioli. His slogan is 'A Fresh Start'. Young persons were dotted around the room. They wore dark suits and crisp white shirts. Fresh start, fresh armpits. He stood at the lectern, wearing what appeared to be a triple-breasted suit, and waved at his claque of MPs. 'They are the future of our party, the heartbeat of our party,' he declared. They looked like an Addams Family reunion to me.

I am now sending in my script to the Disney Corporation. It's an exciting yarn about young Billy Hague. He's being shown round the cockpit of a plane ('Do you like movies about Turkish prisons, Billy?' asks the captain) when a flying saucer appears on the starboard wing. It sends all the adults into a trance.

The plane spins out of control, but the young lad, scared but plucky, hears a crackling on the co-pilot's headphones. He can make out the voice of air traffic control.

'Do you read me?'

'Yes, Lady Thatcher, I read you!'

'Do you see that blue lever on the right, Billy? Push it all the way forward!'

He does so and, with painful slowness, the plane begins to cartwheel, then goes into a nosedive and crashes into the sea, killing everyone on board. So perhaps Disney won't buy it after all.

19.06.97

My predictions are so often wrong that it was nice to get one right for a change.

The result was announced, and in the committee corridor a woman of a certain age, described as a Tory MP's assistant, let loose a blood-chilling cry. 'Y-e-e-e-s! There is a God looking after the Conservative Party!' I was reminded of the famous scene in *When Harry Met Sally*, except that this time the orgasm was real. 'Urghhh! Ohh!' went the woman. 'I don't want what she's having,' murmured a few listeners.

Moments later the new leader marched past us to speak to MPs and peers. His remaining hair was yellow and glossy, his tie was yellow and glossy, and his pate seemed to have been french polished. Give him glasses and he'd look like the comedian Harry Hill, with the same surreal undertow to much of what he says.

After the speech Jeffrey Archer told us, 'I wish you could have been there. He was marvellous. He grew another foot.'

Another foot, to go with the triple-breasted suit! He spoke to us, and our minds rolled back twenty years to that speech in Blackpool. He sounded only slightly younger now. 'The Conservative Party has placed a grave responsibility on me…done me a great honour…road to unity and confidence…collective responsibility…' The phrases poured slowly out, like sludge from a sump. There was a certain frozen look on the faces of his campaign team. Could it be that he is – above all else – terribly, majestically, thunderously boring?

We moved over to Conservative Central Office, where John Major was to make a ceremonial handing over of the leadership. What form would this take? A gavel? A sceptre? A brown envelope full of £50 notes? It turned out to be an exchange of flattering speeches.

'Whichever way we chose today, we could not lose,' Mr Major said.

'Yes, because you weren't standing,' muttered one party disloyalist.

Finally the new leader addressed us. He warned that there would have to be changes. That everyone would need to work hard. That he would sweep away 'a lot of old cobwebs!' (Has anyone ever promised to sweep away new cobwebs?) Then he produced one mighty, resonant line: 'I will tolerate no bellyaching!' If he's so young, why does he sound like an elderly house master in a minor public school?

20.06.97

One week later Mr Hague appeared at his first Prime Minister's Question Time.

Mr Hague persisted with five questions and, I thought, marginally won the exchange with Tony Blair. But there is a problem – his voice is drearily, achingly dull. His longer sentences bump downwards, phrase by phrase, like Pooh Bear being tugged down the stairs by Christopher Robin. His question on Northern Ireland looked, typographically, rather like this:

Searching for (bump)

    A credible (bump)

        Way through the (bump)

           Decommissioning (bump)

          Block

          (bump)

Mr Blair's own tone was, by contrast, hectic. Speed was the

essence. Talks had to start 'as quickly as possible'. The 'settlement train' was leaving. The settlement guard was blowing his whistle and the settlement buffet would be open for the sale of drinks and light refreshments, though not tea or coffee owing to a malfunctioning heater. If Sinn Fein were not on board, they would have to follow in the settlement bus. (Some of these points I might have marginally enhanced.)

26.06.97

But Northern Ireland continued to prove intractable, as Mo Mowlam was the latest Ulster Secretary to find out.

Like young men in 1914, the Northern Ireland Secretaries march off to war, happy to be serving their country, certain it will all be over by Christmas. Then they encounter the tiny-minded, introspective, self-obsessed, mean-spirited, solipsistic, hidebound, pettifogging, miserable, duplicitous, implacable intransigence of the people they have to deal with.

A note of querulous annoyance creeps into the voice. 'The people themselves must decide they want the situation to change,' Dr Mowlam said, 'but we cannot force them to live together.'

This is an improvement on the usual pabulum about the need for goodwill on all sides, combined with government determination to explore all avenues for a possible solution, the whole topped off with an entirely mistaken tribute to the desire of all people in the province for peace.

Even John Hume felt moved to admit ruefully that the problem may not be exclusively the fault of the British but might just possibly have something to do with the folk who live there. The local population had 'failed, as a people' to live together.

This was realistic, but sometimes one yearns for an even harsher realism. 'After 29 years, I implore the people of Northern Ireland to accept that violence is the only solution to their problems. When will they finally realize that it is only when one side has won a convincing military victory over the other that we will see a stable and lasting end to this terrible conflict? I beg ordinary people not to waste their time on peaceful negotiations, which have been the source of so much bitterness and division...' But realism about Northern Ireland has always been thought the height of bad taste.

10.07.97

Dennis Skinner, the Beast of Bolsover, is a much-loved parliamentary institution. Sketch-writers tend, I fear, to ignore him for much of the time, on the grounds that – as the late Jimmy Edwards put it – 'We do the funnies round here.' He tends to be better value when he is being serious.

Dennis Skinner intervened in the British Airways strike yesterday. 'People who work for a living should be treated properly,' he said, 'not by Pontius Pilate!' (Or possibly by Pontius Pilot. 'Good morning, ladies and gentlemen, and welcome aboard. We'll be on our way to Malaga just as soon as I've finished washing my hands...'

Mr Skinner was referring to 'that evil man, Ayling', who had been 'hounding and intimidating the people down at

Heathrow, the stewards and stewardesses who have been on strike, many of whom vote Labour.'

The Tories hooted with glee, not only because Bob Ayling, the BA chief executive, is a Labour supporter, but because of the image conjured up by Mr Skinner's words. To him strikes are not merely a means of bargaining for better pay and conditions, but an affirmation of traditional community solidarity. We could picture the villagers in the old, tight-knit, flight-attending villages of Weybridge, Chertsey and Egham, huddled round braziers, stamping on the snow in their complimentary slipperettes, glugging miniatures of duty-free Baileys to keep out the cold, as their loyal womenfolk hand out plastic trays of lasagne made out of recycled in-flight magazines. These people are engaged in a noble, if doomed, attempt to preserve their traditional, fast-vanishing way of life.

Anyhow, his intervention should be enough to get Mr Skinner a complimentary upgrade if he ever decides to go abroad. (He's tried abroad in the past, but didn't care for it.) 'Our in-flight film presentation this morning is Ken Loach's *The Price of Coal. Songs of Defiance*, with Arthur Scargill, can be found on Channel 7 on your headsets. A protest march against the appalling conditions suffered in economy class will begin from the forward galley shortly after the service of canapés. And can demonstrators please keep the aisles free for the drinks trolley...'

11.07.97

My relationship with Michael Fabricant, the MP for Lichfield, has become symbiotic, a sort of folie à deux *in which we both egg each other on. He both hates and adores being mentioned so often, especially in the context of his extraordinary hairpiece. I feel periodically that I should keep quiet about him and seek new, more deserving targets. Then readers write in and demand more about Mickey Fabb, the reformed disc jockey who once stalked the Brighton and Hove area with his mobile disco. Now and again I ban myself from writing about him at all.*

A friend phoned on Saturday, barely able to contain her laughter. 'Have you seen the *Daily Mail*?' she asked. 'There's piece about Cheryl Gillan, the Tory MP. Apparently she was mugged yesterday, in her own car.

'And there's this quote from her: "They say that in moments of stress, your life flashes before your eyes. But I thought of my fellow MP, Michael Fabricant." '

As regular readers know, I am bound never again to mention the MP for Lichfield, and I will stick to my promise. But Ms Gillan's statement was so arresting that I did some research into this phenomenon, which I learned has baffled scientists down the centuries. Apparently World War II bomber crews who were shot down and later rescued from the sea sometimes described how, as they sank below the waves, the image of a figure with an orange face, an ingratiating smile and bulging eyes flashed before them.

'Blimey, I thought I was a goner and no mistake,' said Airman Reg Tupper of Bow. 'I reckoned 'e was one o' them devils, ready to throw me to the flames, on account of the wife 'ad been fiddling the rations.'

In his book *The Donkeys*, the historian and MP Alan Clark describes the mass hallucination known as 'The Greaser of Mons', in which hundreds of British Tommies, exhausted, hungry and terrified, saw a vision of a gigantic MP in a wig, which changed from grey to strawberry blonde. Though officers assured them that this was merely an optical phenomenon, the men believed they had seen a phantom of the Kaiser and that a German breakthrough was inevitable. Several fled and later faced firing squads.

Records of the Black Death show that, shortly before they expired, many victims believed that a strange, almost human figure was standing over their beds. 'Hysse lockes were notte as menne's hair, but were knotted and sewne from lustrous threades,' wrote Daniel Defoe in his *Journal of the Plague Year*. This apparition was known as 'The Grim Weaver'.

Yesterday there was no sign of Fabricant in the Chamber – he was possibly hanging round hospitals, scaring patients – but that doesn't matter, since I am pledged never to mention him again. He missed a debate in which MPs expressed fury at the suggestion that the BBC might drop *Yesterday in Parliament*, at least in its present form. I thought that showed some nerve, since there were only 54 MPs in the House at the time, or 8 per cent of the total. If the debates aren't interesting to them, why should they be to us?

Denis MacShane was cross about the loss of direct connection between MPs and voters. He wanted debates that were not 'filtered by the distinguished [some sarcasm here, I suspect] cohorts of scribblers and sketch boys'.

This led to more historical musing. In the 18th century, demand for parliamentary sketches was so great that young ragamuffin 'sketch boys' would write them at great speed, then run through the streets, selling the results at a penny a time to silk-hatted toffs who would sit in their clubs and coffee houses, roaring with laughter at jokes about, say, Marchmont Vavasour MP, known as 'the Fabricant of our age', who wore his own hair, cunningly made to look like a wig.

It turns out, I fear, that the only reason Ms Gillan thought of Mr Fabricant at that perilous time was that he had been mugged on the same spot.

15.07.97

Margaret Thatcher might have been forgotten, but she certainly has not gone. Ten days after the death of Princess Diana she turned up in Scotland, speaking to the American Association of Travel Agents, which for some strange reason had chosen Glasgow for their annual conference, and for some stranger reason had picked her as their keynote speaker.

Since the dreadful events of ten days ago, she may well be the world's most famous woman once again. Perhaps that is why her fee is £50,000 per speech, which worked out yesterday at £1,136 a minute. Campaigners for a 'yes' vote in the referendum currently being fought in Scotland were desperately hoping she would speak to the cameras on behalf of the Noes. For years now, her mere existence has been seen by many Scots as the conclusive proof that they need independence. Indeed, she did talk about a proud, hard-working people under the jackboot of an arrogant, distant government. But it turned out she meant Hong Kong.

I settled back to enjoy a treat, since most of her lucrative speeches are closed to the press and public, who cannot afford the £7.57 each word costs at normal talking speed.

She began with a tribute to Princess Diana. This lasted ninety seconds, or £1,704. Then she displayed the breathtaking chutzpah familiar to those of us who are not American travel agents. She launched a paean of praise to herself.

Politicians, she said, always get things wrong. 'There are, of course, exceptions. Ronald Reagan, for example. And, er, there was a woman who worked along the same lines!'

Then she announced that the Blair government was also working along those lines laid down by her. 'That is why we have the lowest unemployment in Europe and, all things considered, the highest standard of living in Europe!'

What? asked the handful of Brits in the audience. Who was she kidding? But it didn't matter. We had reached £6,618 and the meter was running fast. Leadership, she mused, was difficult – for some. 'I know politicians who lead by following the opinion polls. It's called "followership". I prefer to lead myself!' Loud applause; meter reaches £15,904.

She had wanted, she told us, fifty years more on the lease of Hong Kong, 'for which I had the temerity to ask!' Loud and prolonged applause reminiscent of Castro speaking to the party congress in Havana. Meter hits £21,584.

The next twenty grand took us on a *tour d'horizon* including China and the Middle East. The travel agents, having topped up their frequent groveller points, were getting restive and hungry. At £45,440 she quoted Bette Davis: 'I always attempt the impossible; it improves my work!' and they recovered enough to roar with admiring laughter.

Then came the jaw-dropping peroration. We had just reached £48,848, and she got on to the Pilgrim Fathers. 'They didn't go to America for subsidies! There weren't any. Instead, they founded the greatest nation on earth!

'My friends, I salute you!'

Massive, roof-raising applause, cheers, yelling, foot-stamping, with discreet barfing from the Brits. And fifty thousand smackeroonies for her!

10.09.97

That autumn Blair made his first Labour Party conference speech as leader.

The Prime Minister walked on to the music of Saint-Saëns, specifically the part used as the theme of *Babe*. This is the popular film about a shy talking piglet who learns to round up flocks of docile, disciplined sheep. Just a coincidence, of course. We had just seen a video depicting Five Months of Glorious Progress. Election promises honoured! Blair triumphs in Amsterdam! Ragged cheers greeted these declarations, a reminder that Labour has always had trouble distinguishing between a decision and an achievement.

He walked onto the platform and the audience rose to him in a standing ovation which was, perhaps, slightly more enthusiastic than the one at the end. He kept waving them back down. You half expected him to say that the hall was only booked for half an hour, and if they didn't mind he'd crack on. His whole style is muffled and subdued, even the loud bits. It's not so much a speech as a presentation without slides. The audience is like the congregation in an evangelical church. They want to be writhing on the floor in ecstasy but find they've got a Church of England vicar who doesn't even have a tambourine.

By the end he was talking about the importance of giving. 'Make this the giving age...' He sounded as if he was announcing Harvest Festival next week: 'Not too many vegetable marrows this year, if you don't mind.' Soon the congregation realized that they weren't going to get very much in exchange for their giving. He used the phrase 'hard choices' and even 'harsh choices' eleven times. In the past this has always been Labour-speak for 'No more money'.

And so it is today. But under Mr Blair, harshness is also a virtue in itself. 'Ours must be a compassionate society. But compassion with a hard edge. A strong society cannot be built on soft choices.'

Compassion with a hard edge! The razor blade in the duvet! I wonder what it's like at the Blair breakfast table.

'Which cereal would you like, dear?'

'I want the hard choice, and that means Shreddies. But Shreddies without milk, because otherwise they would become the soft choice, and soft choices are no basis for breakfast for our people.'

As well as being harsh and hard, we must be modern. Being modern is an absolute good in itself, and he used the word twenty-one times. 'We must modernize – and take the hard choices to do it.' Civil servants are to be replaced by computers. Soon a quarter of all dealings with government will be performed electronically. Members of the public can be asked: 'Do you want your choice to be (*click on one*) (a) hard, (b) harsh, or (c) downright pitiless?'

There were curious Blairish phrases: 'The gates of xenophobia, falling down', which was almost Blakean. We had anointed him to lead us into the next millennium. 'That was your challenge to me. Proudly, humbly, I accepted it.'

Vainly, modestly, he set to work. Harshly, compassionately, he took the tough choices. Loudly, softly, he spoke to conference and, fascinated, bored, they gave him a standing ovation anyway.

01.10.97

The high spot of the Labour conference is often the merit awards, when two elderly party members get to recount their lifetime's work on stage. This used to come before the leader's speech, but over the years the old stagers, with memories of the Spanish civil war and the General Strike, began to upstage him. So they moved it to the end.

No wonder. Jean Haywood of Norfolk said that the party she had worked for so many years 'has changed so much, I sometimes have difficulty identifying with its policies'. (Loud and prolonged cheers.)

'I still think that progressive taxation is the fairest way of funding,' she added. (Louder cheers, whoops of agreement.) 'Socialism is not something to be ashamed of!' (Delegates rise en masse for spontaneous standing ovation.)

And who was this tall figure striding onto the platform to wrap a manly arm around her frail shoulders? Why, it was the Great Helmsman himself, anxious for some of those billowing waves of admiration to crash over him.

But, we reflected, had he not been the target of some of her words, words that had been, to say the least, rather critical? Why, of course. But the warm clasp did two things. It implied: dear old Gran, we do love her, but she is getting a little dotty these days. And it also transferred some of her magical popularity through touch. Touching is symbolically very important in Blair's Britain.

In forty years it may all be different. Men who are young now will hobble to the platform and say, 'Ah'm old enough to remember a fella, name o' Blair. Tony Blair! 'E weren't afraid to use words like "capitalism" and "global investment". [Hurrahs.] Some of us 'ere still believe in supply side economics, even if it isn't quite so fashionable these days!' (Cheers, rapture, standing ovation.)

Then John Prescott did his rough diamond act. 'During the election I met this chap who said, "You've got to help me John. I've never had sex under a Labour government." If you're listening, mate, I hope the first hundred days were good for you!'

I know you're supposed to end every New Labour speech by saying, 'Do this! Do it for our children.' But I didn't realize they meant it literally.

04.10.97

The Tory Party somehow manages to be triumphalist, even in defeat. But there were some failures at their first post-1997 conference.

Poor John Redwood made a speech of such unremitting ghastliness and failure that even John Major, the man against whom he stood two years ago, might have felt a twinge of sympathy for him. It takes a lot to die on your feet while making a string of anti-Labour jokes to a Tory Party conference. But he managed it.

Those of us who occasionally speak in public know the feeling. The prized routine, delivered with aplomb and flair, yet met with a strained and embarrassed silence. The faint, gutterul, imitation laugh from those members of the audience who are too polite to remain completely silent. The way your stomach begins to heave and your legs start to tremble.

'Whom do we have?' he asked about one Labour industry minister. 'John Battle! Embattled by name, and embattled by nature!' The sound of dead leaves rustling floated up from the audience.

Lord Clinton-Davis, a trade minister, had failed to go on a trade mission to Korea. 'They say time flies, which is more than the minister does!' A low, hoarse noise emerged grudgingly, as if several of the audience had neglected to share their Fisherman's Friends.

Nigel Griffiths, the trade minister, was next in line for a

49

Redwood gumming. 'With his shares in P&O, he has ferries at the bottom of his garden!' At this point his listeners gave up and silence fell like a shroud.

Then, 'My personal favourite, Lord Simon. He thought it would be so easy. But it wasn't so simple, Simon, was it?' He left a longish pause for this joke to fester in our minds.

Then a sound not unlike a frog coughing in a bucket could be heard at the back of the hall. Someone on the platform got up, and so, after a painful wait, did most of the rest of the audience. But then a standing ovation is the least any Tory front-bencher gets at conference time. Maybe one day Mr Redwood will lead his party. But not in this millennium nor, I suspect, in the next.

09.10.97

William Hague, who first came to fame at a Conservative Party conference when aged sixteen, returned as leader.

The foetus has landed. His speech left one mystery: how is it that a party that claims to be proud and independent can rise adoringly as one to cheer a young man they'd barely heard of a year ago, foisted on them against their wishes by a parliamentary party they appear to despise? Still, Mr Hague's was a brilliantly adequate performance, definitively not bad really, thunderously more or less up to it. The effect was helped rather than hindered by his platform voice, which resembles Alan Bennett playing an old sheep. When he announced, 'Conservatives c-a-a-a-re,' you could almost see James Herriot on a windswept moor, up to his elbow in a ewe.

Then there were the elderly school debating tricks. 'So doan tell me this country doesn't need a Conservative Party! Doan tell me Conservative values have no relevance for the future!' he said aggressively, as if throughout the conference people had been marching up to him saying that the country didn't need a Conservative Party.

'And ah'll tell yer summat for nowt, young William. Conservative values have noh relevance to t'future. Sithee, 'appen.'

He played the Yorkshire card as if it were the ace of spades. 'I was born in Rotherham. Around where I lived, people thought a Conservative was something you spread on yer toast!' As a Yorkshire person myself I find this blatant Tykeism rather offensive, playing on a stereotype that makes us stupid, laconic and mean. Which we are, but that's not the point. Just as westernized Chinese people are called 'bananas' – yellow on the outside, white inside – so he is a sort of toad-in-the-hole made with chorizo: Yorkshire on the outside, metropolitan elitist in the middle.

The most important part of the speech was about compassion. Thanks to the Tories we are about to be the most compassionate nation on earth. 'Go to your local NSPCC or Oxfam or hospital visitors, and you'll probably see most of our Conservative branch committee there,' he declared.

Really? Times must have changed.

'How does a round of golf sound, Major?'

'No can do, old boy, 'fraid it's my shift on the ethnic basketware counter at Oxfam.'

Or, 'Dear Lady Marshall-Pugh, I do hope we can tempt you to our bring-and-buy on Saturday.'

'I'm so very sorry, but time and the Somali Gay and Lesbian support group wait for no man!'

11.10.97

The Neil Hamiltons were setting out on their long crusade to prove Mr Hamilton innocent of the charges against him, and also to appear several times on every daytime television show.

There was a steady drizzle outside the Commons. A small queue of glum tourists were outside, hoping to cheer themselves up with a few minutes of the Supreme Court (Offices) Bill, which at least was being debated in the warm. Neil and Christine Hamilton were under umbrellas, waiting for Martin Bell, the man who had defeated Neil in Tatton.

The Commons committee that deals with standards had just produced its report, saying that Mr Hamilton was either guilty as charged, or else not. But that if he wasn't, they had neither the time, the inclination nor the means to sort it out.

Faced with the question of whether, on top of all his admitted wrong-doings, Mr Hamilton had accepted cash in brown paper envelopes from Mohamed al-Fayed, the committee's conclusions were: (1) Search us, squire; (2) Whom would we know, eh? And (3) You're asking the wrong blokes, you are.

Mr Hamilton seemed to believe this amounted to an acquittal. The rain got heavier. Mr Bell could be seen walking towards us.

'Go on, dear, put him on the spot!' Mrs Hamilton said.

'Do you think I should?' asked her husband.

'If you don't, I will, and you know what *I'll* say!'

Mr Bell assumed a strategic position, with a fence between him and the Hamiltons. The rain had turned his celebrated white suit a blodgy grey. He thought Neil – 'He is my constituent' – had been hard done by. There ought to be an appeals procedure.

Mrs Hamilton fumed. 'I won't go near the man,' she said. 'I shall explode! He's a *humbug*!'

Mr Hamilton is now a member of what we hacks cruelly call the Green Ink Brigade, people who have devoted their whole being to some injustice, real or imagined, and who write long letters in green ink explaining every last detail of their complaint. Every time you pitch one into the wastebasket you have the awful sensation that one in a hundred might just be worth investigating. But which?

Green-inkers are pathetically grateful for any response from an apparently normal person, so it wasn't surprising that Mr Hamilton walked up to Martin Bell and shook him warmly by the hand. They went off together, into the dry.

Earlier Mr Hamilton had held a press conference. It was Green-ink heaven! Hacks poised with open notebooks! Camera crews! We even had to wait for Radio Five Live to turn up! No Green-inker could ever ask for more. Imagine – 'We now go over like to 27 Balaclava Terrace, where Mr Percy Snodgrass is marking the 25th anniversary of his battle with Droitwich town council over planning permission for his greenhouse…'

All the familiar features were there. The long list of errors delivered too quickly for anyone to understand, still less write down. The points to be ticked off: 'Ninthly, and tenthly. I now come to my eleventh point…' The constant references to particular sub-clauses within individual paragraphs. The sarcastic references to people and details we know not of: 'So much for the reliability of Mr Bromfield!' And the hyperbolic historical references: 'This is the hoax of the century! Mr al-Fayed is a modern-day Titus Oates!'

I felt deeply sorry for Mr Hamilton, a man trapped in a cage of his own making, rattling the very bars he has put in place.

07.11.97

Labour came to office promising a free vote on a bill to abolish fox-hunting, then spent several years trying to keep the pledge while avoiding the reality.

Fox-hunting is a gut, emotional matter. You loathe it or you don't. It is not susceptible to rational debate. You cannot discuss the pros and cons as if they were interest rates.

But MPs didn't half have a go. The House was almost packed and simmering with excitement. Cometh the hour, cometh the man. Unfortunately the man was Michael Foster, whose bill they were now debating. Mr Foster is a new boy, so there is one excuse. He is also a former accountancy lecturer, and there's another. Unfortunately you can't address the Commons as if they were a group of promising trainee accountants. And Mr Foster had over-prepared.

Even the apparently spontaneous interventions by his supporters were marked 'Intervention' on his script. Beside him sat a colleague who, every few moments, presented him with a fresh sheet of facts, in case he might run short. He used cliché like an aerosol: 'the hand of fate…we must put over our core message and restate our key pledges.' He plonked down truisms like dominoes: 'As many people have pointed out, dying is a natural activity.' At the end he was loudly cheered by supporters of the bill. I know that cheer; it doesn't reward a speech well made, but covers up for a turkey.

This might have mattered more if Michael Heseltine had not, for once, made a bad speech, and if Ann Widdecombe had not made a brilliant one. Mr Heseltine started, as ever, slowly and solemnly. With his bristling eyebrows and bushy hair he looked a little like a fox, but a very grand one with quite the bushiest tail in the wood.

He attacked the bill for allowing 'flushing out'. 'Why do you flush something out?' he demanded, and foolishly left a pause, no doubt designed to add gravity to the reply he was to give us. But it was too late. 'Ask Mrs Thatcher!' shouted Denis MacShane, and the place dissolved into laughter, the kind of nerve-shredding, speech-destroying, morale-deflating laughter that takes away all hope. Heseline ploughed on regardless, but people chattered happily among themselves like mice who've seen the cat locked in its basket.

Soon afterwards Ann Widdecombe rose to support the bill. Magnificent in scarlet and bottle green, she was consumed by a terrifying rage. She didn't just scorn the hunting lobby; she poured whole carboys of nitric acid over them. Their argument about jobs was ludicrous: 'If you abolished crime, you will put all the police out of work. If you abolish ill-health you'll put the doctors and nurses out of work!' Her whole body rocking, she invited the bill's opponents to go and stand near the lions in Africa, 'and see if they enjoy the hunt! I know I would enjoy watching it.'

She sat down to roars of applause from the Labour abolitionists and – strictly forbidden, this – clapping. I doubt if she changed a single vote, but she didn't half cheer up the abolitionists.

We finished with a Home Office minister weaselling his way out of a promise to make time for the bill. But that doesn't matter just yet. In the meantime it will meet its fate in the Lords, where it will be seized on by savage peers, ripped to pieces, its sub-clauses torn out and eaten.

29.11.97

One of John Prescott's jobs as Deputy Prime Minister and environment spokesman was saving the planet. This took him around the world, to visit the places he was saving.

Mr Prescott was apocalyptic. Record drought. The highest temperatures ever recorded. Floods engulfing Europe and deadly pollution blanketing the Far East.

'Our polar ice caps are melting. Only this weekend, Mexico was hit by freak snowstorms…a world of drought and crop failures, rising seas, mass migration and disease. Giant radioactive frogs the size of combine harvesters roaming our cities, eating children as they sit in their strollers.' (I made the last one up, but I feel sure Mr Prescott would have thrown it in if he had thought of it.)

The Deputy Prime Minister was reporting his visit to the Kyoto summit on climate change. It turns out that planet-saving has been yet another of the multitudinous achievements of New Labour in its first few months of office. How had our government managed this, with only a little help from other countries? Well, Mr Prescott had chaired a meeting himself. But the real miracles had been wrought by someone else, someone greater than all of us: 'I would like to praise the efforts of the Prime Minister himself, who was in telephone contact with the other world leaders to secure the final deal.' When it came to averting imminent disaster, even Superman only used a phone booth to change in!

As he rushed to the earth's rescue, Mr Prescott's words came faster than a speeding bullet. The words tumbled out at warp speed. 'Greenhouse grasses' (this may have referred to the police using informers to solve thefts from garden centres); 'so this measure not seen as loopholes'; 'looking at the consequences of being living'; 'Europe had a principle of bubble which allowed for a differentiation within the bubble.'

At one point he said, 'One cannot say too much!' But he himself has the opposite problem. He cannot say enough. The words sheer away like slabs from a melting iceberg.

Using a tape recording, I tried to count the number of words in each sentence, though these figures are necessarily approximate. Some 63 on projected cuts. Then 76 on international co-operation. At least 130 on verification, and a truly astounding 240 on British targets versus legal obligations.

Only Teresa Gorman dared break the mood of anxiety. She pointed out that recent measurements by NASA indicate that there has been no overall increase in global temperatures over the past decade. But nobody takes Teresa seriously, so that didn't matter.

17.12.97

One of my favourite monthly sessions is agriculture questions, taken by whichever department is in charge of the countryside this week. The first New Labour agriculture minister was Jack Cunningham.

You can tell how much the countryside has changed if you attend questions to the Ministry of Agriculture, Fisheries and Food. *Cider with Rosie* it isn't. For one thing, the jargon is almost impenetrable. At one point a Lib Dem MP asked Jack Cunningham about 'modulation'. His jaw jutted out. 'I have made my position *abundantly clear* about modulation,' he said. 'I am opposed to modulation!'

My mind drifted, as it so often does at these times, and I began to wonder how the old rural idylls, those autobiographies that recall a less complicated age, would be rewritten in today's bucolic idioms.

'I was born on ungrazed, native-species-rich grassland on one of England's 32 nitrate-sensitive areas. As I lie abed now, in the silent heart of the city, my mind's ear still harkens to the roar of the combine harvester, the explosion of the electronic bird-scarer, and the haunting whoosh of the cattle feed mill, mashing up another diseased sheep as the cycle of life was repeated once again.

'On a winter morning, we children would tumble downstairs, where Mother was already up and about, stirring a great vat of Ready-Brek, that simple but nutritious food, which sustained generations of country folk. "There baint be no Specified Risk Materials in this here," she would say, a twinkle in her eye. "It's all the goodness of Permitted Additives as outlined in the European Convention," though that meant little to us as we wolfed down the white and creamy puddle in our bowls.

'If we were lucky, Father would return before we left for school, stamping the snow from his boots. "Have you been milking the herd, Father?" we would ask, and he would chuckle, "Dearie me no, my darlings, I've been up at Post Office, mailing my application for Enhanced Suckler Cow Repayments!"

'On Boxing Day the squire would pay us a visit, and would press a crisp green piece of paper into my palm. "What is this, sir?" I would ask, with the wide-eyed naivety of childhood.

' "Why, 'tis a green pound, child!" he replied, smiling.

' "Can I use it to buy sherbet dabs in Mistress Cunningham's shop?"

' "God bless the child," said the squire. "No, green pound is the common name for the agricultural special exchange rate that converts EU Common Agricultural Policy support prices and payments from ECUs into sterling, so you might be able to buy some non-existent olive oil from non-existent Italian olive groves, if you be lucky!"

'They were happy days. Incomprehensible, but happy.'

23.01.98

Tories and sketch-writers alike soon realized that they had a plump, almost stationary target in the Lord Chancellor, Derry Irvine. Surrounded for decades by the obsequiousness that characterizes the law in this country, he arrived poorly prepared for the aggression shown by a select committee of MPs. Nominally they wanted to ask him about constitutional matters; in fact they couldn't wait to get on to the hugely expensive redecoration of his flat in the House of Lords.

Lord Irvine might have adopted the approach humorous, with a few self-deprecating jokes about his £650,000 redecoration. He could have turned up to the public administration committee in white overalls and paint-spattered shoes, carrying an old radio smeared with putty. They'd have loved him.

Instead he took the approach pompous. He had not merely been right to demand his refurbishments; he was working 'in a noble cause', like extending the franchise, or defeating Hitler. 'Future generations will be grateful,' he intoned. (Of course future generations are grateful when we spend our money on them. Sod 'em, is what I say. Let them buy their own £8,000 beds.)

The Lord Chancellor does not so much answer a question as unroll a speech, as if it were precious hand-blocked wallpaper. Nothing is ever so humble as to be merely 'true', but instead 'is the case, across the board, as it were, for all manner of reasons'. He never does anything so mundane as to agree with someone. Instead he examines himself and declares, 'I find myself hospitable to the idea.' Unlike us mortals, he cannot just say yes, but instead informs us: 'Right or wrong, that is the view I took. Other views could, however, be expressed.'

He treated the committee as if they were all junior barristers. Or rather, he spoke to them as if he were the grandest of grand QCs, up before a particularly young and callow judge who might be expected to quail before his admonitions.

'That is a speech, not a question!' he snapped at one whipper-snapper, who just happened to be an elected Member of Parliament. He instructed them to pause for his answers. The more he was attacked, the more blameless he appeared, in his own eyes, at least.

Andrew Tyrie, a Tory MP, asked about the letter the Lord Chancellor had written to Black Rod, explaining that he and Lady Irvine were great connoisseurs and how important it was that great works of art should be shipped to decorate their quarters *instanter*. Had this proved embarrassing?

Embarrassing? What a bizarre concept! A pigeon defecating on his wig, perhaps. That might be embarrassing. But not suggesting the expenditure of huge sums of money upon his official residence. What could be embarrassing about that?

'I was not even setting out an argument. I was setting out the facts, the pros and the cons, as dispassionately as I could... Future generations will agree, and will see this as a storm in a teacup,' he vouchsafed (the style is catching). He could well be right. Peter Mandelson may be sitting in a sperm bank now, canvassing the views of future generations.

Mr Tyrie persisted. Was it not an embarrassment to his party? Heaven forfend. 'I think that people up and down the country believe this has been blown grotesquely out of proportion.'

Mr Tyrie wondered whether his attitude amounted to 'Je ne regrette rien'. Once Lord Irvine had untangled the accent (eleventh-century Norman French is the only dialect Lord Chancellors are allowed to understand), he affirmed: 'I do not think that my apologies are due. I read the commentators who say, 'Three cheers that this work has been done! And three cheers for the committee that chose to make the decision!"'

Suddenly we had a picture of a nation rejoicing. It was like VE Day. There would be school holidays to celebrate the pasting of the last roll on the wall. Marchers would descend upon London, demanding the right to go fox-hunting and for hand-sewn tapestries to line Lord Irvine's bedroom.

But though the Lord Chancellor is as pompous as it is possible for a man to be without actually bursting, he may have a point. When Pugin did the interior decoration of the Palace, he insisted on standards that today cost £4 million to maintain. Either you keep it up as it is, or you go for chipboard and Formica. As Lord Irvine said, 'You are not talking about something down at the DIY store,' though to our delight it turned out that he had never even heard of B&Q. I suspect that the Lord Chancellor has T'ang Dynasty hand-blocked wallpaper in his potting shed.

04.03.98

In the spring of 1998, Tony Blair went to visit the Assemblée Nationale in Paris.

Our prime minister walked informally up the path to the assembly building. A military band, clearly unbriefed in the nuances of Cool Britannia, played 'Land of Hope and Glory'. In

Mr Blair's new 'real entente' they would be replaced by Blur.

His arrival has been big news in Paris, and scuffles broke out between the local press and British photographers jostling for position. It must be strange, wherever you go in public, to find your route lined by men hitting each other.

'You are in Paris, ici, not in Zimbabwe,' yelled one French reporter. 'Azz'ole, azz'ole!'

We trooped into the Chamber, which is a magnificent confection of gold and tapestries and murals and bas-reliefs and statues and enough marble to denude every quarry in Italy – in short, it would make a perfect pied-à-terre for Lord Irvine. Watch for it in the April issue of *Better Chancelleries and Gardens*.

M. Fabius, the President of the Assembly, introduced Mr Blair. We wondered whether he would use his famous verbal twiddles, saying, 'Vous savez,' and 'I mean, guys, voyez!' but apart from a single 'alors', he spoke with a clarity and directness he seems to find hard at home.

He told little jokes. French politicians do not go in for jokes, any more than ours wave pigs' bladders. Jokes are not part of the act. So his jokes were welcome. He invoked Winston Churchill, who famously spoke French like a walrus with a speech impediment, perhaps deliberately. In those days Conservatives thought that having a proper French accent was a sign of moral turpitude, possibly homosexuality.

'Je vais vous parler en français,' said Mr Blair. 'Courage!' They laughed and applauded, because his French is good. You may hear more of the elocution teacher than the streets, but it's about ten times better than that of any previous British leader.

He said that he had worked in a Parisian bar. It was a strict rule that all tips were put into a common pot. After a while, he realized that he was the only waiter who was actually doing this. 'It was my first lesson in applied socialism.'

The Right, who actually do sit on the right of the room, according to revolutionary tradition, and who had turned out in fewer numbers than the Left, suddenly discovered that this was quite possibly the funniest thing they had ever heard in their lives. By the time he had predicted the line-up in the World Cup final *('Angleterre contre Ecosse')* they were cheering and whooping like Texans at a rodeo.

From then on it was competitive clapping between the two sides. When he got to the passage attacking dogma and said that what counted was not whether an economy was left or right, but whether it worked, the Right's cheers were aimed at the Left. 'Gauchiste? Huh, he's one of ours!' they were saying.

Then he got on to the Social Exclusion Unit and the Left decided they could join in. Next we were back with the spirit of small business enterprise, and the Right had nudged ahead once more. But hold on! 'We must recognize the unions' – the Left was back in the lead. 'We must be flexible' – code in French for 'We must sack lots of people' and the Right was on track once more. By now they were willing to applaud anything, if only to attract some of that magical popularity for themselves. Even 'Vive la subsidiarité!' possibly the most boring battle-cry ever cried, brought applause.

I think he ought to speak in French all the time. The voters would get used to it, since few of them actually listen to the words, and it sounds so much better.

25.03.98

Year One

There was something peculiarly nauseating about Prime Minister's Questions, as ambitious backbenchers lined up to praise their leader.

The Beaker Folk were hunters who lived in the Bronze Age, around 1600 BC. They are named after the tall pottery cups found in their graves. Possibly, like New Labour beakers, they were adorned with slogans of the day: 'Tough on Mammoths, Tough on the Causes of Mammoths', perhaps.

The Bleeper Folk now live among us. They are Labour MPs. They rely on their bleepers to tell them what they should think. No doubt many will be buried with them. Otherwise, how would they know what to think in the afterlife? The other day I had lunch with a Labour MP. 'Bleep, bleep' went his bleeper. He pulled it out and showed me the message: 'Members are reminded not to take part in newspaper or television surveys, polls or questionnaires. These are often damaging to the party.' There was no reason why this admonition should have been sent to him at lunchtime; it was merely a reminder that at no time at all are Labour MPs permitted to have any views of their own.

When they sit in the Commons Chamber, the bleeper people are obliged to make their bleepers silent. Instead they have them in vibrate mode. This means they can receive a stream of messages from Millbank Tower, until the time when the party finds a way of injecting instructions directly into their brains.

Martin Bell, the independent MP for Tatton, raised the point yesterday. Would Labour MPs have a free vote on the predatory pricing of newspapers? 'Disregarding their pagers for a while,' Mr Bell said, to happy laughter, 'they could enjoy a vibrant democracy instead of a vibrating one.'

It was Mr Blair's birthday yesterday and the bleeper folk had brought him lots of presents. It was also local elections day, and the bleepers had brought instructions to ask sycophantic questions about Labour councils. David Crausby of Bolton was outraged that Tory councils were not passing on education funds. Ian Pearson of Dudley listed 'three incontrovertible facts about education spending in Dudley'. By coincidence Mr Blair had all the figures to prove these incontrovertible facts. The bleeper makes every man a master of his brief.

Anne Campbell of Cambridge had warm words for Cambridge's Labour council. Someone from South Tyneside felt an urgent need, an overwhelming passion, to put on the record the fact that South Tyneside had a Labour council which, through its wisdom, efficiency and promotion of human happiness, rivalled ancient Athens. He demanded an apology from Paddy Ashdown, the Lib Dem leader, who, 'on a visit to South Tyneside, openly criticized the leader of South Tyneside council!'

For some reason, this outrageous example of lèse majesté merely raised titters rather than horror.

It was quite the most sickening sycophancy we have suffered since Labour came to power. Just as I reached retching point, Gordon Prentice stood up. Not him, surely not! He of all people could not join the Choir Obsequious. He didn't. He only wished to say that he planned to meet local dentists to discuss the politics of dentistry.

But even there, his bleeper will tell him exactly what to say: 'Vote Lay-burr for a be'er Bri'nn, and for a gummunt wiv teef!'

07.05.98

The British intervention in Sierra Leone created a great deal of controversy.

Sir John Kerr, the permanent secretary at the Foreign Office, is someone who would make the grandest grandee look like a tea-boy. Yesterday he gave evidence to the foreign affairs committee about the Sierra Leone crisis. It was not an unmitigated triumph.

(In the crisis, the government claims that it did not knowingly break a UN resolution against the export of arms, but that if it did it was all in a good cause, but if it wasn't a good cause, the arms arrived only after the fighting had ended. Got that?)

Normally when someone as astute as Sir John appears before any committee of MPs, it's like the Napoleon of Crime being interviewed by a rural constable.

('Thang 'ee, thang 'ee fur cummin' into the station, zurr.'

'It's entirely my pleasure, you silly little man.')

This time they gave him a rougher ride. You can tell when a grandee is in trouble because he resorts to British, a language that is different from, yet eerily similar to, English. It uses much of the same vocabulary and many of the same grammatical structures. Except that in English you might say, 'I don't know,' whereas if you were speaking British, like Sir John yesterday, you would say, 'Once again, you are probing the depths of my ignorance.'

David Heath MP quoted Sir John back at himself. He had said about the first allegations of British complicity, 'The situation was well short of counter-allegation,' which a glance at my English-British dictionary suggests means 'true'.

Sir Peter Emery wanted to know why a minister, Tony Lloyd, had been fully briefed on the situation, but when asked about a newspaper article that covered the same ground had told the Commons that it was 'ill-informed and scurrilous'. How so?

'I really don't want to be drawn into a choice of adjectives,' said Sir John, smiling his secret little smile, 'but I would say that in the Foreign Office, "ill-informed and scurrilous" was a pretty mild form of debate.'

I thought Sir Peter might pop. You'd have imagined that Sir John had suggested that 'Well, shag me three times sideways' was a suitable form of address to a foreign plenipotentiary. 'That was *not* the case when I served in the Foreign Office,' he said.

Sir John smoothly moved into the Grandees' Defence, which is that there is an awful lot of paper around the place and nobody can be expected to read it. If it were all kept, 'You would not be able to get into my office for paper.' Much of the *stuff* was handled at low level and did not make its way up. He hoisted an arm to help any members who might have been unclear in which direction 'up' could be found.

'You are obfuscating!' shouted Sir Peter, using the British term for 'talking rubbish'.

Sir John ended a masterpiece of obfuscation in his own tongue with a final extract from *Brewer's Dictionary of British Phrase and Fable:* 'You are tempting me into dangerous territory here.' This is British for 'You don't seriously expect me to answer that, do you, you silly little man!'

15.05.98

Robin Cook, who was Foreign Secretary at the time, never really got on with the highest and mightiest of the Foreign Office. Derek Fatchett, a minister of state, was by contrast very well liked. He died suddenly, at the height of the Serbian crisis. I cannot possibly say which Foreign Office personage said at his funeral in Leeds, 'It's like the bombing of the Chinese Embassy. Right idea, wrong target.' Mr Cook's embarrassment was the source of much satisfaction to one of his colleagues.

Considering what a wonderful fortnight he has enjoyed, Gordon Brown looked rather glum. But then he usually does. Most people would be delighted to see their enemies laid waste, destroyed, riven, their political careers salted over so that nothing can ever grow there again. And it has been a dreadful week for Robin Cook, Gordon Brown's old rival. Theirs is an enmity that makes Celtic and Rangers look like Tristan and Isolde. What is its cause? Nobody seems to know, not even the two antagonists.

It appears to go back into some dark, mist-shrouded, Caledonian past. Some say it is due to Mr Cook's belief that, as the older man, he should occupy the senior post. Mr Brown was a humble canvasser for Mr Cook when first they met.

Others allege that Mr Cook was once thunderously rude to Mr Brown and has never been forgiven. There are those who suggest that it is connected with the great devolution debates of the 1970s when the two men were on different sides. This sounds improbable since theirs is a feud that transcends mere political disagreement.

One version has it that when Mr Cook relinquished the post of secretary of the Scottish Young Socialists, Mr Brown hoped to succeed him and asked for his endorsement. Mr Cook said he was willing to wish him good luck, but would not make a public statement on his behalf. This sounds more like it. We are all very sensitive in our student years.

Now and again a mutual friend or acquaintance will arrange a meeting and try to patch things up. Frequently one of them doesn't appear. Or if they do shake hands, then they are spitting nails about each other minutes after the meeting is over.

Recently Mr Brown has been offering public sympathy to Mr Cook in his travails. But in the meantime his satraps and envoys have been busy pleading with journalists not to print anything about the Chancellor, since this would use up valuable newsprint that might otherwise be devoted to the Foreign Secretary's failures.

Of course Mr Brown could not say any of this at Treasury questions yesterday. But he did have the joy of a Tory split on Europe.

'The Conservative Party is in complete disarray,' he chortled, or rather came as near to chortling as Mr Brown ever does. It was a sort of chuckling scowl. You could say that he *chowled* the words out. All that was needed was for Peter Lilley, his Tory opposite number, to make a fool of himself, and this he duly did. I have often compared Mr Lilley to Niles Crane, the precious brother in the hit sitcom, *Frasier*.

Apparently Mr Lilley never sees the programme. So why does he sound more like Niles every day?

'Every time he [Mr Brown] goes off into auto-rant, he alienates thousands of people who listen to these exchanges,' said Mr Lilley in a mimsy, Niles kind of voice, to the loud laughter of the studio audience – sorry, his fellow MPs.

He wondered aloud why Mr Brown seemed well disposed to the euro but unwilling to rejoin the exchange rate mechanism. 'Isn't it like being willing to paddle in the shallow end while being ready to throw the pound into the deep end? [Loud laughter, mostly unkind.] And I will have large mocha frappé, thank you Frasier!' (I made the last bit up, but you get the idea.)

22.05.98

By the end of June 1998, the opening of the Millennium Dome was getting alarmingly close. The minister in charge at this stage was Peter Mandelson.

Yesterday Peter Mandelson was attacked, as usual, over the contents of the Millennium Dome. How, asked Tim Loughton, a Tory from Worthing, could anyone enjoy contemplation in the Spirit Zone, with the roar of the Blackwall Tunnel underneath, a circus nearby 'and not a crucifix in sight'?

Mr Mandelson said solemnly that there would be, somewhere in the Dome, a place for private prayer. (Though if it's like other theme park attractions, the queues will be endless, with signs saying, 'At this point you are ninety minutes away from the Lost Orison Experience.') Mr Mandelson added, 'Churches are setting up many events, centred on Pentecost 2000.'

Pentecost 2000! It's a perfect New Labour name, being pure PR-babble and also quite inaccurate, since Pentecost happened thirty years after the birth of Christ. (Though of course 'Pentecost 1970' wouldn't work, since it would make everyone think of flared trousers and Sweet records, and the time when Michael Fabricant was one of the top disc jockeys in the Brighton and Hove area, appearing as Mickey Fabb.)

You could rename all the events in the Christian calendar. Christmas would become Nativity Year Zero. Good Friday would be the Hanging On In There '33 Tour, and Casting the Money-Lenders from the Temple would be entirely rethemed and launched as In Partnership with the Business Community.

Mr Peter Ainsworth is a man of whom I had not heard before. He has a magnificent head of hair, like a female American TV newsreader, and surprisingly he appears to be the member of the shadow cabinet concerned with culture, media and sport. He complained about the lack of government support for seaside towns. Indeed such places were suffering from tremendous over-regulation. 'Far from receiving a Kiss-Me-Quick hat, any minister visiting the seaside this summer is likely to be told exactly where he can stick his rock!'

I wondered briefly what Harold Macmillan would have made of Mr Ainsworth. I suspect he would have told his gardener to spray him with something.

30.06.98

The Princess Diana Memorial Bill was rushed through the Commons yesterday. It wasn't called that. Its technical title is the Landmines Bill. The Princess hovered over the debate – not the real woman, of course, but the Sainted One who appears on the limited edition, fine bisque porcelain commemoration plate designed by noted award-winning artist Magnus Shagbladder, a lifetime heirloom available in five easy instalments.

Robin Cook opened the debate, speaking in a manner suitable for Rouge Dragon Pursuivant: 'Her Majesty has placed her royal prerogative at the command of Parliament for the purposes of the bill,' he said or, rather, intoned.

He faced a sprinkling of Tory members. Many of them had been all in favour of landmines until a few short years ago. 'Look at that British craftsmanship,' they would say. 'You don't see filigree brasswork like that on a pressure-sensitive detonator any more.'

Michael Howard, the shadow foreign secretary, replied. It was disgraceful, he said, that the government had not made more time for debate. He wished to place on record his disgust... This would have had greater effect if there had been more than three Tory backbenchers listening to him. Labour, who had several dozen, chanted 'Three! Three!' sounding like starlings at dusk.

'If they think that numbers are the correct way to judge scrutiny,' said Mr Howard, 'then they have a lot to learn about scrutiny,' so rather missing the point, since if you want scrutiny, you have to have people around to do the scrutinizing. For some of the debate there were no backbench Tories at all.

Mr John Reid, a defence minister, appeared to insist on Clause 5 of the bill, which makes it legal for British soldiers to be associated with landmines, provided they're being laid abroad, and provided they are being laid by our allies, i.e. the Americans. However, a British soldier might build a bridge, which would then be crossed by an American truck loaded with landmines. He could in theory face fourteen years in jail.

Mr Reid lurched forward on the Despatch Box, his head weaving from side to side, like a paratrooper halfway through his weekend leave. You really wouldn't want to mess with him. 'We can't send men into battle,' said the veteran of a thousand vicious battles in the Scottish Labour Party, 'with a rifle in one hand and *Archbold's Criminal Pleading* in the other.'

True. But the effect was that some landmines are all right, sometimes. I wondered what the Princess would make of the debate as she watched it from that Great Paperweight in the Sky.

11.07.98

I had an important appointment yesterday. I missed it – I'd made the mistake of taking a privatized train – but at least I was in time to catch John Prescott say that if present trends continue, we will soon need 'a motorway 150 lanes wide between here and Leeds'. He was speaking in London.

This is an example he has used before, though over the months the number of lanes needed has risen from 100. Assuming a three-second gap between vehicles and an average of two people in each car, this would permit the entire population of Leeds to reach London in just four hours, and allow everyone in London to move to Leeds in just under two days.

It's a classic example of politicians' hyperbole, being both inaccurate and meaningless. You might just as easily say that, since the temperature yesterday was 20 degrees higher than it was on 1 January, 'If present trends continue, the temperature will reach 49 centigrade in December, and we'll all die of heatstroke.'

The Tories had decided to barrack Mr Prescott, which was a mistake. It's like hooking Frankenstein's monster up to the lightning conductor: every jolt renews his energy and aggression. 'Bus passengers have fallen!' he cried. (They certainly have on our route. Since modern drivers have no idea of clutch control, every time the bus starts three pensioners collapse on the floor.) 'Car drivers sit in congestion for hours!' he yelled. 'In their Jags!' shouted the Tories, referring to the Environment Secretary's official limo and his private runabout.

He wanted better training for bus drivers. 'The one I met yesterday could benefit from a visit to charm school – perhaps the one I attended,' he said, puzzlingly. Perhaps he didn't realize; you're not supposed to take your Jag *on* the bus. And when he declared, 'Let no one say we are not putting our money where our mouth is!' they rolled round in ersatz laughter, because they know that what we really need is an Integrated Syntax Policy for John Prescott.

Listeners to the Deputy Prime Minister need to be assured that once a noun has arrived, a verb will be available very soon afterwards. They are fed up with words that are too short for rush-hour demand – and it is always rush hour in a Prescott speech – so that priority becomes 'prity', ownership is 'o'ship', and his attempts to pronounce 'hypothecation' make him sound in the grip of an asthma attack.

It is infuriating to have to wait for one pronoun, then have a convoy of four all pull up in the same place in the same sentence. One thing is for sure: privatization (or 'prizun' as Mr Prescott calls it) cannot be the answer. The Treasury couldn't afford the subsidy.

21.07.98

The long summer was followed by the long party conferences. The Liberal Democrats always come first.

Britain's trendiest think-tank, Demos, held a fringe meeting at the Lib Dem conference yesterday. Demos are the people who are always telling us to strip away our boring old traditions, to 'remake and rediscover our national identity'. I take this to mean euthanasia for Beefeaters. Here is an actual and typical Demos research work: 'Freedom's Children. Drawing on extensive new data from the British Household Panel Study and the MORI Socioconsult, this report details the lifestyle and values of the 18–34 generation.' Mmm, great beach reading! I can see the suntan oil on the pages already!

I had hoped to encounter one of Demos's most famous members, a person who goes by the name of 'Perri 6'. Mr 6 is the author of a number of works, including 'Holistic

Government', whatever that might be (does it mean government by crystals and aromatherapy?), and 'Restricting the freedom of choice of charities' – about time too, Demos people no doubt say. Sadly there was no sign of Mr 6 on the platform. Perhaps he exists in virtual reality, as in '6, Lies and Videotape'. Or maybe his number is up.

The debate was titled 'The Third Way and Beyond'. It's a measure of the audience's sophistication that when Ian Hargreaves, the chairman, announced this, they groaned. He recovered lost ground by telling jokes. 'What is President Clinton's third way? It's when you have sex with someone, but they don't have sex with you.' There was much talk of 'social democracy and neo-liberalism', 'the Rhineland model', 'the Swedish Third Way', which sounded fun, and something Baroness Nicholson called, 'La Troisième Force'. There was no mention of 'La Troisième Reich'.

The Baroness is a good speaker, but she has an alarming use of metaphor. 'The Third Way is not just a blob of cream on a Christmas cake which has been stuffed with all kinds of things that we cannot digest and which will be unpalatable to a modern electorate…and I have a massive example up my mental sleeve if anyone doubts me.'

I had a vision of future Lib Dem conferences at which we would debate the Nineteenth Way with Perri's grandson, Darren 27. It was time to slope off for lunch.

23.09.98

The first Labour conference session yesterday was closed to the public, though I turned on the TV feed anyway. You could see the hall, but all you could hear was a bored technician somewhere, repeating over and over again, 'I have been asked to say "This is the BBC control room, identifying conference sound." ' A few minutes later he said it in Robin Day's voice. Then he did the gormless people from Monty Python: 'Diss. Ish. Durr. BBC. Control. Wooomb!' Then he did an excellent John Cole.

An hour later we got a brilliant Tony Blair impression. So it took me a while to realize that this was the real thing. Like many politicians who are insecure in their style, he has begun to copy his imitators. The long legs (he is much taller than you think if you've only seen him on television) march forward to the front of the stage, then back again, like Michael Flatley in slow motion. He is beginning to sound like Margaret Thatcher, though with 1960s diction and a mid-Atlantic vocabulary. He never meets a man, but always a 'guy'. The conversational tone is 'aw shucks' and self-deprecatory. He had, he told us, been made overconfident by the success of his speech at the French National Assembly. Afterwards, he said, 'Ah got me French muddled up and said, "I desire Lionel Jospin." '

The line 'No backing down. Backbone, not backdown, is what Britain needs' must surely have deliberately echoed 'The lady's not for turning.' He is becoming a cross between smiley, cuddly, toothy Richard Branson and Miss Whiplash.

Most of all, the verbs disappear. The number of verb-free sentences rises every year. Yesterday there were 112 syntactical orphans in the speech. Verbs are cut down like earthworms under a lawn strimmer.

As my old English teacher used to tell us, a verb is a doing word. Leaving verbs in your sentences implies a promise of action or a record of achievement past. But no verbs, so no pledges. Instead, fuzzy, well-meaning word pictures. New investment. Holding firm. Modernization. Reform. The best in the world.

These sentences tell us nothing. They are the equivalent of the copy in ads for expensive cars: 'Luxury. Prestige. Performance. A promise of the future, with you in control.' There is no commitment, nothing concrete, nothing to attack or to demand. Instead we are offered a vague evocation of a better world, as if the fantasy were the reality – a trip to Utopia without a map.

After the speech, Alastair Campbell, the Prime Minister's press secretary, stopped by our part of the media room to tell us that it had been a 'self-spinning speech'. What a technological triumph that is, along with the self-cleaning oven and the self-basting turkey! What he meant, I suppose, is that it was written in terms so simple even mere voters would be able to understand it, and did not need to rely on hacks to interpret it as 'Blair's triumph' or 'My pledge to our children – by Tony'.

Afterwards I eavesdropped on the delegates, many of whom seemed genuinely moved. 'Wonderful' and 'truly uplifting' were among the remarks I heard. And indeed it was uplifting, in the same sense as a Wonderbra, creating a marvellous appearance with the minimum of raw material.

30.09.98

The Conservatives always end the conference season.

The Tory conference found a new heroine yesterday. She is a replacement for the disgraced Michael Heseltine, whose face has already been airbrushed out of the official histories.

If Heseltine could always find the party's clitoris, Ann Widdecombe gives the party a big stinging smack on its plump red rump. They adored it. But first, we were captivated by the stage set. This includes, to one side of the platform, eight informal Ikea chairs in different colours. In a magnificently snobbish remark, Heseltine was once accused by the chief whip of being 'the kind of man who buys his own furniture'. The Tories have now descended to being the kind of people who assemble their own furniture.

The effect is to make the platform party look very ill-at-ease, as if an officers' selection board had to meet in a suburban sitting room, or as if they'd all turned up to what they thought was a Tupperware party and the hostess had suddenly offered them split-crotch panties and vibrators.

Behind them is the conference slogan: 'Listening. Learning. Leading.' Speakers repeat this mantra at intervals. The MC introduced a video about listening. 'So whenever you see that video, you'll know we've got our ears cocked!' (Unlike the last Tory government, who had their cocks earmarked, by the press at least.)

Listening. Learning. Leading. As it went on, the mind began to spin. 'Shaving. Showering. Shampooing.' By mid-morning the conference was getting distinctly torpid. 'Drooping. Dozing. Dying.'

Then suddenly Ann Widdecombe was before them. She was magnificent. It was electrifying. She had learned her speech off by heart, so she needed no autocue and could stalk about the stage, her arms flopping up and down maniacally, like a drowning porpoise, if such a thing could exist. Hattie Jacques had become one flesh with Rosa Klebb.

And what flesh! Like my late great-aunts, Ms Widdecombe does not have breasts, but one single, unicameral bosom, as vast and lavishly upholstered as any Ikea armchair. The hands swerved wildly from side to side. Hectoring. Haranguing. Harassing. The wagging finger waved and, having waved, wagged on.

And the voice – the voice ran out of control and peaked alarmingly like feedback from a microphone. 'Just because…' she squeaked, then 'just because…' and she soared into an unwonted falsetto, as if she were about to begin some dreadful Andrew Lloyd Webber song, backed by a hundred dancers, all dressed like William Hague. Now and again she got carried away and said things that made no sense at all: 'And other things have been banned, including varicose veins!' She was cheered dementedly. 'Every time you provide for your own health care, you are freeing up the NHS to provide for someone else's health,' she cried, and the delegates applauded themselves frantically for queue-jumping.

She spoke of the hospital matron. 'She was a dragon and she was a champion. We want her back!' You could feel the sexual frisson charge around the hall, goosing the patients as it ran. Matron! Bed baths! Traction! Catheters! They cheered and shouted and whistled and yelled. With friends like these, who needs enemas?

Finally, spent but happy, the delegates trooped off to the innumerable receptions where they could eat free food and drink free wine, while skulking in the corner and ogling any woman under the age of sixty. Ligging. Lurking. Lusting.

07.10.98

One of the great Tory conference traditions is the arrival of former leaders on the platform, to be cheered or ignored, as the case may be.

The Prime Minister who gave away our national sovereignty to Europe sat on the platform yesterday. Ted Heath was a safe ten feet behind her. Margaret Thatcher sat serene and poised, receiving plaudits from speaker after speaker, who have each remembered her triumphs and forgotten the disasters. Ted Heath sat at the back, scowling and sinking as deep into those nasty Ikea armchairs as it is possible to go. I was put in mind of one of those beached whales who turn up at seasides now and again. You half expected Greenpeace to send a crane to pick him up, load him onto a boat and offer him a hearty lunch of plankton. Speakers would say the kind of weird, dysfunctional things people say at Tory conferences, and his arms would stay still, draped along the sides of the chair.

'We say no to Labour's nannying attitude to British beef and the meat-eating public!' someone said. The conference whistled and cheered. Ted sat still. Even his eyes were motionless. Like the stranded whale, he is in a wholly alien environment.

The speakers attacked Europe. Some imperceptible muscular movement caused the expression on his face to register faintly more distress and contempt than it had before. 'How ebsolutely splindid it is to si Margaret Thetcher and Tid Heath on the plitform,' said Michael Howard. This compliment to himself was greeted by Sir Edward with what, for him, amounts to wild applause: that is to say, he placed his palms together twice, very slowly indeed.

'We votid overwhilmingly to support William Hague's policy on the single currincy,' said Mr Howard. Lady Thatcher applauded. Mr Hague tried to look stern and resolute. In a frantic burst of activity, Ted turned his head three degrees to the right. For some reason I formed an image of Lady Bracknell taken hostage in Beirut, determined to give no satisfaction to her captors.

'Tin years ago, Margrit Thatcher lifted our eyes...' said Mr Howard. Liddy Thatcher's own eyes, always gleaming madly, seemed lit from within by a phosphorescent glow. Sir Edward's eyes widened sceptically by a millimetre, which, for him, is the equivalent of leading 10,000 people on a protest march to Downing Street. The speech ended and the conference rose for a standing ovation. Faced with the prospect of being the only person seated in the hall, Ted was obliged to stand, which he did with unwilling yet stoical lethargy, in the meantime flapping his hands together like two dying flounders twitching on the dockside.

At that point, Michael Ancram, the new party chairman, started to execute a curious little dance, a sort of stately onstage gavotte, which puzzled me until I worked out that he was trying to steer Lady Thatcher out to the exit while simultaneously blocking Sir Edward's progress, so they wouldn't have to be in proximity to each other for even a few seconds. He did this with such success that I half expected him to sweep off a tricorne hat and bow in triumph.

Soon afterwards John Redwood made his annual rabble-soothing speech. It must be hard to fail at a Tory conference by making an attack on Peter Mandelson, but the shadow trade secretary managed it. The biggest laugh, evoking a sort of ghastly rattle like a rat trapped in a dustbin, came for this line: 'For Peter Mandelson, Dome is where the heart is.' It got the biggest laugh because it was the best joke, and that tells you all you need to know.

08.10.98

The committee on culture, media and sport met yesterday to consider the timing of the ITN News. I don't know why they bother. This session has become a sort of horrible, aggressive chat show from hell. It could be entitled 'Gerald Kaufman – Who

Else?' Almost no one else gets a look-in. Mr Kaufman, as chairman, asks a series of questions in a low, menacing tone. Since his victims have to strain to catch his assaults, they must feel even more uneasy than before. They are then allowed to respond, briefly, before Mr Kaufman returns to the attack, firing off statistics, tripping them up with their own words, triumphantly seizing apparent contradictions in their arguments.

It was hypnotically boring. One longed for Oliver Reed to appear, waving a half-empty whisky bottle. Or a stuffed emu to attack the chairman. Or anything at all to break the monotony. Why should the nation be so appalled by the prospect of ITN bulletins being put back an hour? Apparently Tony Blair is opposed to the idea. Tony Blair? Here is a man who is merrily ripping up half the British constitution, who regards the fact that something has lasted for hundreds of years as an excellent reason to abolish it, but who treats *News at Ten* as if it had more majestic permanence than the royal family, Magna Carta and Stonehenge.

The hapless ITV executives yesterday told Mr Kaufman that the changes they propose would actually increase viewing figures for the news. But they also admitted that the real reason for the change was to increase audience share. Apparently nearly a quarter of viewers switch off as soon as they hear the first *bong!* A later start would allow ITV to show longer films, interrupted by fewer commercials, as Channel 5 does.

But if you look at Channel 5 listings, they're all for films that sound familiar but which you've never quite heard of, such as *Terminal Vengeance*, *Total Weaponry*, *Lethal Action Force*, *Death Race Fury*, *Fatal Rage Revenge*, *Deadly Attraction*, *Co-Ed Frat Party*, *Dragon Slayer* and *Bunny Boiler III*. Or if it's not some grisly, straight-to-video movie, it's a grisly, cheap panel show such as *Hung out to Dry*, the wacky quiz based on dry cleaning in which panellists have to guess the mystery stain, or

Celebrity Hunt the Thimble, or *Up for it with the Stars*, in which you can win a night with someone who once appeared on *Big Brother*.

I did feel sorry for the executives. They kept saying piteously that they wanted viewers who would be attractive to advertisers – 'a new young metropolitan audience', as they put it, as if the only people who now watch Trevor McDonald are Eddie Grundy and a pair of sick piglets.

23.10.98

In October 1998, Ron Davies, the Welsh Secretary, resigned over what he called 'a moment of madness'. He had been walking on Clapham Common where he had encountered a Rastafarian who had invited him to his flat for a meal. Perhaps unwisely, Mr Davies accepted, and so set in train the series of events that obliged him to leave his job. As Linda Smith said later, 'You go for a walk, you think, "Gosh, I am a member of the Cabinet, and I'm about to become the first-ever Prime Minister of my homeland! Haven't I done well! On the other hand, I could murder a dish of rice and peas."'

There are three stages to a scandal. The first is shock. How could he be so stupid? Of course, people add, I had my suspicions, always wondered, something wrong with the cut of that man's jib. The second is regret – what a shame that an essentially good, hard-working person should be brought down by a single, tragic error.

The third stage is jokes. As someone said after Mr Davies's convoluted confession, in which he explained roughly what had happened but not why it should have caused him to resign, 'That's Tony's new policy: tough on crime, tough on the victims of crime.' Or as someone else said, 'That Rastafarian must have promised to take Ron to meet Elvis. Because if it wasn't sex, and it wasn't drugs, it must have been rock and roll.'

The Commons was packed for Mr Davies's personal statement. These can be thunderous parliamentary occasions: Sir Geoffrey Howe began the events that forced Margaret Thatcher out of office. Norman Lamont's farewell to John Major's administration – 'They are in office but not in power' – was almost as potent. And most MPs would find confessing to their colleagues a greater agony than telling the police, worse than informing the Prime Minister, harder even than facing one's wife.

Yet Mr Davies appeared cool, calm and relaxed when he arrived in the Chamber. A few members shook his hand, one gave him a glass of water, and he sat smiling, waiting for his turn.

We soon learned why. This wasn't a *mea culpa* so much as a whinge. He admitted making 'a severe error of judgement', but that's about all he did admit. Even that turned out to be less than met the eye. The error of judgement that he was admitting to was 'failing to protect my personal safety' (or as he might have put it, 'If I have a shortcoming, it is my reckless courage'). And he offered no reason at all why the fact that he had been 'the victim of a frightening and shocking crime' should have obliged him to resign from two jobs.

The incident itself having been covered thus, he could set about enlisting our pity. His week had been 'unremittingly agonizing…a nightmare'. It was, as ever, all the fault of the media, 'reporting as fact a stream of rubbish'.

This arbitrary abuse of power is not just an attack on me, but on all our rights,' he claimed, a line of argument that MPs usually find deeply appealing – as they did this time, cheering him at the end. Who would want to run for office, he asked, 'in the knowledge that one mistake may result in the whole of their lives being picked over and twisted?' The message was: your turn next. The statement then took on a surreal tinge: 'You can't allow powerful people to bully the weak,' he said, as if a member of the Cabinet and the future Prime Minister of Wales could be an enfeebled victim of oppression.

Yet there were darker hints, secrets that lay only half concealed within his words. 'We are what we are. We are all different, the product both of our genes and our experiences.' Was this him admitting he was gay? Later he said: 'This is not the first time I have been badly beaten and hurt.' Clearly he was hinting at something from his past, some dreadful formative experience which, years later, dragged him out into the wind and rain on Clapham Common.

03.11.98

Later, members of Mr Davies's family said that he had been badly treated by his father. His wife wrote a memoir, which, though bitter, provided a sad account of a gay man who was trapped by his office and by his desire for family life into pretending – as much to himself as to anyone else – that he was straight.

The Chancellor yesterday brought to the House what he called his pre-Budget report. In the past we had budgets roughly every twelve months. Now we can have them all year round, like Cadbury's Easter eggs. The Tories had billed their reply in advance as the great onslaught on the Labour government. Groggy, bleeding ministers would reel around the ring, their brains dislodged inside their skulls, pleading with the ref to stop the fight.

Unfortunately they gave the job to the shadow chancellor. Francis 'Mad Frankie' Maude would like to make the teeth rattle in your head. Instead he creates the impression of a peevish hamster.

As usual he began at a pitch of hysteria and proceeded to get more excited. The Chancellor was guilty of 'fantasy forecasting' and 'Peter Pan economics'. (Why does Peter Pan always get so much verbal from politicians? Would they prefer Captain Hook economics?) As the Chancellor gazed back at him with amiable condescension, Mr Maude's rage reached new and frenzied heights. 'He sits there! Grinning! And smiling! It is disgusting complacency!' Labour MPs laughed in his face. Fury always looks feebler than scorn.

Finally there was the inevitable metaphor. 'They are just moving the deckchairs on the *Titanic*. There is a £40 billion hole below the waterline of British business!

'They are painting nude portraits in the staterooms of industry while the ship of state sails inexorably towards the iceberg of the Chancellor's arrogance and indifference, and soon the economic revival will be just a stream of bubbles under the icy depths of the Atlantic as the Prime Minister, played by Kate Winslet in a fetching and surprisingly undamaged dress, struggles, weeping, to pull it to the surface.'

(I made the last paragraph up, but only to help Mr Maude. If we must have *Titanic* metaphors, why can't we have some new ones?)

He sat down to jeers from Labour, a self-satisfied little smile from the Chancellor and a sense of vague embarrassment from his colleagues. Mr Brown's reply was, as ever, anally retentive. Stability and prudence are his watchwords. The phrases, such as 'A government that is steering a stable course, prudently investing in our future', are repeated over and over, as if the more he says it, the more he will make it so.

As I listened I had a vision of young Gordon, aged eight, unbolting his piggy bank from the floor and counting his bawbees repeatedly, just to make sure they were all still there.

04.11.98

Austin Mitchell MP yesterday winkled out the month's most fascinating statistic so far. The member for Great Grimsby enquired what the effect of Viagra has been on the financial assets of the Church Commissioners. This is the body that runs the Church of England and is answerable to Parliament via one of their number, Stuart Bell, the Labour MP for Middlesbrough.

Mr Mitchell wanted to know how the commissioners' investment in shares of Pfizer, the company that makes Viagra, had improved their portfolio – or, as he put it, what has been the effect on the Church's standing?

According to Mr Bell, Viagra had made the Church £3 million richer over the course of three months. It would take an awful lot of cream teas and jumble sales to raise the same amount. I'm sure the source of this money won't trouble the Church at all. In fact, I could write the sermons now.

'You know, when we get married, we say that wonderful little phrase: "With my body, I thee worship." Well, as it happens, an awful lot of chaps find that with old age, and one thing or another, they're just not able to worship in the same way as they once did. It can be embarrassing. Imagine not being able to get your advent candle lit, or turning up at the Harvest Festival without your vegetable marrow? So at Holy Communion this week, instead of wafers, I'll be handing out little blue pills. As well as helping you in your day-to-day worship, you'll be supporting the splendid work of the Church...'

You could almost see MPs' brains spinning as they tried to top Mr Mitchell's little joke. But few ideas sprang to mind. Once you've done the one about 'the gang of hardened criminals' and asked what happens if you take Viagra and Prozac at the same time (if you don't get a fuck, you don't give a fuck) there's not much left. However, you could make a jolly arresting poster for the steeple restoration fund.

10.11.98

The Lord Chancellor continued to delight and amuse us all, at least all of us parliamentary sketch-writers. He occasionally deigned to appear before committees of MPs, in this case the one that considers home affairs.

As I waited for Lord Irvine to appear – he finally arrived with a cohort of no fewer than eight advisers – I gazed up at the massive group portrait on the wall of committee room no. 6. It shows Gladstone's Cabinet of 1868. Fifteen men, all superb in mutton-chop whiskers, several of them dukes. I wondered how many of them were gay.

'Pargiter, it says in the *Morning Chronicle* that I have been "outed". What in damnation does that mean?'

'It means, ahem, that Your Grace is not as other men are.'

'Of course I'm not. I'm a duke.'

The Lord Chancellor took his seat with infinite dignity. He was wearing a blue suit, a blue shirt and a blue tie, with a scarlet poppy to match his scarlet face. He looked cheerful. At least this time nobody was going to ask him about his wallpaper. He could leave that to the Master of the Rolls (who presumably is also charged with replenishing his official toilet).

The first topic was legal aid and how it can be more fairly dished out. He moved straight into management-speak. 'Our basic vision is of a network of quality providers, supported by co-ordinated funding delivery services,' he announced. Perhaps he is looking for a job at the BBC.

'Improved focus and co-ordination of funding…improved standards through achieving a more standard means of evaluating service quality…' On and on he went with this gobbledegook. Did his most famous predecessor, Saint Thomas More, ever talk like this? I suspect not.

The subtext, as ever, was money and how it can be saved without actually reducing lawyers' fees. 'Getting a reduction is not the point,' he announced, which I translated as 'The gravy train will continue to call at all Inns of Court.' He said that the cost of legal aid was now £16 million a year, which sounded barely enough to buy a case of decent claret for every lawyer who signs up.

Moments later, after a discreet cough from one of the multitudinous advisers, he came back. 'I may have inadvertently said £16 million a year. Of course the real figure is £1,600 millions.'

Phew! They can afford the odd bottle of champagne as well! Next we got on to the subject of his clothing and in particular his wig. 'It weighs a ton,' he said. He had nothing against wearing 'the full kit' on state occasions, 'but I feel that for male adults of sound mind, like myself, the days of breeches, tights and buckled shoes ought to go'. He wanted, he said, to be able to take part in debates 'free of my outer garments and my wig'.

A frisson ran round the room as members of the committee pondered the image of Lord Irvine, free of his outer garments.

Soon after that he announced that he had decided that applicants for high judicial office would not have to declare their sexuality. He said that until now there had been a question on the application form that was clearly designed to elicit this information.

It was curiously phrased. Applicants were asked: 'Is there anything in your private life which, if it were to become public, would be of possible embarrassment to the Lord Chancellor?'

But why to him personally? The correct answer might be: 'Yes, I met him once on Clapham Common and freed him of his outer garments...' Now, that would be embarrassing.

11.11.98

MPs these days use more and more jargon, stripping the magic away from so much of our lives.

Why do so few British roads have any romance? Nobody has ever written a song called 'I Get My Kicks on the A66'. The French have L'Autoroute de l'Est. US 1 may be the most beautiful road in the world, seeming to fly over cliff tops, past the sun-soaked spray of the Californian coast. On I 95, you can crash into a moose near the Canadian border and be mugged in the comfort of your car, 1,500 miles south in Miami, all on the same road.

Yesterday the Commons discussed the possible improvement of the A303. This is the road to my mother-in-law's house, so it obviously has a special significance for me ('I get my glee / On the A303'). But there is a resonance to this highway. Winterbourne Stoke, Long Sutton, Over Wallop, King's Somborne, Coombe Bisset, Sedgemoor. What could be more mellifluous? These are names that sound as if they should belong to something else, such as Othery.

'What's your village like?'

'Well, it's sort of *othery*...'

There's George Nympton, famous for his character roles, usually as policemen, in so many British films of the early 1950s. Most of all, there's Stonehenge, now absorbed into England HeritageWorld, but still heart-stopping when you just round a bend and see it there.

So the A303 is Druids, sweaty Celtic labourers dragging the stones with hide ropes on the last stage of their terrible journey; it's peasants with jugs of cider resting against hayricks under the summer sun, with church bells ringing across water meadows. It's a positive pleasure to be stuck behind a fume-spewing lorry if you know that Melbury Abbas is just over that hill. None of this has reached the junior transport minister, Glenda Jackson. It is astonishing that someone who has played so much Shakespeare cannot see the A303 as a highway through our history. To her it is merely a 'corridor study'. 'We are committed to improvement, and to the bypass at Winterbourne Stoke. The strategic role of the A303 will also be considered.'

Why? So Roman legionnaires can march against the Saxons at Tiverton? Or will tanks thunder down it in case the Cornish independence movement ever turns nasty? David Heath, a Lib Dem who has the good fortune to have the A303 running through his constituency, tried, somewhat plaintively, to stand against this tide of jargon. Wouldn't a wider road save lives as well as time? he asked. But nothing would stop Ms Jackson, who could only rave about the A303 being part of a 'major, multi-modal study'.

18.11.98

Yesterday morning I ran into a Labour MP. He was just back from New York where he had bought, he said, a New Labour doll for his granddaughter. I said I was surprised that such a niche product should be on sale in America. 'Oh, it's not labelled "New Labour",' he said. 'But when you pull the string, it goes: *I love you / You love me / We're a happy family!*'

And in that happy family we are beginning to get the hang of New Labour. I popped along to the committee on public administration to hear Jack Cunningham, the minister for the Cabinet Office, or Lord High Everything Else, as he might be termed. Dr Cunningham was at pains to remind us that he works very closely with the Prime Minister, close to Number 10. Perhaps he puts a glass up against the wall to eavesdrop. He has certainly caught Mr Blair's style, which I would describe as a blend of baffling management jargon, combined with folksy mateyness. He told us about the 'substantial refocusing' of his work and said he was giving 'strategic direction to the Prime Minister's programme'. He and his chums are 'overcoming institutional boundaries', ensuring 'effective delivery of the government's central message' and 'underpinning collectively agreed priorities'. At the same time they are going round calling each other by their first names, chuckling cheerfully at nothing in particular, and, like Dr Cunningham, talking about fly-fishing, as if we cared.

Blair people never discuss a problem but 'target an issue'. They don't change anything, but 'bring direction and impetus to modernizing the government's agenda', as he said yesterday. The troubles arise when the jargon runs out. (It is the verbal equivalent of Lego; you could create a building with it, but you wouldn't want to live there.) And calling your interlocutor 'David' instead of 'you Tory bastard, Ruffley' doesn't help when he's asking you about the astonishing cost of refurbishing your workplace.

Dr Cunningham said that the new Cabinet Office accommodation would cost, over four years, some £60 million. You might think this was a lot of money, but you would be wrong. It is a mere nothing compared to other departments: £104 million for the DSS, a majestic £105 million for the Home Office – even £65 million for the Northern Ireland Office.

A quick piece of mental arithmetic told me that this amounted to more than £100 for every one of the 600,000 households in Northern Ireland, all paid for by us, the UK taxpayer, purely to accommodate their masters on the mainland. I hope they're grateful. Only a politician, I thought, would seek to excuse the fabulous sum spent on his behalf by comparing it to the even more fabulous sums spent by his colleagues.

10.12.98

Who needs preventative medicine when we have Ann Widdecombe? A speech by the Tory health spokesperson acts as a tonic, sending blood coursing through our arteries, promoting a healthy glow and skin that is a-tingle. She is the oratorical equivalent of a five-mile walk in a stiff breeze.

As I sat in the press gallery, however, feeling gusts of rhetoric blowing past my cheeks, I was reminded of something else. It was like watching a child playing a video game. Ms Widdecombe reminds me of Sonic the Hedgehog, the cute little cartoon critter who braves monsters and other perils while gathering rings to give him energy, and a force field, which grants temporary immunity from danger. As I watched her thump on the Despatch Box, pirouette round, sideways and upwards, forward and back, arms flapping as she made each point, I had a vision of a thirty-foot-tall schoolboy jabbing buttons and twisting a joystick.

Like Sonic, she operates on several levels, being allowed to advance to the next-higher after completing a series of tasks. So she started on level Angry, then moved up to Fury. She had reached the level called Blistering Rage before her lives ran out and she flopped down on the bench, while the thirty-foot boy shouted, 'Mum, what's for tea?'

Like a video game she emits various strange noises, which only experienced players can recognize. 'I *squeak* to say that the Liberal *squeak* amendment is almost word-for-*squeak* our amendment!' Or, 'There is pressure on hospitals to force through *squeak* waiting list cases...' What does the squeak mean? A life lost? An energy pill absorbed? Any eight-year-old could tell you.

Actually, she doesn't need energy pills. She absorbs energy from her own umbrage and from Labour interventions, which galvanize her, rather as other strong women throughout history have needed the blood of young virgins.

'Patients *squeaking* from potentially fatal infections... conditions are worse than in India.' Clearly the force field had come on. Like Sonic, she should have been surrounded by an eerie blue light, emitting a throbbing noise. And there was a throbbing noise. It came from Conservative backbenchers. 'I am going to be very kind to the Health Secretary,' she said at one point, with heavy irony. 'No, no, no!' throbbed the Tories.

She announced she would not take any more interventions, but it was no use: the rules require that she needs them, or the dreaded 'Game Over' message would appear. She gave way to David Hinchcliffe (Lab., Wakefield) purely in order to suck the life force from him. He, emboldened, tried to intervene a second time.

'I've had enough!' she raged. 'Now sit down! It wasn't good

enough the last time. Nurses regard this government as the worst masters they have ever had!'

'Look behind you,' said Mr Hinchcliffe.

'*Why*?' fumed Ms Widdecombe. 'Are there *nurses* behind me?'

The boy with the control panel was on a roll. Nothing could stop Sonic. In front stood the biggest, scariest monster of them all, the Health Secretary Frank Dobson. She launched her final, ferocious assault.

'I really wish he would look at me, just occasionally! He is *quite incapable* of meeting my eyes. He looks this way. He looks that way. But he never looks at me. He just turns his face from me as he turns from the real problem!' But of course he doesn't look directly at her. He fears that she is a Gorgon, and if their eyes meet, he will be turned to stone.

At this point her anger was so great that I feared she would undergo some terrible internal collapse, and would have to be choppered to a non-existent emergency bed hundreds of miles away, until I remembered with relief that she was only a collection of pixels on a screen.

19.01.99

Even before the foot-and-mouth crisis we had the BSE scare, and the consequent ban on selling beef on the bone.

Agriculture questions in the Commons and a full discussion of beef on the bone. The Bull at Ambridge it isn't. 'Will the ACNFP test cross-pollination for novel foods?' someone asked. Somebody else wanted to know about notifying retailers that they could be included in the 'chain of product liability, attaching obligation for full insurance indemnity, ooh, aar!' (I made the last exclamations up.) They also debated 'MBM controls', 'interim edicts' and 'market-distorting state aid for pig meat'.

On the TV commercials we see ruddy-faced farmers in weskits striding across meadows in dappled sunlight, golden grains of wheat streaming through their honest if gnarled fingers. In the Commons we learn about the 'new chemical surveillance programmes'. These days 'something nasty in the woodshed' is a tray of genetically modified parsnips.

Nick Brown, the Agriculture Secretary, announced that he would not be lifting the beef on the bone ban for at least six months. The Tories were furious. Even as Mr Brown stood up, they were handing out leaflets stating that there was only a 5 per cent chance that a single British person might contract CJD in any one year. 'This means that the risk of an individual dying of new variant CJD via the Dorsal Root Ganglia in 1998 could be one in *1 billion*,' the press release said.

(Did you catch *Cider with Rosie* at Christmas? I particularly liked the bit where Juliet Stevenson produced a steaming dish of beef bones for her hungry family. No beef, only bones. 'Now, my dearies, which of you is to have the lucky dorsal root ganglia? Which of you has done as I bade you, and mucked out the cow byre this Yuletide morn?'

'Me, Mam, me, 'twas me, I do swear it...')

The Conservatives added more statistics to put this all in context. 'Risks of an individual dying in any one year: smoking ten cigarettes a day, one in 200. Salmonella poisoning due to poultry meat, one in 5 million. Hit by lightning, one in 10 million.'

These are amazing figures. If my calculations are correct, the average adult British woman is *four* times more likely to have a love child by Tory agriculture spokesman Tim Yeo than to contract CJD through beef on the bone.

05.02.99

There was a scandal when it turned out that some of the 'real people' appearing in the daytime TV talk shows were actors, drafted in for lack of sufficient amateurs with exciting personal problems.

The House of Commons has always been in the vanguard of shock television. Kilroy himself used to be an MP in the 1970s and 1980s, under his stage name, Robert Kilroy-Silk. Oprah is no more loveable than Diane Abbott, and Vanessa Feltz is just a self-effacing version of Teresa Gorman.

To boost the ratings they should give the Speaker (renamed Betteeh) a roving mike, so she could wander round the Chamber, eliciting opinions and encouraging members to hit each other. But recent scandals have had their effect. Faced with a problem such as genetically modified foods, researchers would normally go out and recruit a professional actor who could play any part. So Jack Cunningham was rarely off our screens. 'I Was an Enforcer for the Blair Mob' was one of his great roles. So was 'Daddy was in Jail, But I'm a Survivor'. Recently he's been seen in a lab coat, persuading us that injecting the genes of scorpions and jellyfish into our food is not going to hurt us. (Apparently they can also put human genes into animals, so that John Gummer can now feed his daughter tasty morsels of himself.)

The minister, Jeff Rooker, told us about the tough safety procedures that surround what he called 'novel foods'. How many memories that brings back, some happy, some less so! Proust's tea-soaked madeleine. The chicken legs in *Tom Jones*. The scene in Huysmans' *À Rebours* where the hero eats steak and kidney pudding in the Gare du Nord, then decides there is no longer any reason for him to visit London. Less cheerily, the piece of liver in *Portnoy's Complaint*. After what happens to that, most of us would prefer to eat broccoli modified with scorpion genes. Or starve.

Mr Rooker got off lightly. He was fortunate in his opponent, Mr Tim Yeo, who has spent much of his adult life putting his own genes where they don't belong. He tried to imply that the row over genetically modified food was created at the behest of the American President. 'President Clinton is close to Monsanto!' he exclaimed, to Labour giggles. Was he referring to Monsanto Lewinsky, famous for having tobacco genes inserted in her by a live president?

Mr Rooker happily pointed out that all the GM foods now available in Britain – including tomato paste, soya beans and maize – had actually been approved by the previous government. On shock TV shows it is quite all right to attack your opponent viciously for doing exactly what you've been doing.

Loyal Tories leaped up in the studio to complain. Michael Fabricant, red-faced and silvery-haired, the result of inserting human genes into a half-peeled lychee, failed to be called by Betteeh.

'There is no such thing as safe food,' said Mr Rooker. 'Crossing the road isn't safe.' This was roughly the height of scientific sophistication we reached yesterday.

19.02.99

Every year, MPs have to update their entry in the Register of Members' Interests. This document is meant to deter corruption. Often a member is charged not with taking wonga, but with failing to declare it. Like most of the paperwork at Westminster that is meant to be seen by the public, it has become a convenient method of grandstanding.

I spent several happy hours leafing through the new edition of the Register. It's often hard to work out exactly what the entries mean. For instance, an MP might admit to taking money from 'Mondrexal'. What does Mondrexal do? I have no idea. It could sell burial space for toxic waste under school playgrounds. It might act as a liaison facilitator for paedophile rings. Who can say? And when the MP concerned speaks passionately in favour of using salmon rivers as conduits for the effluent from nuclear power stations, how can we know if he is representing Mondrexal's highest-paying clients?

But mostly MPs use the Register to tell us how wonderful they are. Their favourite section on the form is 'Unremunerated Interests' in which they list all their fabulously worthy activities. So there's Mike Foster: 'Patron of the Maggs Day Care Centre for Homeless People in Worcester'. Or Tony Baldry: 'Adviser to the Shrimati Pushpa Wati Loomba Memorial Trust, to educate the children of poor widows in India'.

Another trick is to demonstrate your amazingly punctilious conscience by listing every single thing you receive, no matter how valueless. Melanie Johnson logs 'carpeting for my constituency office provided by Mr Kevin Daley, a carpet supplier'. Fiona Mactaggart got a 'Fortnum & Mason hamper which I passed on to SHOC, a housing group, and other voluntary groups in the Slough area'. Lucky them.

'Sperrany change?'

'No, but here's a tin of truffled goose liver in a rich Madeira jelly, courtesy of your local MP!'

Jack Straw got a 'space available upgrade on a flight to Delhi', calling to mind the old joke about the bossy BA stewardess: 'Eat your food up. There are children starving on Air India.' Sadly, Jacqui Smith got nothing at all, other than 'the loan of a Ford Focus car for one week from 14 to 21 December

1998'. A Ford Focus, the ultimate naffmobile, and only for one week! The unluckiest of all may be Ann Widdecombe: 'Overnight stay plus dinner plus small gift (timepiece) at the Imperial Hotel, Blackpool, after I performed the opening of a newly refurbished function room.' But worse was to come. She also received 'one BBC teaspoon, bent and signed by Uri Geller. Intrinsic value, nil. Added value, according to Geller, considerable.' So it's worth nearly 3p, then.

The most ghastly free trip, in reverse order: at number three, several MPs went 'to Kazakhstan to see Karachaganak gas field, and meetings with the Prime Minister and Foreign Minister'. At number two, 'with all-party freight group to study intermodal rail freight facilities in the Chicago area.' And at number one, the grisly winner, Clive Efford's 'Visit to Universal Studios, Florida, as guest of Mr Bob Hope'.

Runner-up in the politically incorrect category: David Curry who 'attended a trilateral conference at Chevening, partly funded by Monsanto [genetically modified food] and Générale des Eaux [owners of worst privatized commuter rail service in UK]'.

Winner, Edward Garnier: 'A day's shooting near Warlingham, as guest of the Tobacco Manufacturers' Association'.

26.02.99

'I want new clichés!' Sam Goldwyn allegedly once demanded. He should have heard Gordon Brown introduce his Budget yesterday. 'A Budget for Britain to succeed, to lead in the new century!' he raved. 'Work, Enterprise, Families First!' he added. He never admits to mere financial tinkering like other chancellors. Instead, everything he does has its own inspiring title. You feel that the Budget speech should not be printed so much as turned into a vast, hand-stitched tapestry showing the glories of British economic life, with a frieze of admiring workers and peasants round the edge.

He doesn't just change the tax arrangements, he announces 'Family-Friendly Employment in Action'. Nobody merely gets a tax break for having a baby; instead they receive the 'Sure-Start Maternity Grant'. Even boring old charity has been abolished. 'Instead of the rich bestowing favours on the poor, I want A Democracy of Giving.' (This sounds suspiciously as if the poor may have the democratic right to give money to the rich, though even New Labour might baulk at that. So far.)

This wasn't just a Budget; it was part of the Great March of Our Island History. 'Children are 20 per cent of Britain's people. But they are 100 per cent of its future!' Tories, who knew that, jeered merrily. In the past, Budget speeches were heard in a respectful if sometimes sullen silence. No longer. The old traditions are dying. No frock coats. No beaker of brandy and water to soothe the Chancellor's throat. And lots of noise.

To be fair, Mr Brown knows how to construct a speech. At the start he is dour, the Presbyterian minister explaining why pocket money will be down this year. The talk is of 'stability', 'following the rules', 'a lock in fiscal tightening' and the Chancellor's great love, Prudence, whose name is evoked with a husky voice and – was it my imagination? – a moist eye.

But then he warms up and relaxes. The stern, unbending dominie is replaced by a smiling Mr Cheeryble. Winter allowance for pensioners up, he declared to great applause. And there was more. 'There will be no tax rise on alcohol this side of the millennium!' he announced, and a cheer arose as loud and full throated as that which greeted VE Day, England's winning goal in 1966, and the news that *Noel's House Party* had been axed.

It was a warming moment. That's how we remember Old Labour – a bunch of tender-hearted drunks.

There was a slight hiccup, so to speak, when he announced the end of mortgage relief, but then he was back with a 22p standard rate of income tax. 'Ish zatt all?' slurred one Tory who, it turned out, had been beating the Budget, quite unnecessarily, by getting pissed at lunchtime.

10.03.99

In the spring of 1999, we attacked Serbia from the air. Most, though not all, MPs were broadly in favour.

Tony Blair made his first Commons statement about Serbia. The pacifists were, as usual, bellicose; the war party quiet. After half an hour I worked out the tone of the occasion. It was a late night phone-in on a provincial radio station.

The presenter is a mild, affable fellow. All he wants to do is play Carpenters records, but the lines are humming with loonies. Few of them are first-time callers; most ring in every night, and the DJ must groan to himself when each familiar voice comes on the line.

Take Sir Peter Tapsell. Sir Peter is the opposite of a stealth MP. If ever he appeared on Serb radar, they would assume they were being attacked by Zeppelins. Massive, overbearing and overweaning, swathed in yards of the finest suiting, face permanently tanned as if lit from within by the furnace of his self-esteem, Sir Peter would be a majestic figure if he were not quite so silly.

Just when the Prime Minister was trying to calm things down ('...and for those of you who are in love, or who have ever been in love, here's that great romantic number, "Close To You"'), Sir Peter phoned in, booming slowly and portentously. In the gallery, the Hansard reporters were replaced by a crack team of monks, frantically scribbling his words down on vellum, to be illuminated later.

'Does the Pwime Minister wealize how twagically!' (Sir Peter has a slight speech impediment.) 'Apt. It was for him to go to Berlin. To explain. Why he is the leading European advocate of.

'A histowically ignowant.

'Politically inept.

'Internationally illegal!

'And half-botched policy, which is already thweatening to incwease and extend the carnage in the Balkans!

'Is he determined. To prove himself. As STUPID! As the *Kaiser*?'

Sir Peter sat down to Labour jeers. I almost felt sorry for him, an elderly man beset by louts, though I suspect it is an occupational hazard for those who believe themselves to be the Foghorn of History, warning that the Ship of State is about to hit the Rocks of Misguided Foreign Entanglements.

Like many DJs, Tonee does tend to witter. His sentences start out with flair, but no one is quite certain how they are going to end. 'There is no doubt about what is happening, you know, the idea that this has only been going on since the NATO bombing, it has been going on and on…' (That was a verbatim quote.)

Brng brng! 'Yes, you're on the air, caller!'

'Tony Benn, yer old mate, back again. Look, what I say is, Tonee, I reckon we oughta bring in someone with, like, international status, like that Nelson Mandela, to bring the sides together. Catch my drift?' (I have slightly adjusted Mr Benn's actual words to convey the flavour of what he said.) This was presumably Mr Benn's reply to the question he is always asked – what would he do instead? But the idea that Mr Milosevic would pay any more heed to Nelson Mandela than to Bill Clinton or, come to that, Jerry Springer or Zoe Ball, was sufficiently ludicrous to make several members titter.

It was Martin Bell who brought a distinct, cold, dark, small-hours feel to the phone-in when he said in his understated but pessimistic way that it was inevitable that ground troops would be needed. 'If the political will is not there, let us admit it is not there, hang our heads, and walk away in shame.'

Tony Blair always responds to Mr Bell in a way that he never could to Sir Peter. He put aside his CD of 'Gilbert O'Sullivan's Greatest Hits' and said firmly and clearly: 'I have no doubt at all that we shall succeed in our objective. We must have complete and total resolve to see it through to the end.'

30.03.99

As, to be fair, he did. Ground forces were threatened, Milosevic fell and was put on trial. A fortnight later, Tony Blair took a tremendous risk and left the country at a time when Prime Minister's Question Time was due.

The Prime Minister was in Brussels, working with Kofi Annan on the plight of the Kosovo refugees. Back on the government front bench another humanitarian disaster was unfolding. His deputy, John Prescott, had taken over Question Time.

It was terrible. It was also ghastly, chaotic, miserable and floor-staringly, mouth-puckeringly, gaze-avertingly awful. In any civilized country a trained SAS squad would have abseiled down the Chamber walls, tossing smoke bombs, grabbing Mr Prescott and hustling him to safety.

As it was, many people felt sorry for him. He is, after all, a working-class lad who has got where he is by dint of hard work, dedication and political flair. Others take a sterner view. He is, nominally, the second most powerful man in the land, and should at least be able to patch a sentence together. Or be vaguely aware of government policy on the kind of vital, world-changing issues to which the rest of us devote slightly less thought than whether we want salt 'n' vinegar or original salted flavour. Being a soggy, *Guardian*-writing liberal, I agree with both points of view. Yes, it was hilarious. Yes, but only an arrogant, boorish oaf would not feel a twinge of pity for the man.

He began by flannelling well enough. Labour's David Chaytor asked him about the role of the Russians in the Balkan war. 'I think that on a number of occasions there has been a concern and it has been a subject of discussion in these discussions,' he said, in what was basically pidgin Prescott. He was reading from a script, and though he skipped several words, the average brain, accustomed to the Prescottic dialect, supplies the missing syllables.

At this stage, Labour MPs were calmly discussing whether Peter Lilley (William Hague's deputy and the Niles Crane of the Conservative Party) was wearing make-up for the cameras. Things were calm. They had no idea of what was to follow.

Then nemesis arrived in the unlikely shape of the genteel Alan Beith. The Liberal Democrat deputy asked him to confirm that average class sizes are, in spite of Labour's promises, actually increasing.

'I can confirm that we are on target for reducing class sizes,' Mr Prescott said, to Tory jeers.

'But that is not the same question,' said Mr Beith, who rattled off a series of figures which seemed to make his case.

'You asked if we were on target,' said Mr Prescott, changing the subject again. 'And that is the answer you are going to get!' The Tories were chortling, even glistening with pleasure.

Then Michael Spicer demanded a guarantee that the withholding tax would never be introduced in this country.

Mr Prescott scrambled desperately through his notes but couldn't find the page. 'Well, as someone who is now the secretary of state for the environment, that disastrous poll tax is one that I am constantly having to deal with. You should bear in mind that what we have now settled with the local authorities is the most generous settlement they have ever received!'

The Tories suddenly realized that he was talking not about withholding tax (which is to prevent people using offshore holdings to dodge tax) but about the council tax. He probably didn't even know what the withholding tax was.

They collapsed in tucks of mirth, some genuine. Ann Widdecombe kept clutching at her own face, as if to hold the hysteria in. 'More, more!' the Tories yelled.

Soon afterwards, Mr Prescott paused for thirty agonizing seconds, then answered the wrong question. 'There are different ways of doing this at different times,' he said in reply to a query about a new National Forest.

'It's the way I tell 'em,' he said plaintively. 'I have caused some confusion.' (More confusion was caused by Labour's David Taylor, who asked for 'the government cavalry to ride to the rescue of a scheme which is becoming becalmed in a quagmire'. Oh, those poor horses!)

Mr Prescott stalked angrily from the Chamber to further Tory cries of 'More!' Am I just imagining the quiet glee with which this debacle will have been welcomed by Mr Blair and his staff?

15.04.99

The House of Lords debated its own abolition yesterday. Gosh, it was dull. Gary Gilmore, the first person to be executed in the United States after the return of capital punishment, was allowed to choose the manner of his death. If he had adopted the same approach as their lordships, he'd be alive today. The firing squad would have fallen asleep on their rifles before they'd even heard the order.

As did I. Drifting briefly into the arms of Morpheus, I was being chased round the Lords Chamber by Lady Young, armed with a giant fish. Just before she caught me I woke up, to find that whoever had driven me to slumber was still speaking.

The debate was kicked off ('dropped off' might be more accurate) by Lord Campbell of Alloway. He wanted a referendum, so that the people could democratically show their overwhelming support for the hereditary principle. Listening to him is rather like riding on a privatized train. Every now and again he grinds to a halt, for no apparent reason. On the railways, something usually happens while we wait – a train loaded with nuclear waste rumbles past, or a leaf is rescued from the line. With Lord Campbell there is merely a judder and off we go, a few more yards down the track, the end of our journey nowhere in sight. 'Participatory deprivation of parliamentary entitlement!' he exclaimed, or rather mumbled.

The public gallery, originally full, began to empty, until only six people were left. I don't know what's wrong with today's tourists. No stamina. In the old days they'd have listened to five hours of speeches, then gone to Lyons Corner House for tea. Now they expect to be entertained, for heaven's sake. Soon the authorities will have to launch the House of Lords Experience, with animatronic peers falling off the benches.

After a while an astonishing fact became clear. These guys actually think the public is behind them. Lord Campbell called the abolition of the hereditary peers 'a great denial of democracy'. The trifling fact that it appeared in the Labour manifesto was airily dismissed: 'Only 2 per cent of the people have any recollection of it,' he said.

Lord Strathclyde detected a great popular movement. 'The abolition of hereditary peers is not wanted. We do not want it. The public does not. The outside world does not.' So even foreigners were in favour! Lord Waddington said: 'I refuse to imagine that we do not have the public on our side.' Did he think that those great parades that march down Whitehall every day were ordinary workers and peasants demanding the preservation of the hereditary principle? And if so, why do they all carry Serbian flags?

21.04.99

Year Two

The party conferences herald the season of mists, mellow fruitfulness and even more absurd speeches.

John Prescott was on the platform with Tony Blair, and they were soon joined by Gordon Brown. The three sat for the cameras like lads waiting for the start of the match, smiling, joking and laughing. You'd almost imagine that they liked and respected each other. Perhaps they do. When you reach that level you can employ people to do your hating for you, and a very good job they make of it too.

The Chancellor started. At first he was all twisted and hunched together, as he usually is. Mr Brown stands at the rostrum like a man who, for security reasons, keeps his bus pass jammed up his backside.

But the speech was a roaring success and as the conference cheered and shouted, Mr Brown relaxed. His arms began to wave wildly as if he was being controlled by a puppeteer with Parkinson's disease. His oratory took off, and grew wilder and wilder as the reception got louder. To those of us who have heard Mr Brown speak many, many times, it was quite weird: like suddenly seeing train-spotters do the conga down the platform at Crewe. At one point he seemed to imagine he had become Martin Luther King. 'I have a dream!' he cried.

I would love it if a politician, just once, followed up by

saying: 'In my dream I'm standing at a bus stop in my underwear and the bus comes up and it's driven by Nicole Kidman, and she's smoking a huge cigar…' Instead it always turns out to be the usual boilerplate about a vision of peace and justice for all.

There was plenty of the vision thing. What there wasn't was any reference to prudence. Not a mention of the poor girl. She has been binned, like one of Mickey Rooney's wives. Then he started the audience participation, like Buttons in a panto. This came when he reminded us that the Gordon Brown recession had, against predictions, failed to materialize. Who had opposed the tax cuts? he enquired. Why, it was 'Hague, Widdecombe, Redwood and Maude!' Who had called his growth forecasts 'fairy-tale figures? 'Hague, Widdecombe, Redwood and Maude!'

Finally the audience caught on. When he asked who had opposed the pensioners' £100 allowance, they chanted the names for him. How lucky he was that the four Tories that the government wants to demonize all have names that scan perfectly in whichever order you arrange them. Try it: 'Widdecombe, Redwood, Hague and Maude!' or 'Hague, Redwood, Maude and Widdecombe!' Magnificently resonant, every one.

Mr Brown had begun by saying that he affirmed 'the values that brought our party into being – the same values, yesterday, today and tomorrow'. This is usually New Labour-speak for cuts in public spending and tax reductions for the well-to-do. But not yesterday. There was very little about economics or finance, but there was a great deal about enterprise and modernity and radicalism and conquering the forces of reaction and privilege.

If you closed your eyes, you realized that this wasn't really a chancellor's speech at all. Like Michael Heseltine, Mr Brown has grasped that conferences don't want to hear about stuff. They want to be aroused, tickled, stroked and brought to a climax.

He finished like this: 'Join us. Join with Labour. Join us. Join us on our journey. Join us.' It wasn't a speech but a mantra, suitable for performing down Oxford Street, a reminder that to belong to New Labour is to lose your soul in the universal consciousness of Tony Blair's thought.

His very last words were: 'We've only just begun.' (This, and eleven other great hits, can be found on the K-Tel album 'Gordon Brown Sings the Carpenters'. Not available in stores. Or anywhere else.)

28.09.99

The highlight of the Labour conference is, of course, the leader's speech. In the distant mists of Labour history, this was merely called the 'Parliamentary Report' and always came on the Tuesday. It still does, meaning that the whole conference climaxes just after it has begun. This particular speech, which appeared to blame everything wrong in the world not just on the Conservative Party but on conservatives in general, aroused a great deal of annoyance.

It wasn't so much a leader's speech as a product launch. There was a video depicting a hundred years of Labour achievement which, oddly enough, includes the 1966 World Cup. Then in the dramatic fashion of someone unveiling the new Ford Fellatio to an audience of sales reps, the chairwoman said: 'Conference, Tony Blair!'

But instead of running out from the wings, the Prime Minister emerged from the side of the hall, which looked tremendously modest but in fact obliged everyone to get up in order to see him, thus awarding him a standing ovation merely for walking through a door. It also gave him the chance to say to the cheering multitude: 'I hope it's like this at the end!' which won him double points for lack of pretension while actually getting a reception that would have pleased the Emperor Trajan.

At the end he stepped back from the podium and stood alone for what was probably only a few seconds, but felt like for ever. John Prescott moved towards him, but an invisible force field, possibly controlled by Alastair Campbell, prevented him getting near to the leader. The message was plain: 'This is about me, and only me. Everyone else is irrelevant.'

Soon he was back on the master plan, or the sales strategy as we call it in marketing. This is nothing less than the complete abolition of the Conservative Party – a party that had 'spent two years in hibernation, shaping a new image, and had come back as the Addams Family'. This is a cunning way of reminding us of the curious appearance of so many senior Tories, so that, as their names are chanted, 'Hague, Redwood and Widdecombe', we can think 'Ah yes, the slaphead, the alien and the bag lady.'

He outlined a Manichaean world in which progress and modernity were ranged against 'the forces of conservatism', a phrase he used over and over again. He told pensioners that the Tories would take back their £100 winter allowance 'if ever they were elected back to office', as if this was as horrible and yet as unlikely a prospect as the return of the slave trade. 'I say, "Roll on the general election,"' he declared to a mighty cheer, which was pretty ludicrous as he is the only person who can decide when that is.

Round about the point that he got on to the subject of DNA testing – we are to have a national computerized DNA data bank – he began, ever so slightly, to foam at the mouth, sending an almost invisible spray of his own DNA over the front row, which will be useful if Tony Blair ever nicks your car radio.

It's a cliché, but like many clichés it's true: that Blair speeches resemble revivalist meetings. You could fit in a few 'Hosannas' and tambourine tinkles between each line. He uses the language of religion: 'Social justice is the nation's only hope of salvation,' then a little later, 'Liberating the talent of the people is the nation's only hope of salvation.' They can't both be the sole hope of salvation, but that doesn't matter – other political parties offer jobs and prosperity; only Tony Blair pledges eternal life.

His last words, before he staggered back from the lectern, were: 'Set our people free!' We were supposed to be inspired, enthused and uplifted. Certainly the audience gave that impression. But it didn't really work. This was, after all, a sales conference. The echoes of Moses and Martin Luther King were drowned out in my mind by the smaller, piping voice of John Inman: 'I'm free!'

29.09.99

After the anticlimax of the leader's speech, it is often left to John Prescott to stir the conference up again.

John Prescott was furious. Mr Angry. Kebabbed. Off his trolley. Out of his pram. This is a man who has brought bad temper to a fine art. He should be the author of a self-help book: *'Oo You Lookin' At? – How to Liberate your Inner Consciousness through Constructive Rage*. Think of Victor Meldrew seeing the last bus of the night sail by his stop. Visualize Basil Fawlty when a guest with a nose ring arrives at reception. Nikita Khrushchev at the UN. John McEnroe debating a line call. Truly, seriously cross.

Mr Prescott is often tetchy. He has threatened in the past to kill me, or at least so I am told by kind friends, who look forward to the memorial service, followed by drinks and a wide range of canapés in the church hall afterwards.

But for heaven's sake, what has he got to be angry about? This is a man with two Jaguars, one chauffeur-driven. He went to Oxford. He earns a salary that would make most former members of his profession, barmen on cruise ships, drool with envy, though there are fewer tips. He is even – in name at least – Deputy Prime Minister of the United Kingdom, which is, as Labour ministers never tire of reminding us, the fourth-largest economy in the world.

As I watched him yesterday, shouting furiously at the conference, bellowing from the podium, I decided that he is angry because angry is what he knows how to do. For years he raged against the iniquities of the Tories. Now, more than two years after coming into government, he has to rage about the successes of New Labour. He has no other style. Urghhhhh! Gosh, he was angry. 'Under Labour, our air is getting cleaner. Our rivers and beaches are less polluted!' This is appalling, I thought. Where can we all march to protest in favour of all this?

Gak! 'Five billion pounds of capital receipts to help improve 2 million homes!' No wonder he was beside himself. The better the news, more spittle poured from his mouth. Aaarghhh! He announced the creation of two new national parks the way you might declare the annexation of the Sudetenland.

He told the railway companies, which have been left almost entirely alone during his stewardship of the Transport Department: 'You! Are! Still! On! Probation!' He really stuck it to hypothermia – 'an obscenity': that was telling them. All those in favour of hypothermia must have been shaking in their shoes. As for asbestos – 'Britain's biggest industrial killer' – if I were a lobbyist trying to persuade schools to offer asbestos spread in children's sandwiches, I'd be really worried now.

Everything made him furious, even the new miracles of public transport. 'The Docklands Light Railway crossing the river to Lewisham!' he barked before scowling at the audience. Not since Caesar crossed the English Channel have we had such cause for alarm. Rage, rage against the crossing of the Docklands Light Railway!

'We have a name for it! We call it "democratic socialism"!' And having daringly used the S-word, he sat down. Tony Blair led the applause – so no threat there, then.

30.09.99

It later emerged that to make this speech, in Bournemouth, John Prescott had used his ministerial car to ride the 250 yards from the hotel to the conference centre, where among other topics he railed against the way we rely too much on the car. His excuse, 'The wife doesn't like having her hair blown about,' made the whole episode seem even more ridiculous. When a politician becomes a national figure of fun, there's usually one particular incident that crystallizes our hitherto vague and diffuse feeling; for John Prescott this, I think, was it.

The year's Conservative conference was held in Blackpool.

The Tories launched their new campaign yesterday under the title, 'The Common-Sense Revolution'. What an amazing revolution that will be. 'Let's not build any barricades, lads, they'll only make people late for work.' Or, 'Don't burn those buses, they might come in handy later.'

Mr Hague appeared at the Imperial Hotel, Blackpool, to read out his declaration of common-sense revolutionary principles. The Tories get worried about appearing in front of the press on their own, so they had arranged for a claque of Tory delegates to sit behind the media and clap his strange speech patterns, which include barking the first part of each sentence, then producing an unfeasibly long northern vowel. 'Our! Principles! Doan fall ad-a-a-a-awl by the wayside!' (Loud and prolonged applause, from the claque at least.)

The cover of the new policy document shows a different Hague, three-quarter length, turning to the camera with an unnerving gleam in his eye. He looks very like Dr Frasier Crane in the TV series, though of course Frasier would never have sacked his brother Niles, played by Peter Lilley.

(The common-sense revolutionaries come down from the hills in their trademark Thermawear headbands and Clarks shoes.

'What do we want?'

'Loft insulation!'

'When do we want it?'

'As soon as the builders have finished that job in Sutton!')

Mr Hague started offering us guarantees. There was the Sterling Guarantee, the Parents' Guarantee, the Can Work, Must Work Guarantee. And, what's more, the guarantees were, themselves, guaranteed. 'As anyone who knows me knows, that is guaranteed!' he said.

(Crowds line the streets as the common-sense revolutionaries march through the capital. Their placards declare: 'Regular dental check-ups, now!'; 'Keep eggs in a cool place, not in the fridge!' and 'You're not wearing that coat in this weather, are you?')

I went into the conference hall. The stage is truly weird. It consists of a series of gigantic blue 'thinks' bubbles in the shape of William Hague's head. The podium itself is a set of random geometric shapes, resembling the Cadbury's Smash robots. There is a desk to one side but chairs to the other, so that the Tory dignitaries sit like the defendants at a show trial.

(The common-sense revolutionaries revere Michael Fish, with his common-sense revolutionary thought and sensible glasses. Their Rosa Luxemburg is Delia Smith.)

A young man of seventeen, Alex Lee from Worcester, spoke in the defence debate. 'Good Lord,' you could see people thinking, 'he could be our leader in less than twenty years.' Then he opened his mouth. 'Let us cut our aggressive military commitments,' he said. 'Let us dispense with our outdated military past, and use the money saved to improve people's lives!' The applause at the end was distinctly lukewarm. Common sense is one thing, but being revolutionary is another. No doubt he was taken away to be shot, or at least given a friendly ticking-off.

(Meanwhile the mobs have reached the presidential palace. The leader of the Common Sense faction climbs onto the wall. 'Comrades!' he cries. 'The time has come to storm this citadel of privilege and oppression! But be careful not to step on the flowerbeds!')

05.10.99

It's hard to recall now, but for many Tories, the only issue that really mattered at this time was the fate of General Pinochet, who was being held in a comfortable house set among the rock stars and TV presenters of Virginia Water.

This was the big event of the day. Lady Thatcher felt so strongly about General Pinochet that she planned her first Tory conference speech for nine years – and had even waived her usual £50,000 fee. We were a deeply privileged group, for we were to get the old bat gratis. Mad cow would offer comfort to mad dictator.

Delegates fled the main hall to make sure they had seats for her meeting. Many even skipped the debate on agriculture and so missed hearing their spokesman, Tim Yeo. ('We plough the fields and scatter the good seed wherever we get the chance.') Off they went to the ABC Cinema, Blackpool, which had even cancelled its regular showing, *The Haunting*.

We waited. For a long time. On the screen was a picture of General Pinochet, smiling and laughing, surrounded by happy grandchildren, many of whom had never been tortured. The Tories are beginning to resemble the Labour Party of the early 1980s. Ranting. Bonkers. Obsessed by single issues. Out of touch with everyone except themselves.

On the sides of the cinema was the slogan, 'Free Pinochet – Britain's only political prisoner'. This poor wretch, we were led to believe, had been imprisoned in the Surrey Gulag, where he survived on just three meals a day and was forced by his captors to sit in a comfy armchair watching daytime television. Finally there was a loud cheer and prolonged applause – and that was just for Denis Thatcher. When the President for Life and Global Leader of the World Institute of Thatcherology appeared, they went berserk. This, you could almost hear them think, was a real leader – not the wimps we've had to put up with for the past nine years.

Norman Lamont, the chairman, moved forward to welcome her. We were at a meeting of the Death to John Major faction of the Free Pinochet Movement. Don't go near any football stadiums, John!

'General Pin O'Shea,' (as Norman Lamont pronounced it – the real pronunciation is 'Pea – no – CHETT' but none of his admirers here has bothered to learn that) 'helped make the world safe for Tony Blair, but he was in CND at the time!' To these people Tony Blair is the Salvador Allende of Britain, leading an irreversible Marxist revolution through highly motivated, desperate cadres of businessmen who are prepared to pay £500 a plate to eat with him.

Finally it was her turn. 'My friendsh,' she said (she's beginning to get the sibilant s, like Tony Benn) 'it'sh nine yearsh shinsh I shpoke at a Conshervative Party conference. A lot hash happened shinsh then – and not much of it for the better.' A reference, we assumed, to the three great enemies in her life, in ascending order of wickedness: Tony Blair, William Hague and John Major, the Trotsky of her own revolution.

She described how Pinochet had helped the British in the Falklands by offering airborne intelligence. On the day they switched it off – 'for overdue maintenance' – we lost two ships. They switched it off for maintenance? That's the kind of excuse London Transport offers.

Her words were full of fury, and her hatred of so many people came through. Yet the voice has begun to fade. The heat remains in there, but the fires are now banked.

07.10.99

One thing that most of us agreed on was that, however poor his poll ratings, however unsatisfactory his image with the general public, William Hague did, as often as not, worst the Prime Minister at Question Time. One particularly difficult session was ended by a mysterious voice who apparently gave Tony Blair the desperately needed chance to cap Hague. Exactly what had happened baffled the press gallery. Luckily my favourite detective, Rex Stout's Nero Wolfe, was on the case.

The great Norway mystery consumed the Commons yesterday afternoon. Parliament was abuzz with the rival theories. All we could say for sure was that no Tory leader had been so troubled by that sea-girt, pine-clad, troll-infested land since Neville Chamberlain was obliged to resign after the Norway debate of 1940.

It had been a good session for William Hague. But who left it in ruins? I handed the conundrum over to my old friend Nero Wolfe, the gourmet detective who solves most of his cases without even leaving his brownstone mansion in New York. Wolfe's legman has always been the hard-bitten, fast-talking Archie Goodwin.

'I decline,' the great detective said, 'to have lunch interrupted by the exigencies of mere business. I shall attend to the client's request after we have eaten.'

When he had added another inch to his waistline so that he looked more like the Goodyear blimp than ever, which is saying plenty, he grunted at me, which I knew meant it was time to talk.

'Proceed, Archie, and kindly err on the side of brevity.'

'OK, boss, here's the story. Prime Minister's Questions, almost over, the chief is getting both barrels from Hague, the Tory capo – for now. Usual story. Europe. Big turf row going on there.

'Hague swears he can renegotiate the deal. Blair says five gets you twenty he's talking through his fedora.'

'Be so good as to spare me some of the more colourful details, Archie,' Wolfe said, pulling on his beer and closing his eyes. This is the only guy I know who gets paid more for being asleep than Michael Jordan gets for shooting hoops.

'So Blair goes nuclear. "You can cut a deal with the EU mob, huh? Name one other country in Europe supports you. There isn't one."

'Next thing, it's hell on a skateboard in there. "Norway?" shouts Blair, 'cos he's heard some bird yell it out. "Norway? Norway isn't even a member of the European Union!"

'So the Labour gang collapses in a heap like a girls' school outing who just spotted Brad Pitt through the bus window and Blair gets himself cheered out the room. He looks great, and Hague looks so damn dumb that if you took off his baseball cap his head would fall off.

'So who yelled "Norway"? That's what the client wants to know, and he'll pay fifteen big ones to find out.'

'Eyewitness reports, Archie. You know the procedure.'

'You'd get more reliable eyewitness reports if you put LSD in the coffee at St Dunstan's. But here goes.

'Some say it was Forth, the guy who has his ties run up out of boarding house curtains. A couple reckon it was Bercow, the bird who took a 'copter to his selection meeting to make himself look stacked, though the bag lady on our stoop has more; at least she's got pizza coupons.

'Some of the reporters figure it was Hague saying "No way!" He likes American talk; he's going to tell Blair "Eat my shorts" over tax rises next week.'

'Pfui!' said Wolfe. 'Folderol and balderdash. It was none of those things. The mystery is that there is no mystery.'

'OK, even for you, that's crazy. You sat here, you didn't go outside the house, no one came by and you didn't pick up the phone. But you know the answer, right?'

'The answer,' said Wolfe wearily, 'is that nobody exclaimed "Norway!" Blair claimed he heard it in order to use a line he had, no doubt fortuitously, arranged to deploy. It worked satisfactorily; he won a round of applause at the end of a difficult session. He invented it.'

'You certain? The hacks say he doesn't have the smarts to pull a stunt like that.'

'Possibly so,' said Wolfe. 'But there is one man who is quite cunning enough to construct a foolish heckle in order to facilitate a crushing riposte. He is a tall, sinister individual with a perpetual sneer.'

'You mean…?'

'Yes, I refer to Alastair Campbell. I think you will find that he was present throughout the exchanges in order to make certain that his "boss" did exactly as he had been instructed.

'You may bank the client's cheque tomorrow. Meanwhile, Fritz has prepared beluga caviar blinis with a juniper-scented sour cream mousse, and I suggest we proceed to supper before Inspector Kramer eats them all.'

21.10.99

Alastair Campbell was certainly capable of doing what Nero Wolfe suggested. The contrast with the last Labour Prime Minister's press secretary – Jim Callaghan's Tom McCaffrey – could hardly have been greater. When Mr Campbell is displeased, which is often, he phones up the miscreant hack, sometimes an editor, at two in the morning if needs be, or during dinner, or the school run, or whenever the mood takes him. 'That's complete crap, that is!' is one of his gentler remonstrations, though it could be called his catchphrase by now. By contrast, Sir Tom was never less than affable. 'Story you wrote this morning,' he would murmur at a lobby meeting. 'The one about the Slaughter of the First-Born. Prime Minister asked me to point out that you may be confusing it with the bill to permit the eradication of diseased ducks in the High Wycombe area. No, don't bother to correct it, Jim just wanted you to know…' Alastair Campbell would regard that as the kind of niminy-piminy attitude that lost Labour so many elections. If you make a mistake like that now you can expect a hit squad to arrive at your home with sawn-off howitzers and red roses in their lapels. Or something like that.

Like a fabled mediaeval beast, eating itself from the tail inwards, the House of Lords yesterday debated for the last time its own abolition. Things got off to an exciting start when a tall, bearded man leaped up on the Woolsack and began to harangue them. 'This bill, drafted in Brussels, is treason!' he shouted.

Peers looked up anxiously. He could have been a murderous mad anarchist, except that the face foliage, though luxuriant, had been neatly trimmed. This was not a bomb-thrower's beard.

But the peers never get too troubled about anything, even their own suicide. The mild hubbub they made was roughly the same as you'd expect in a public library reading room when somebody rustles the paper too loudly. 'Get him out,' said someone, but quietly and without much conviction.

'Treason!' repeated the belligerent. The Earl of Onslow, who once threatened to behave like a football hooligan in defence of the hereditary principle, tried to tug him down, though not very hard.

'It is treason! Stand up for your Queen and country!' Finally Black Rod managed to talk the fellow down, possibly by offering to buy up all his *Big Issues*, and he disappeared to give a press conference. He turned out to be the Earl of Burford, who is son and heir to the Duke of St Albans and who will now presumably never take his father's seat. Both are descendants of Nell Gwyn, and it seemed somehow historically apt that a person who was in the House only for that reason should be loudly asserting his divine right to stay there and so help do to the country what Charles II had done to his famous ancestor.

The debate finally got under way. The government has conceded that there will be by-elections if any of the ninety-two elected hereditary peers dies or resigns. This will make for some fascinating campaigns.

'Can I count on your support, Lord Malfeasor?'

'Certainly, we're all Conservatives in this castle.'

'Splendid, splendid. And would you like 289 posters for the windows?'

The Tory leader spoke in his usual fairly ameliorative fashion. His full name is Thomas Galloway Dunlop du Roy de Bliquy Galbraith, which is only the second-longest name in the place. The winner is John David Clotworthy Whyte-Melville Foster Skeffington, Viscount Massarene and Ferrard, known to his friends as 'My Lord'. (Lord Strathclyde's address is 'Old Barkskimming, Ayrshire'. That's not so much a house as a hobby.)

Lord Clifford, who, as well as the day job, is a count of the Holy Roman Empire, wanted privy counsellors to keep their place in the House, and put it to the vote.

'Contents?' the peers were asked, and a few mumbled.

'Not contents?' was met by a huge roar from the benches, like a reverse panto. 'Ooh, we can't 'ave you not being content, can we, ducks? 'Ere, 'ave some of these Wispa bars!'

The finest put-down of the day came from Lord Longford, now 94. He rose to speak at the wrong time according to the rules. Lord Carter pointed out with great courtesy that 'the only peer who can speak after a minister is the peer who moved the amendment...'

'I do not *know* what the relevance of that is,' said Lord Longford, with magnificent aplomb and disdain. When the peers are all Tony's cronies – bland, think-tanky, fettucine-munching, Pinot Grigio-swilling automatons – I shall miss the old lot. Treason to get rid of them.

27.10.99

Almost unnoticed, whole areas of parliamentary life have been ethnically cleansed of the English tongue. Take education and employment questions yesterday. These are not conducted in the language of Shakespeare, or even Radio 1. MPs utter words and phrases that might, on their own, have a meaning, but which when combined with others seem to signify nothing at all.

David Blunkett, the secretary of state, told us that he hoped 'to extend the intensification of the gateway'. Something or other was 'co-terminous with the learning and skills councils'. In the world inhabited by Mr Blunkett and his junior ministers, nobody ever borrows more books. Instead there is a 'massive take-up of the library service'. We are not merely enjoined to treat disabled people as our equals; instead we take part in the 'See the Person Campaign'.

Mr Michael Wills, another junior minister, was asked about 'enhanced services at the gateway stage'. He replied, to everyone's apparent satisfaction, that the government had 'established trailblazer projects'. This delighted a backbencher, Rosie Winterton, who said that she supported trailblazer initiatives 'because of the help it will give in best-practice coalition with employers'.

You expect someone to shout out: 'For Gawd's sake, speak English, can't you?' But no one does. To them it is as straightforward as the Gettysburg Address. Mr Wills continued, 'The point is to promote best practice for the roll-out when they emerge into their own gateways, promoting the soft skills that employers want to see.'

Soft skills? What on earth was he on about? Origami? Lap dancing? Pillow plumping? Or perhaps soft skills have to do with 'the sensitive interface for job seekers'.

Of course jargon has its purposes. You can't expect people to describe at length every time what each new 'initiative' or 'roll-out' or 'programme' or 'disabled pilot' or even 'soft skill' is when there's a snappy phrase to put it in capsule form. The trouble is that the cant catchwords pile up on top of each other, as if a toddler were playing with Lego; it all fits together, but the result resembles nothing at all.

Ordinary words turn into jargon by acquiring phantom capital letters. Thus, otherwise sensible people such as the new minister, Jacqui Smith, promised 'support through the Small Schools Fund, which exists to support small schools'. Mr Blunkett praised the 'Voluntary Sector Option, which is funded by the voluntary sector, voluntarily'. Initials tumble out like alphabet soup. There was even a reference to Mr David Willetts, the shadow secretary of state for social security, or the SSSSS as he is now known in the trade.

29.10.99

The jargon that infests New Labour extends everywhere, including the Queen's Speech. Her Majesty opened Parliament, as usual, in November.

What is the point of having all these ushers and courtiers and heralds in Parliament – including Fitzalan Pursuivant Extraordinary, Maltravers Herald Extraordinary, Clarenceaux King of Arms, the Cap of Maintenance (does Queen Beatrix have a Dutch Cap of Maintenance?) and Gold Stick in Waiting, which sounds like a breath freshener you keep for emergencies, but which turns out to be Princess Anne, all of whom seem to have been saved from the tumbrils that carted all but 92 hereditary peers off to the guillotine last week – if not one of them can say to the Queen: 'Don't read out this stuff, Your Majesty, it's complete and utter garbage'?

At one time the Queen's Speech at the State Opening used to be couched in dry, flat, dull language and contained brief descriptions of coming legislation.

After 1997 it began to be padded out with New Labour jargon about – as it was yesterday – 'a dynamic, knowledge-based economy', 'transparency', 'providing people with the opportunities to liberate their potential' and 'meeting the challenges of the new millennium' – just some of the cringe-making, jaw-sticking, tooth-furring drivel that the poor woman had to read out from the throne.

I've been going to these occasions on and off for twenty years, and whilst the Queen has always read out the speech as if it were slightly less fascinating than the used tools section of the *Exchange & Mart*, this time she seemed to be infected with a greater ennui than ever. Her voice droned on unhappily like someone who, the moment she has finished, will have to come to terms with some terrible sorrow.

But then this year's speech was worse than ever before. It

was without doubt the worst Queen's Speech I have ever heard. It wasn't even a royal speech at all, but a party political broadcast.

'More people are in work in Britain today than ever before, with employment up by 700,000, and long-term unemployment has been halved,' she intoned.

'Education remains my government's number one priority,' she said, like a Dalek with a head cold, and I half expected a video clip to be broadcast on a giant screen, showing bright, attentive children with nice clean hair sitting in a sun-dappled classroom.

'My government are helping people back into work. The New Deal has helped 145,000 young people [this would normally be a cue for a shot of a cheery black teenager with an acetylene lamp, pushing up his goggles to smile at the camera in gratitude for New Labour]…inflation is now historically low …the income of working families [mum, dad and two children walking hand in hand down an improbably clean beach]…my government will continue to manage the public finances prudently.'

It was awful, dreadful and horribly embarrassing. The Queen is supposed to be a national symbol, above party politics, not re-created as the latest on-message Blair babe. Next year someone at the Palace should crisply tell Downing Street to spin itself up its own fundament.

18.11.99

I've finally worked out how to follow a John Prescott speech. You have to think of the speech itself as a chap who is taking his large, bouncy dog – a Great Prescott perhaps – for a walk in the country. Prescott is on a lead, of course, because there are sheep in the fields. But he can't just stroll along. He tugs and pulls at the speech, trying to force it to go the way he wants. Some of these tugs are just small twitches: 'That is something we are particularly, and proud of,' he said. On other occasions, he bounds away, with the speech left running to catch up.

'I think you'll see that the confidence in the public transport as shown by this side of the House in that they think it is an important part of the transport system,' he shouted, and you could hear the poor old speech – no younger than it used to be – panting to catch up without tripping over the lead.

We moved on to the Conservative attitude to local government – 'or their idea of democracy', to 'bolish the GLC' as he put it. So fast was he charging towards a dozy-looking ewe that he couldn't spare time for mere vowels. On we raced. 'Repeating this' meant 'repealing this'. Tenants were suffering because of 'unscruppolous' landlords, which sounds like a disease that sailors catch.

Suddenly he was off the leash and away into the fields. The speech was abandoned, left standing in a cold muddy cart track. 'There are difficult legal complexes – our draft bill this House can take first steps, which is creating a great deal of social injustice in our housing situation.'

The speech tries to whistle him back, but he's still running round in circles. 'The actual people in areas have pointed out that all these things definitely was worse for the taxpayer. I would think they are a body to be actually claimed on our side to welcome best practice.'

'Prescott, back here, boy!' cries the speech across the fields, but the dog hardly notices.

'All have a contributory contribution to congestion,' he barks over his shoulder as he chases the increasingly anxious sheep.

Finally he trotted back to heel and allowed the lead to be clipped back on. But then he was off and running again, tugging the speech frantically to the end of their walk. 'I think there is umanimous support,' he said, pulling onwards. 'It is the issue of our preferred consideration!' Deterioration became 'deteriati'; environment, 'envymen'. 'We are unpacking the damage they have done!' He was going to bring back a paper, 'so the House can look it at!'

Mrs Prescott looked on, smiling, from the Strangers' Gallery. Her famous hair was certainly not messed up, but after listening to her husband, I cannot speak for her mind.

19.11.99

Every year a group of us meets to select the Spectator *parliamentary awards. We also get to go to the lunch at which they are presented. The Blairs' baby son, Leo, was born in late 1999.*

Off to the Savoy Hotel for the awards ceremony. It's always embarrassing to be a judge, as you sit surrounded by scores of MPs, all united by a single thought: why the hell didn't they choose me?

This year we had a real superstar on our list. Thirty months ago, John Major was a wet, clapped-out, discredited, feckless, incompetent, petulant, weasely Prime Minister, who had not only led his party to its most humiliating defeat ever, but was also a close friend of Jeffrey Archer.

Now he is a much-loved, twinkle-eyed elder statesman as welcome at any festive gathering as Father Christmas or Dame Vera Lynn. Indeed, his speakers' agency quotes a personal appearance fee of between £40,000 and £50,000. We got him for free.

And he was good. He said how moving it had been to write his autobiography and learn the history of his kinfolk. 'Before I wrote it, I could trace my family back only as far as my father. Which was further than some of my colleagues.'

We strolled down memory lane, back to a meeting with the Russian President. 'I asked Boris Yeltsin to tell me briefly what the situation in Russia was like. "Good," he said. I asked for a longer version. "Not good," he replied.'

I enjoyed these gags, but was glad I hadn't had to shell out ten grand to hear them. In fact, the biggest shout of laughter greeted a true story told by Robin Cook, who a week ago had been at the Foreign Ministers' summit in Istanbul, discussing Chechnya with his Russian opposite number, Igor Ivanov.

'London was buzzing with news of a certain baby. I left the meeting to be confronted by an ecstatic Bertie Ahern, the Irish Prime Minister. He asked me to give my warmest congratulations to Tony Blair. Naturally I assumed there had been a breakthrough in the Irish peace talks.

' "Of course I will," I replied. "Tony's been working hard on this for a very long time." '

25.11.99

One of the great problems in Ireland has been the way that language drives the conflict forward. 'No surrender!'; 'Ireland unfree shall never be at peace'; 'A terrible beauty is born'; 'Ulster will fight and Ulster will be right!' The combatants have a tremendous ability to encapsulate their raw emotions into words that make retreat and reconciliation impossible.

So it is to Tony Blair's credit that he has managed to damp

down this inflammatory rhetoric with a great asbestos, fire-proof blanket of jargon. Yesterday in the Commons he paid the usual tribute to people who have taken part in what he terms the peace process. Then he mentioned 'the appointment of an authorized representative to discuss the modalities of decommissioning with the independent commission on decommissioning'.

Aha! 'The modalities of decommissioning with the independent commission on decommissioning'! Try picking the bones out of that piece of cod. Imagine if Padraig Pearce had stood over the grave of O'Donovan Rossa and called for a review of further decommissioning modalities. Or if Edward Carson had harangued the crowd at Stormont, bellowing: 'Ulster demands modalities, and Ulster will have modalities, or else face without flinching the prospect of further talks with expanded parameters!'

Nobody could have fought under those banners. If Mr Blair can keep this up we may finally see peace, marked by the establishment of a commission to supervise the decommissioning of the independent commission on decommissioning.

02.12.99

In January 2000, it was finally decreed that General Pinochet should be allowed to leave Virginia Water in the Surrey Gulag and return home.

One of the most prominent campaigners against General Pinochet made his sorrowful way to the Commons yesterday. You had to feel deep pity for the man. All those years of protest, the cold, wet vigils outside the embassy, the visits to Chile for clandestine meetings with activists risking their lives so that their passionate demands for justice might be heard – all dashed by a single announcement, smuggled out to the media late on Tuesday night, made by a right-wing Home Secretary who apparently cares nothing for those Chilean people who suffered for so long under the rifles and jackboots of the Pinochet regime.

The fact that the activist and the Home Secretary are one and the same person, Jack Straw, can have brought him scant consolation. You kept feeling that he would have been much happier standing outside the House with a banner, shouting: 'Hey, Straw, what's that for? How about the innumerable innocent victims of Pinochet's secret war?' Or something along those lines.

(You have to remember that, basically, Jack Straw, for all the revolutionary fervour of his past, is a Goody Two-Shoes. At a time of life when Mo Mowlam was toking merrily away, he, as a students' union official, was busy campaigning against the use of pot at Leeds University. And possibly picketing Rolling Stones concerts, shouting: 'Druggies, druggies, druggies! Out, out, out!' while holding up placards reading 'we want Cliff! And the Shads, waving their legs in unison, because they know how to have fun in a clean, manly fashion!')

So one way or the other, the last seven days must have been difficult for Mr Straw. He intends to restore to his family a man who gave orders for his political opponents to have their bellies slit open before they were thrown from planes. He must have been sorely tempted at times to throw eggs at himself.

13.01.00

Yesterday the great jargon slick, which has spilled from this government, spread even farther, taking over and covering what had once been pristine language. Much of the session on environment questions was devoted to incinerators, or 'Energy from Waste' as we are supposed to call it now. Many MPs are angry that these furnaces are pumping out poison straight into the lungs of their constituents.

Michael Meacher, the minister, was sanguine. 'There has been some small increase in primary liver cancers,' he said, 'but it is not yet clear if this is due to the incinerators.' That must have mightily cheered everyone who lives downwind of a pile of smouldering tyres and chemical by-products.

'Currently, no more than one nanogram per cubic metre is released into the atmosphere,' Mr Meacher went on. I had vaguely assumed that a 'nanogram' was a stripper dressed up as Mary Poppins who comes to Tory MPs' birthday parties and spanks them on the botty with a hairbrush. Apparently it's something much worse.

Hilton Dawson wanted to help. He was hugely enthusiastic about new bus schemes. 'Isn't it marvellous,' he chirruped merrily, 'that local councils are going to be able to meet new targets under Objective Two, and under SRB 6, and 7!'

The environment, bizarre new jargon, impenetrable terminology – our thoughts naturally turned to the Deputy Prime Minister, John Prescott. Yet, after one brief, bland answer at the start of the session, he said not a word for forty-four minutes. I suspect they are shutting him up. His understrappers are told that their hopes of promotion depend on keeping the boss quiet.

'I think I can field this one, John!' junior ministers say eagerly. 'Stamp duty on large-scale voluntary housing transfers? I'm your man!'

'Gosh, you'd really make my day if I could tackle that tough question on the Garstang Super 8 minibus service!' As a result Mr Prescott sat happily and silently on the front bench.

None of this mattered because yesterday a new star was born. Keith Hill, the Labour MP for Streatham, now handles transport in the Commons and found himself matched against John Redwood. Mr Hill is definitely not gay, but he has developed a manner reminiscent of Larry Grayson in the old *Generation Game*. The voice dives and swoops. His fingers flutter, or occasionally come to rest on his hips. Asked a fierce question about road building, he pirouetted round and said: 'Madam Spe-e-e-ker!' in a way that might have brought a blush to all of Julian Clary's cheeks.

Mr Redwood asked a convoluted question about the Dome and enquired why 'the Big Top is being written off as the Big Flop'. Mr Hill paused briefly, then squeaked, 'More, more! I read an article about you talking about making the trains run on time. Ooh, yes, our home-grown Mussolini. The Il Duce of the Home Counties!'

Mr Redwood raged on. Why, on New Year's Eve, he demanded, had there been no ministers in London telling revellers how to get home? But what on earth did he expect? Keith Hill on the platform with a clipboard, saying: 'Take the Jubilee Line to Swiss Cottage, and while you're in there, give my regards to Hans. Whoops!'?

12.01.00

The Mussolini line is a good one for incompetent departments. It implies that anyone who cares about a decent train service is necessarily a fascist tyrant. Sadly Mr Hill became a senior whip, and we heard very little more from him after that.

There's a programme called Powerhouse, *which goes out on Channel 4 at weekday lunchtimes while parliament is sitting. They often have guest presenters, many of them politicians.*

I popped down to 4 Millbank, the building that is the real centre of our national debate now that so few people pay attention to the House of Commons. It's where the BBC, ITN, Sky and local broadcasting stations have their Westminster offices. Even when the Chamber is deserted you can find a clutch of pols there, all desperate for an appearance on *Good Morning, Oswestry*! Yesterday's draw was Ann Widdecombe, who has been presenting *Powerhouse* all week. She was to meet her own leader, William Hague, in what was billed as 'an exclusive interview – his first of the year'.

I admire Ann Widdecombe. Working in a political world that prefers appearance to reality, image to substance, she sticks by real convictions. I don't care for many of her convictions, but that is not the point. Here is a woman who refused to change her bra style under instruction from Central Office. What you see is what you get. If she had had a spin doctor, he would have been struck off by the BMA a long time ago.

However, when it comes to no-holds-barred, gritty, in-your-face interviewing, she will not have Jeremy Paxman too worried. Indeed, as I felt obliged to tell her after the programme, she reminded me of those interviews conducted by the late Robert Maxwell with various East European despots and apparatchiks. 'Tell me, President Ceausescu, what is the secret of your great popularity?' he would probe. Or, 'Just why are the people of Albania so content, President Hoxha?'

Of course Mr Hague is not a blood-soaked tyrant. But he could not have been any more fearful than them. The Labour

Party was pleased enough with the event to issue us with a transcript afterwards, so that we might enjoy it time and again.

'Thank you for joining us,' she challenged.

'I'm very pleased to be here,' Mr Hague shot back.

'Last year we had quite a good year in terms of election results,' she insisted. 'Yet we've still got our critics, particularly over keeping the pound. Does that matter?'

William Hague confessed that, all things considered, it didn't. 'We stick up for the British people,' he said.

Then she wrung out of him: 'You go round sticking up for the British people yourself.'

She was pitiless, intransigent. 'You've been setting out your vision of the Conservative Party, and I have to say it's a vision that I think will encourage people.' We leaned forward to see if the sweat was pouring from his forehead, the veins pulsing on his cheeks. 'Yesterday Tony Blair described Blairism as "winning elections". What's Hagueism?' she demanded.

Phew. Luckily he had a response ready for that. 'I want to win elections in order to govern. He wants to govern in order to win elections.'

Like Cardinal Fang in the Monty Python Spanish Inquisition ('Bring on – the comfy chair!') she showed no mercy. 'One of our traditional areas has been law and order, but we see Jack Straw making quite a sizeable mess of that, don't we?'

By now, he was stretched on the rack. Somehow he managed to choke out these defiant words: 'Our response to that would be to put in a much better Home Secretary, which is why I hope you will do that, unless you're going to go into full-time TV presentation, which you also do very well.'

Politicians would love to be grilled like that all the time, and of course thirty years or so ago, they usually were.

14.01.00

It was one of those dreams that make ministers wake up at 3.30 a.m., sweating and perhaps even whimpering with fear. 'Darling, what is the matter?' ask anxious wives and mistresses, as their menfolk wipe the clammy moisture from their brows and crawl downstairs for a cup of tea and twenty restoring minutes of Judge Judy on all-night television.

The dream is always the same. There they are in the Commons, confidently beating off Tory attacks, poised, assured, the facts disposed in well-marshalled files, the arguments deployed like a chessmaster's pawns. Their quiet glow of satisfaction sends serotonin, the happy drug secreted by the body, into the correct receptors of the brain.

'The whips are listening,' murmurs the serotonin. 'They'll be telling Number 10 about how brilliantly you laid about the Tories. Margaret Beckett, Jack Straw, Robin Cook – who knows what will happen to them in the next reshuffle? Tony's bound to need someone as intellectually nimble as you to promote to the Cabinet. You only need to keep going.'

John Spellar, the defence minister, dreamed on as peacefully as any child. In his nocturnal lucubrations, he was being assailed by Robert Key, a Tory spokesman. Mr Key had made rather an ass of himself on the *Today* programme by saying: 'We can't be held responsible for things that happened ten years ago.' In that case, whom can we hold responsible? In any event, this was not a man whose debating skills were going to cause Mr Spellar much difficulty. He could cope with him while fast asleep.

Mr Key was complaining about a cut in the amount of money being provided for service hospitals. 'How is it that when I asked you what had happened to the £1,500,000 allocated for orthopaedic waiting lists, you replied that there were no cuts?

'We then discover that as long ago as last December Admiral Sir John Brigstock confirmed that there had been £1.5 million cuts. I for one feel misled. Who is right – you or the admiral?'

Mr Spellar grunted gently and rolled over. Outside the first notes of the dawn chorus could be heard, and the soft whine of a milk float wafted from a nearby street. A distant shriek told of urban foxes fighting over scraps of rubbish. In his dreams he formulated the perfect reply.

'We recognized that these cuts in defence medical services had gone too far,' he said – except that horribly, unimaginably, nightmarishly, he had inserted an extraneous letter N into the word 'cuts'.

The mistaken word was clear and crisply spoken. What made it even worse was that the sentence as it came out made just as much sense as what Mr Spellar was trying to say. There was a short but terrible silence. Mr Spellar must have felt like a man who dreams he is falling out of bed, then realizes that he is, and that his bed is on a clifftop mountain bivouac.

Then the Tories exploded, laughing riotously, slapping their thighs amid a barrage of stage hilarity. Front-benchers scanned the gallery to make sure we had caught the words he had used.

At the end you could say that the government had survived a damaging assault on its credibility. Or you could argue that the opposition had mercilessly exposed its shortcomings. Or, as I beg Mr Spellar never to try to say, you could take your pick.

25.01.00

Homosexuality was a common feature of many debates in the early days of the Blair government. The peers in particular seemed to take great relish in debating buggery.

Lord Waddington, near the start of the Lords' debate on

Section 28, enquired: 'Who cannot see, from their knowledge of anatomy, that sodomy is an unnatural act?' This is the 'Lego legover' theory of human sexuality. Something is perfectly moral provided the bits fit together snugly. The trouble is that it would also excuse incest. Or shoplifting, since our hands are well adapted to that purpose.

His lordship went on to say that it was, of course, 'wrong to be intolerant of homosexuality', so provoking that rarest of sounds in the Upper House, sarcastic laughter. In a way his speech was quite refreshing, a fine example of beautifully polished, hand-chamfered, traditional British bigotry, as much at home in the smoking room of a gentleman's club as a leather armchair, as welcome in the saloon bar of a pub as a gin and tonic.

He was especially distressed by a leaflet recently issued by a South London borough on the subject of 'cottaging etiquette', cottaging being random gay encounters in public lavatories.

In fact, cottaging etiquette has been long neglected by the experts. 'Dear Mr Morgan, if a single tap on the cubicle door is ignored, is it courteous to knock again? Or should I wait for the occupants to emerge? Also, I was raised always to send a handwritten note of thanks afterwards. However, many of the people I meet seem unwilling to tell me their names and addresses...'

Lord St John of Fawsley, who I consider the thinking man's Dale Winton, said that there was no moral problem, since all sexual activity outside marriage was wrong according to the 'Universal Christian Church', which is what the rest of us call the Roman Catholics. 'These problems are best dealt with in the confessional, not the public hall,' he said. At last! A perfect solution for unhappy Labour MPs who carry with them the miserable knowledge of their own perversion. Now they could mumble what they really believe to a priest, rather than have to vote against the dogma of the Universal Church of Tony Blair.

Next came Lord Longford, addressing us briefly before he beetled off, perhaps to be at the side of Dr Harold Shipman in Strangeways prison. The difficulty for us admirers is that half of what his lordship says is inaudible, because of his extreme age. But he could try speaking a little more slowly. Presently it all comes out like a stream of consciousness filled with rocks and dead branches.

'Too clever by half, yes, that was Cranborne's grandfather …gay lobby referred to Lord Boothby as unpaid leader of the homosexual lobby. I've got homosexual medals [sic]… homosexism is against Christian rules, deprives people of the supreme joy of having children [sic]…maybe not homosexism, having five mistresses, sinful, sinful, hmmm, sinful…I know two young men, one serving ten years for attempted buggery, leanings, leaning, should be resisted, hmmm…'

08.02.00

That was, I think, the last speech I ever heard Lord Longford make. He was never a man to conceal his talents, nor his own estimate of their value. On one occasion I met him in the Gents in a pub in Warrington where I was covering a by-election. Somewhat startled to see him at the next urinal, I said rather rudely, 'What are you doing here?' He replied: 'I'm here on behalf of the Universe!' which I thought was pretty much, even for Longford, though it turned out he meant the Roman Catholic newspaper of that name.

William Hague, meanwhile, decided it was time to take his message directly to the people and cut out the media middlemen. He set off on a tour round Britain on a lorry, from which he intended to harangue the crowds. Most of them, naturally, turned out to be members of the media.

Ashley Stewart, a dark, jut-jawed, freelance van driver, steered William Hague's 'Keep the Pound' battle lorry into the main street of St Albans, displacing the Dinky Donuts van, which was moved out of camera range. The juxtaposition of Dinky Donuts and the Tory leader's head might have set up unwelcome resonances in the voters' minds.

On the left was another van selling French pancakes. It's not the first time Mr Hague has found himself in competition with a load of crêpes.

Just why the battle lorry was there at all seemed unclear. Except for a few balloons, the back was empty. Mr Hague was coming by car, and when he finally arrived, he chose to stand on a platform instead, having no truck with the lorry, which seemed to be little more than a mobile backdrop.

A medium-sized crowd had assembled, though most seemed to be local Tories, a few were puzzled tourists and a lot were media folk. Mr Hague had promised to get outside the M25 – that perimeter fence that rings all the inbred, metropolitan, chattering classes – and get out among the real people; and, indeed, St Albans does lie about one mile beyond that Highway of Hypocrisy.

There was a sudden loud screeching noise, so we assumed Ann Widdecombe had arrived – though it turned out to be feedback from the mikes. Michael Ancram, the party chairman, assured us he was on his way. 'Yes, he is coming!'

'What a plonker,' remarked one of the real people, standing outside Boots.

Finally Mr Hague was among us, wearing a brown, rustic sort of jacket, suitable for gassing badgers on a chilly night. He put his hand in his pocket and pulled out a pound, which he waved at us. 'Yes, this is a pound!' he told us, as if we were a particularly thick school class. 'Put up yer hands if you have a job or run a business!' he shouted. No one did. 'Yes!' he exclaimed, undeterred by the absence of hands. 'Hundreds of you have a job or own a business! Now, hands up everyone who pays taxes!' About six hands rose. 'Yes, almost everyone pays taxes, and under Labour you pay more taxes!' Nothing would stop him. 'How many of you have a pension fund?' About seven arms rose. 'Hundreds of people!' he raved.

Question time next. This consisted largely of Mr Hague repeating the question, then adding, 'Vote Conservative.' Michael Portillo gazed up at his leader, alternately smiling adoringly, or else jutting a determined jaw, like a man who is looking forward to having several teeth extracted. Another real person shouted, mysteriously, 'Do you wear dresses?'

Mr Portillo spoke grimly about the day in 1992 when we crashed out of the European exchange rate mechanism. 'Some people may have short memories, but William and I have long memories,' he said.

As do we all, of that dark, humiliating day when the Chief Secretary to the Treasury was, er, Michael Portillo.

16.02.00

The following day Charles Kennedy, the Lib Dem leader, said that the whole meet-the-people tour was a rare example of dodgy goods falling onto the back of a lorry.

Theresa May arrived for education questions in the Commons. She is the Tories' shadow minister and, like most of her colleagues, is largely unknown to the public.

However, there is a porn star, who appears on the cable channel Granada Men and Motors, or Boys and Boobs as it should really be called, and so is slightly better known. Her name is also Teresa May, spelled without an H. Apparently this has caused some confusion, with phone calls and letters being forwarded to the wrong Tess.

One protested in a recent radio interview: 'I was disgusted at the sleazy world these letters revealed. My namesake was asked to expose herself in public, to do things with men that most of us wouldn't consider doing in the privacy of our homes, and to force herself into weird, unnatural positions in front of the cameras.

'She was told to blank out her fears and anxieties, and just do it. They said, "It will make a lot of middle-aged men very happy." Thank goodness I'm not a Tory MP.'

I myself am not acquainted with the oeuvre of the thespian Ms May, but from my limited knowledge of porn films, they are all much the same. Typically a woman is in bed with her lover. They copulate. He goes to work and the pool maintenance man comes round. They copulate. He goes next door where he finds a topless housewife… Well, you get the general idea.

So the plot hardly exists, and the dialogue is both banal and predictable. Which makes it almost identical to parliamentary questions. The trouble is that once an event as dull and workaday as education questions takes on an erotic tinge, it becomes hard to make serious and sober political judgements. For example, John Bercow, a troublesome Tory right-winger who always looks as if he ought to have a rottweiler on a piece of string with him, is now a front-bench spokesman on education. Mr Bercow looks exactly like the heroes of those chirpy 1960s British sex films, which generations of schoolboys used to watch furtively: Education Spokesman on the Job, perhaps. ''Ere, darlin', wanna get acquainted wiv my differential top-up?' (Education questions are conducted almost entirely in jargon. Speaking about schools with specialist status, Mr Blunkett, the education secretary, promised to 'cascade both their resources and their work outwards', whatever that might mean.)

Finally Theresa May got up – this was the politician, but she was wearing alarmingly pointed shoes, which I doubt she obtained in Dolcis – to complain about the teachers' pay award. 'This government is all mouth and no delivery!' she shouted, as I silently corrected her; 'Trousers, the word is "trousers".'

Mr Bercow asked why grammar schools might have to be made non-selective just because of 'ten local malcontents'. Estelle Morris, a junior minister, seized on this. 'Aha, the new Tory word for "parents" – "malcontents"!'

Mr Bercow looked glum as his phantom rottweiler slumbered beside him. The four female ministers then filed triumphantly out of the Chamber for the obligatory final orgy scene – and yes, I did make that up.

18.02.00

Oddly enough, shortly after writing that I found myself sitting next to the other Teresa May on a commuter train. I wasn't sure it was her until she pulled out the Daily Star *and not only perused the page 3 picture carefully but actually read the caption. Probably no other woman in Britain would do that.*

In 2000 we had the first election for Mayor of London. I did an interview with a journalist from an American TV network who wanted to know why we were electing a Mayor of London when we already had one. I explained that the existing one was the Lord Mayor of the City of London, which was of course quite different from London, the city of that name. They stopped the interview at that point.

Frank Dobson, the Labour candidate, called for a new blitz on London. He was, of course, mistaken. The difference between Ken Livingstone and a doodlebug is that with Ken, the time to duck is when the whining noise begins.

Which it did yesterday afternoon when Ken launched his attempt to become Mayor of London. His should be renamed the Stuff Blair campaign. In the absence of a serious Conservative Party, Ken is standing on behalf of everyone, right and left, black and white, sane and bonkers, who can't stand New Labour.

Meanwhile, Labour MPs, who split roughly into two groups over Ken – those who loathe him and those who detest him – were asking each other: 'What are the two worst things about Ken Livingstone?' Answer: 'His face.'

The launch was at BAFTA, the film and TV association. There were posters on the wall for great British films, such as *The Bridge on the River Kwai* (man commits suicide rather than see his life's work destroyed) and *Brief Encounter* (after months of indecision, man decides to call it a day), so they seemed very appropriate.

The microphones were many and highly sensitive, and Mr Livingstone has a nervous way of grunting while he listens to a question, so the alarming effect was of a bear that has just spotted its lunch hiding up a tree.

But there is no doubt about it: the man is a great performer. From the relaxed opener, 'Is everybody ready? Then I'll begin,' to the line near the end, 'I've almost reached the Buddhist plane where there is no ego,' he was calm and in control. (No ego? Ken without an ego? His ego could survive a frontal assault from the parachute regiment.) He faced head-on the charge that he had broken his promise never to stand against an official Labour candidate. 'It is for Londoners to decide what is the greater crime. I'm not looking for a weasel way out. I am not hiding the fact that I am backing out of commitments I have made.' This strategy – 'Trust me, I'm a liar' – may prove hard to break down.

And would he be allowed back into the Labour Party? He flashed us the sweetest of smiles. 'I take heart from seeing all those people in Tony Blair's office who left to join the SDP and were welcomed back. I hope that generosity of spirit can be extended to me.'

It will be hard for poor Dobbo to fight that sweet smile.

07.03.00

In 1999, it was revealed that Lord Archer had persuaded a friend to invent an alibi for him, in order to win a libel case against the Daily Star. *The news caused him to be dropped as Tory candidate for London Mayor and to be expelled from the Conservative Party. In 2001 he was convicted at the Old Bailey and jailed for this offence.*

On my way to the Lords to attend the debate on their future, I stopped to pick up one of the guides printed for tourists from exotic lands, the latest being in Welsh. Apart from learning that the Woolsack is *y sach wlan,* and that the Liberal Democrats are the *democratiaid rhyddfrydol*, I discovered that the Lord Chancellor, Derry Irvine, is known to his Welsh subjects as *Arglwydd Ganghellor.*

The Great Lord Gangler! What a superlative title! I watched

him with increased reverence, as he gangled around in his pocket, appeared to pull something out of his ear and put it in his mouth, then gangled round inside his wig, rummaging as if trying to find a small woodland creature that had got lost.

I was so wrapped up in this display that I failed to spot someone who had slipped unnoticed into the Chamber and was sitting behind the Gangler on the steps to the throne – not just on the steps, but bang in the middle in front of the throne, in such a position that if Her Majesty were in place she would be able to kick him swiftly and painfully in the kidneys. Jeffrey Archer was back.

Only four months after what we assumed to be the terminal disgrace of his career, he was there, among his colleagues in what is still nominally our Upper House, not just listening in a concerned, sage sort of way, but – given that he can no longer sit with the Tories, having been expelled from the party – in the most prominent position the whole Chamber has to offer, short of perching on *y sach wlan* itself. I have seen giraffes with less neck than Lord Archer. Short of asking the Queen to pretend she had had dinner with him, I cannot imagine a greater display of nerve.

Unless perhaps it was Lady Jay's speech on the reform of the Lords themselves. The Leader of the House was leading the discussion on a royal commission report. The government wants an appointed House but with a few – a very few – elected members.

Now we know the real reason, which is that if you start letting the electorate decide who represents them, you get all kinds of non-New Labour riff-raff succeeding – look at the result of the vote for London Mayor, where the electorate is about not to choose the candidate personally chosen for them by Tony Blair! But nobody can make this point in public.

Instead, Lady Jay announced gravely: 'Any proposal totally to elect the second chamber, under the mistaken view that it would increase the democratic base of Parliament, would in fact undermine democracy.'

This was breathtaking stuff. I sat slack-jawed through this display of sophistry without sophistication. Lord Strathclyde, the Tory leader, confined himself to saying that he wanted more voting: 'We do not think there is anything to fear in an election.' What a wonderful turn-up: a hereditary Tory peer telling a Labour government that they ought to trust the people. I never thought I would live to see it.

At this point, 'Lord' Archer slipped away to – who knows where? Beside Lady Jay, a look of truculent innocence on his face, was Lord Irvine, gangling happily away to himself.

08.03.00

Tony Blair gave an important talk to the newspaper conference yesterday. Not for the first time, I was struck by the way that a Blair speech is closer to a musical composition than to mere rhetoric. Like a piece of music, its aim isn't to inform but to create good feelings.

It's no more about facts and policies than the Pastoral Symphony is an examination of the common agricultural policy. And, like a piece of music, it has a definite structure, based on internal rhythm and repetition. A theme is introduced and merged with the earlier ones. The repetition brings a satisfying familiarity, so that by the end the listener's brain vibrates with all the interwoven passages.

Nobody ever listened to a Blair speech and came away saying, 'Well, I learned something there.' Instead they praise the bravura performance and enjoy the afterglow created by the mood.

He began, 'My argument today is this.' That was the equivalent of the conductor tapping his baton. Next he announced: 'Britain is stronger together than separated apart.' How we might be separated together he did not explain.

'True Britishness lies in our value, not unchanging institutions,' he continued. This was Beethoven's technique: state the main themes crisply and boldly at the start and then refer back to them at different tempos and in different settings. So 'Britain' or 'British' appeared 49 times in the speech, a rate of almost five times a minute.

'Values', usually integrated into a longer phrase, such as 'a clear sense of shared values' or 'our core values as a country', cropped up 17 times. And there were 16 variations on 'change', or the invariably pejorative 'unchanging'.

In his third sentence he introduced another powerful theme: 'The constitutional changes we have made...are the means of strengthening Britain for today's world.'

The fourth paragraph bound this theme to the earlier ones: 'Standing up for our country means standing up for what we believe in. It means standing up for our values, and having the strength...to stand up for the core British values.'

As the themes circled round and disappeared up their own treble clefs, the orchestra was in full flight. The violins were soaring, the harps created a loud glissando, and the brass was about to crash in.

'To fail to modernize would be to fail Britain. But we must modernize according to our core values.' So after just two minutes, all the main motifs had appeared. Then three minutes later, we heard of a 'Britain that is stronger, fairer, modernized...modernization based on values'.

Then a great surge of woodwind, drawing together all the

earlier themes: 'Standing up for Britain means fighting for British values.' Next the kettledrums began their climactic pounding.

Except that a Blair speech does not end with a crescendo. Instead we were reaching a diminuendo, a soft, gentle coda in which the main themes were gathered together in verbless sentences, creating mood music, which sends the audience away in a soporific reverie. 'An economy gaining in strength. Pride from a modern constitution which strengthens the nation. We are rediscovering our strength and values. We are uniting those values...to make Britain stronger.'

And so the listeners leave, no wiser or better informed, but with the music echoing round their heads.

29.03.00

What is the point of Archie Norman? One of my colleagues believes that William Hague appointed him environment spokesman to make John Prescott look good by comparison, and so help to preserve one of the Tories' best election assets.

My belief is that Mr Hague is a 'sleeper', a closet Labour supporter who was recruited in his fiery, left-wing, Rotherham youth to infiltrate the Tory Party and has been successful way beyond his controllers' wildest dreams.

So you can imagine him saying to his advisers, 'Look, manufacturing is in a bad way, Byers is bound to be in trouble soon. Let's put up a really big hitter. How about...Angela Browning!'

The advisers groan inwardly, but there is nothing they can say. Mr Hague adds: 'John Prescott, old "Two Jags", eh! He's a bit of a national joke by now. I know who'll cut him down to size. Archie Norman!'

The advisers contort themselves over the table, apparently to take biscuits from the plate, but in fact to roll their eyes covertly at each other. In Rotherham an old, wheezy man takes out an ancient radio transmitter from his pigeon loft and taps out a secret message to a Bakelite receiver hidden in Tory Central Office: 'Tha's done greet, lad. Kep it oop.'

Yesterday Mr Prescott outlined to the Commons the housing plans in his new Green Paper. Or, rather, he outlined his housing aspirations. Things, he announced, were to be 'taken in action'. He had 'a wider ambition' to support sustainable communities. He promised 'consultation' and to 'seek responses'. There was a consensus that the rent system was in a mess, and he wanted to 'build a new consensus on that consensus', so that a great, rickety, jerry-built tower of consensuses would stretch to the sky.

And what would he do about all this? Well, the government was 'to examine a range of options' and 'invite proposals' for 'fresh initiatives'. He proposed a 'stronger, more forward-looking, strategic role' for local authorities. ('Strategic' translates as 'taking a long time'.) 'We aim for a step change,' he added ('step change' means 'taking even longer than that'). In short, he promised to do everything except take action.

The Green Paper has a beguiling entry on page thirty-four, announcing the establishment of the 'cowboy builders working group'. One imagines the members of this quango putting their paint-spattered radios on the table and saying, 'Sorry we're late, 'ad another consultative document to finish up in Purley. Now, 'oo did that last report for you? Blimey, wot a botch job that was...'

Then it was Mr Norman's turn. It's not his fault that he sounds like a dying wasp, though that is no excuse for his droning on and on, his voice rising, falling sometimes, making that awful whirring noise that means that the fly-killer has kicked in.

After thirty seconds he was banging on about rail safety, then leaks to the press, then on to air traffic control. 'What about housing?' asked Mr Prescott, a huge grin circling his huge face. Tory MPs were hurling themselves around the benches like sand fleas, all part of a desperate attempt to stay awake.

'Now, eighteenthly…' you expected him to say. He wagged a finger at Mr Prescott, who looked happier than ever.

'In conclusion,' he said, and Labour MPs cheered wildly. He looked thunderous, or at least mildly peeved. 'I repeat, in conclusion!'

'Yet another impressive performance,' said Mr Prescott, sarcastically, though having watched Mr Norman dig a mantrap, then fall in it himself, he proceeded to follow him down. 'I can think of a whole paucity of things to say,' he began. But it didn't matter. He was safe. From Rotherham a message crackled south over the short-wave band. 'Slap tha'self on t'back, lad, tha's done a reet gradely job!'

05.04.00

Year Three

After lunch is the most dangerous time of day for Nicholas Soames. What he likes to do is to come to the Commons and shout endearments at the lady members. 'Splendid, absolutely splendid!' he will say, especially when the woman in question has just asked a particularly toadying question.

Yesterday he placed himself at the very back of the backbenches, as if in hiding. He was even behind the lavender-clad figure of Julie Kirkbride, a Tory MP so comely that she causes male Labour members to leave criss-cross trails of drool round the Chamber, like snails.

It was culture questions, which are usually dull, being for the most part Tories saying what a failure the Dome is, and other MPs moaning that too little lottery cash has been spent in their constituencies. ('Why was the excellent and costed proposal for Elastoplast 2000, celebrating the history of the plastic-backed bandage, which would have brought scores of jobs to my constituency, turned down?' That's the sort of thing.)

'The government is sitting on £480 million of lottery players' money,' said the Tory spokesman, Peter Ainsworth. Mr Soames began to study his nails, very carefully, one by one.

Janet Anderson, the junior minister, declared that the Dome was the most popular tourist attraction in the country, and she for one was very proud of it. Mr Soames began a tricky operation: he started to pick the dirt from under the fingernails of one hand with the fingernails of the other.

'The halo effect of investment in the Dome is widespread all over the country,' Ms Anderson went on. Mr Soames began to – 'pick' would be an inadequate word – he began to excavate his nose, with all the fastidious care of an archaeologist who has just started work on a hitherto unknown Minoan dig. Possibly this was because, as wine writer for the *Spectator*, he needs to get rid of any nasal substances that might interfere with his appreciation of the most subtle bouquets.

Or perhaps, like motorists at traffic lights, he imagines that on the backbenches he is invisible. Nick, old chap: when folk are listening to Geoffrey Howe's resignation speech, all eyes are on the speaker. When Michael Fabricant is discussing the seating arrangements in his local rep, our eyes roll round the Chamber in a desperate attempt to find something interesting. That is why they lighted on you.

Nigel Waterston tried to find a way to blame Chris Smith, the culture minister, for Labour's poor local election results. Mr Soames, having attacked his nails too vigorously with his other nails, discovered blood on his hand, and pulled from his pocket a gigantic handkerchief, the size of a mainsail, to staunch the flow – not, I am happy to report, a Quentin Tarantino-style geyser of gore, but a sort of dark red splodge.

'Tourism should be at the very heart of government,' said Ms Anderson, and Mr Soames began work on his teeth, one by one, using some of his seven uninjured fingers to scrape away deadly plaque.

'We have a quality product in our tourist industry,' Ms Anderson went on. Mr Soames ruminatively sucked the last drops of blood from his maimed forefinger.

Ian Bruce, a Tory, launched into a dreary whinge about the state of the tourism industry. Mr Soames found an interesting object on the end of his finger – who can say whence it came? – and he flicked it, so that it landed somewhere on his front-bench colleagues.

Now, perfectly groomed, all extraneous matter cleared from his system, both within and without, he was able to join the rest of us. 'Quite right!' he bellowed at the top of his voice, and sank back on his seat, as clean and glowing as if he had just spent the previous week at an expensive health spa.

09.05.00

Stephen Byers has had an awful few weeks, much of it his own fault. But you would need to be a miserable curmudgeon not to feel a twinge of pleasure on his behalf when he rose yesterday to say that Rover, or at least some of it, had been saved. Perhaps. For the time being.

Mr Byers is the ultimate Blairite. He lives in relation to the Prime Minister as Baldrick does to Blackadder – he doesn't merely need his support, but without Mr Blair he probably would not exist.

Even he could not praise the Prime Minister for personally saving Rover Cars. Instead he paid tribute to the Third Way, which is the political equivalent of Scientology – another meaningless jumble of gobbledegook – and a crafty means of allotting the credit to our great leader, L. Ron Blair.

'The corporate state has been tried and it simply did not work. But neither did a naive reliance on laissez-faire, which led to a crippling obsession with what the government should not do,' he said.

My mind began to drift. 'We cannot rely on heads,' I seemed to hear Mr Byers say. 'Equally we cannot sit back and hope for tails.

'We will never order chips. On the other hand, we know it is frequently right to reject mash. We cannot approve of

Reggie, but at the same time we must not say no to Ronnie. Instead, we should opt for the Third Kray…'

Well, of course he didn't say the last bits, but when ministers launch in on these self-admiring platitudes, you expect similar drivel to issue forth at any minute.

Angela Browning, the Tory industry spokeswoman, made a graceless little speech in which she did not even express pleasure at the planned rescue. Mr Hague must be feeling now a bit like the management of BMW: he made a big investment in Mrs Browning, he rescued her from the backbenches, saving her and all her suppliers – researchers, secretaries, etc. – from destitution, only to see the credibility of his core business drain away. But I don't think they will find a consortium to deliver Mrs Browning from her fate.

She was not the only Tory woman who suffered for the cause yesterday. For some time this column has had a kindly eye open for Anne McIntosh, MP for the Vale of York, not least because she carpet-bombs our Commons office with faxed press releases about every event that happens in her life.

It hasn't yet reached the stage of 'Anne McIntosh takes cue from Nick Soames: flosses teeth regularly', but that cannot be far off.

'Stop Press!' reads a recent despatch from the front. 'MP welcomes further inquiry into pylon line!'

Later, 'MP stands up for the countryside. Venue and time change for photo op!' In March, we were delighted to learn that she had visited a chocolate factory: 'MP samples sweet success.' Days earlier she invited her fortunate constituents to meet her while she ate a hamburger: 'Little Mac to meet Big Mac for Millennium Mac.'

But there is something engagingly ingenuous about Ms McIntosh. Yesterday she called John Prescott 'the Deputy Speaker' instead of Deputy Prime Minister, and confused the new deal for the unemployed with the new deal for communities – as most of us would, except we're not Members of Parliament. The fax reading: 'MP screws up badly in environment questions. Was my face red! Photo op and cringing apologies available…' has not yet arrived. But no doubt it's on its way.

10.05.00

Fans of A. A. Milne will recall that a heffalump trap is a pit that you dig for a heffalump and then fall in yourself. Yesterday William Hague dug a beautiful heffalump trap, scooped it out, stuck sharpened stakes in the bottom, covered it with branches, leaves and moss, paused to admire his work, then walked slap dab into it.

Ka-poom! The sound of him crashing down reverberated round the Commons for minutes, if not seconds.

Poor William. He has been doing quite well lately. I've always thought that the boy had an inner calm that has helped him in difficult times, which is to say since he became leader of the Conservative Party. With Labour's poll lead down to the lowest since 1992, he might have expected a triumphant Prime Minister's Question Time. Instead he found himself trying to climb out of a heffalump trap.

It all began with stuff about ministers disagreeing over the euro. 'Will the Prime Minister get a grip on his Cabinet, and stop them fighting like ferrets in a sack?' (Fighting ferrets in a sack might have been a childhood diversion in the Rotherham of his youth. 'Young William Hague took on five ferrets at once before leaving the sack, hurt…' More fun than memorizing parliamentary majorities, which is what he actually did.)

Mr Blair pointed out that the Tories were also divided.

'But I lead my party, and he follows his,' said Mr Hague.

This braggadocio was greeted with wild cheering, at least from the claque seated behind the Tory leader. At a greater distance I noticed expressions on the faces of Tory MPs that were rather more thoughtful, perhaps even mildly embarrassed.

It was then that he started to dig the trap. He decided to quote the private memo from Mr Blair's mentor, Philip Gould, the one in this week's press that said that 'TB' was lacking in conviction, unable to stick to a position and out of touch.

'Does TB himself agree with this, or is it just the rest of us?'

'Well,' said the Prime Minister mildly, 'if he's not careful, I'll start to read what the focus groups say about him.'

This is why Amanda Platell, Mr Hague's personal spin doctor, ought to have radio-controlled cattle prods sewn into his Y-fronts. Sitting in the gallery, she could press a button – left for 'Carry on, you're doing fine', or right for 'Shut up, for goodness' sake, shut up, *now*!' We would know that she had hit the button because the opposition leader would start to twitch madly, which we would all enjoy.

Lacking this high-tech guidance, Mr Hague blundered on towards the trap he had prepared. 'We'd be delighted if he'd read what the focus groups said, because then we could have the whole document placed in the Commons library,' he said, going on to add what was meant to be a mighty peroration: 'He has run out of steam, run out of time and, if he carries on like this, will be run out of office!'

Mr Blair smiled amiably. 'He challenged me to read out the focus groups, so I will. This is what they say about him: "Boring, false, he irritates me greatly, pathetic drip, nonentity, no substance, no personality, complete waste of time, no policies and a very unimpressive team, particularly William Hague".'

Labour MPs, who had been fearful a few moments before, erupted in glee. Tories were deeply, deeply glum. Mr Hague began smiling and laughing, in the strained, half-demented way that any of us might, but only if we were sitting impaled on spikes at the bottom of our own heffalump trap.

15.06.00

Experienced vulcanologists know the signs. The slight rumbling, the occasional spitting noises, the almost imperceptible earth tremors. These tiny events, unnoticed by most bystanders, indicate to the expert that an eruption may be imminent.

Mount Widdecombe is much the same. She sat on the bench before yesterday's law-and-order debate, growling gently. The odd harrumph escaped her. The green leather of the bench could be seen shaking like the millennium bridge. As an old hand who has often stuck his seismograph onto the flanks of this great natural phenomenon, I knew that a terrible event was about to occur.

Suddenly it did. The Speaker called the debate and a mighty roaring noise filled our ears. The sides of the mountain bulged alarmingly. A shower of debris, or at least the shadow home secretary, crashed onto the Despatch Box.

'The more desperate the Prime Minister and the Home Secretary become, the bigger fools they make of themselves! Gimmicks! On-the-spot fines for drunken yobs! Senior police officers are queuing up to call the idea ludicrous and ridiculous!'

By this time the mountain was spouting fire from its crater. 'When the said yob has straightened himself up enough to say that he doesn't have the £100, and the policeman has accompanied him to the cashpoint, and in his drunken state he has recalled his pin number, and produced his bank card, and instantly got out the £100…' she spat, and a river of contempt flowed like lava towards Mr Straw. 'If that is the best he can manage in the face of rising crime, it is pathetic. Yes! It. Is. *Pathetic!*'

Here I must briefly abandon my extended metaphor, since Ms Widdecombe does not only erupt. Unlike a volcano, she can also make gestures to enhance the effect of her words. 'They sound tough for the headlines,' was accompanied by a terrific flapping motion, as if she were shaking out a crumb-infested tablecloth.

'I noticed none of them is leaping up to defend this policy,' she cried, and made sinister beckoning signs, rather like Count Dracula: 'Come to me, my beautiful creatures of the night.'

'What is the point in condemning the courts for over-lenient sentences when even those they give are not serviced?' she yelled, while pointing furiously at Mr Straw ('Yes, that man is the father of my baby!'), then smashing her hand down, like Joe Grundy finishing off a ferret.

Allegedly there are some 4,000 vacant spaces in British prisons. 'Are there indeed 4,000 spaces? Why are there 4,000 spaces? Where are the 4,000 spaces?' She makes Edith Evans's 'A *h-a-a-a-nd-bag*?' sound like the merest sotto voce aside.

'A shambles! It is a shambles! Yesterday we even heard of one criminal who was let out, having been electronically tagged on his wooden leg. He simply substituted the tagged leg for another false leg and went out drinking! Until all hours!' She delivered a series of karate chops to a pile of imaginary bricks.

Jack Straw pointed out in his earnest way that the Tories

had cut prison sentences too. He kept trying to intervene. He would place one foot in front of the other and start to rise from his feet, but the hot, sulphurous blast from the mountain and the furious, frantic finger hurled him back down again.

Even when she had finished and he was allowed to reply, she remained, like Vesuvius after an eruption, still muttering and shouting and spouting, fitting in a second speech by way of her spluttering, rumbling commentary on his.

Now no flowers or trees will grow at her feet for many years to come.

04.07.00

There is a cartoon story by H. M. Bateman called 'The One Note Man'. A series of beautifully detailed drawings shows a chap waking up, having breakfast, going to work with his instrument case, joining the orchestra and, at the climax of his day, playing a single note on the oboe. The tale ends with him going home and tucking himself into bed.

Yesterday Michael Fabricant became The One Word Man. We can follow his day because it is described minutely on his brand-new, freshly overhauled website, which for some of us holds even more interest than the likes of hotbabes.com.

He gets up, brushes his teeth, feeds his hair from a bottle of Baby Bio, goes to the House, answers his mail, then ponders the state of his stomach. 'Sometimes I have lunch appointments, but more often than not I take a sandwich back to the office.'

Fascinating! (Though I fear I might have invented the bit about the Baby Bio.) Next he makes his way to the Chamber and leaves a card marked 'Fabricant' at his favourite seat. So later he was in his place and poised as Prime Minister's Questions began.

Mr Blair was having a hard time. In the gallery were five Australian Prime Ministers, in town to celebrate one hundred years in the Commonwealth. Our own Prime Minister paid tribute to the relationship between the two great countries, only slightly spoiling things by calling the premiers 'Americans' – though they seemed to be amused rather than offended.

Mr Hague had decided to attack him over the scheme to have on-the-spot fines for drunken hooligans. This is a typical New Labour wheeze, in that it was worked up in a panic over the opinion polls and bunged in to grab the headlines, without any reference being made to the people who would have to enforce it.

'Can you tell the House which person in government came up with this brilliant idea?' Mr Hague asked, adding: 'Who came up with the obviously fatuous idea of getting drunken criminals to form orderly queues at cashpoints around the country?'

Mr Blair did what he always does when caught out like this: he pretended Mr Hague was opposed not to the batty scheme itself, but to the very notion of controlling yobs. 'If we introduce fixed penalty notices, on the spot, for disorderly conduct, will you support it?'

Mr Hague was enjoying himself. Like a yob, he had found a victim and was not going to let him go. 'You spend your time clutching for another empty headline instead of getting a grip on your divided and shambolic government!'

The Prime Minister was getting seriously rattled. The yob was shouting at him and there was no bobby in sight, no cashpoint within half a mile. Passers-by were scurrying along with their eyes averted. 'Let's deal with spin, rather than substance!' he yelled, getting it the wrong way round as people will in a panic. 'The truth is that when the debate turns to policy, we shall see who is standing!'

For some reason, at this point, time stood still. There was a sort of muted hubbub. But into the comparative calm came a single manic shout of 'Resign!' It was Mickey Fabb, making in just one second the finest oration of his parliamentary career.

That one second was enough for the Speaker. She barked at him, 'Any more of that and you will be out!' But that didn't matter. Teresa Gorman bent over and gave his shoulder a squeeze. He went scarlet with pleasure under his silky white hairpiece. Then, I assume, he went home, had his tea, put on his jim-jams and went to bed, a full day's work well done.

06.07.00

'Order! Order!' shouted Betty Boothroyd. Most MPs did not even know that this was one of the last times she will have cleared the tubes with her famous catchphrase. What I've always liked is the way that when she is genuinely angry, the genteel voice fades, and her Yorkshire accent returns, like a barmaid saying she will put towel back on taps and chuck all you buggers out if she doesn't get a bit of hush. Sue Lawley turns into Annie Walker.

She then announced that, after eight years in the job, she would retire as Speaker just before the next session begins. It was a tremendous shock. For some Tories, it must have been like hearing that Nanny is leaving to get married. They'd pretend to be pleased for her, but inside they'd be screaming, 'What about me?'

She then also said that she would resign as MP for West Bromwich West. A startled 'Ooh' swept round the Chamber, and you can bet there were plenty of MPs who at that point could actually recall her majority when she was last opposed by a Tory (7,830).

But she clearly thought the 'Ooh' was of dismay, because she departed from her script and said passionately, 'Be happy for me!' – and for the first time I have ever heard, the House of Commons started clapping.

It was an extraordinary sight and an extraordinary sound. Clapping is not what MPs do. You are simply not supposed to clap, in the same way you are not supposed to throw toilet rolls.

You can go 'year, year, year' like a manatee with indigestion. You may shout and jeer and yell. You can wave your order paper in the air. You can even, like Le Pétomane, fart 'Frère Jacques' and you will find nothing to forbid it in Erskine May.

But against all the rules they clapped, wildly, with warmth and gratitude and affection, as if she were an ageing film star receiving a lifetime's achievement award at the Oscars.

Betty does not – how can I put this? – have a serious problem with her self-esteem, and I suspect she was awfully pleased to find that the announcement of her departure was greeted by a total breakdown in parliamentary order.

13.07.00

The low spot of the government's first spell in office came with the petrol protests in the autumn of 2000. These ended when the government sort of gave way...

It was the Prime Minister's third press conference in as many days. He was nearly forty minutes late, possibly because he had just heard that some petrol companies had decided that yesterday was the perfect time to stick another 2p on each litre – timing that even Mr Peter 'Dome' Mandelson, who appears to have all the public relations skill of Pot Noodle, might have eschewed.

The Prime Minister appeared, quickly and silently. He was in the State Dining Room, in front of a portrait of George II, the last English king to lead his troops into battle, an example that Mr Blair seems to have decided not to follow. But there is a link. King George was famously out of tune with the mood of the people. However, he had an excuse in that his first language was German. The Prime Minister himself speaks Blairish.

Actually Blairish is not so much a language as a cast of mind. Blairish is inclusive. It seeks consensus. Nothing is asserted; instead the speaker of Blairish precedes his wisdom with remarks such as 'I think everyone will agree…' or, 'You know, I hope people will reflect carefully on events…' Someone asked if he saw the apparent ending of the crisis as a defeat of 'the forces of conservatism', which play the same role in the present government as the Daleks did in *Dr Who*.

But there was no gloating. 'I don't think it's a question of defeating anyone,' he said vaguely, in an emollient phrase lifted straight from the Blairish lexicon. His eyes constantly roamed round the room, looking for agreement. Thatcherish was the language of confrontation, or as your Latin teacher might have put it, 'A question expecting the answer "Sod off".' A sentence in Blairish, by contrast, is supposed to evoke a low rumble of agreement.

He refused to sound triumphant. He realized that the hauliers had had a hard time lately, owing to their increased costs. (Was there a hint here that his life would be a lot easier without having a cackling Silas Marner figure next door, grabbing every bawbee he can from the lorry drivers, farmers, manufacturers, widows and orphans of Britain?) He even refused to pretend that he was protecting the environment, always a temptation for politicians. 'In a rural area, the price of petrol is an issue, and it's no good us saying that it isn't.' I was reminded of a man rediscovering the joys of not hitting his head against a brick wall.

19.09.00

As the Labour Party gathered for its annual conference, two problems seemed to loom over ministers – the fuel protests, which had seen the party fall behind the Tories in the opinion polls for the first time in eight years; and the Ecclestone affair, in which it appeared that in their account of dealings with the millionaire Formula One racing chief, the Prime Minister and the Chancellor had been somewhat economical with the truth. Mr Ecclestone had given £1 million to Labour Party funds, and we were invited to believe that this had nothing to do with the decision to exempt Formula One from the proposed ban on tobacco advertising.

Gordon Brown sat down to a massive ovation after a dazzlingly successful speech. He had tackled the twin problems of the Ecclestone fib and the petrol crisis head-on – by ignoring them. Was he contrite? No, he was not. His speech was as packed with contrition as a frog is full of toothpaste. But the Labour Party has decided it adores him. The stamping and applause and cheering continued for ages, and became even more hysterical when his wife Sarah ran to join him on the platform.

As they descended, a vast, heaving mob of cameramen climbed up on top of each other.

The Browns saw the tottering, lurching phalanx advance towards them. They fled backstage, and finally the cheering stopped.

The reception was as demented as the Prime Minister can expect, and possibly more so. And it can't be coincidence that he ended with the last words John Smith uttered in public: 'The opportunity to serve: that is all we ask.' (This is politician-speak for 'The chance to grab power: that is all we demand.')

Mr Blair sat on stage clapping and beaming as if his life depended on it, which it possibly does. One imagines him saying sibilantly to Mr Brown afterwards, 'That was jolly, jolly good, Gordon. Now I'm afraid I'm going to have to kill you…'

Earlier we heard from Peter Mandelson, who spoke about Northern Ireland. For most of the delegates this was the equivalent of having a guest speech from Beelzebub on the subject of flower arranging. He did not receive a standing ovation; instead the applause resembled the sound of empty crisp packets blowing across a deserted playground.

By contrast, John Prescott's speech was received with rapture. Under Labour, he said, you'll have noticed – 'no water bans or hosepipe crises'. That's because we've had all that rain, I wanted to shout. It's certainly a first – even this government has never before taken credit for the weather.

'Citizens make cities and cities make citizens,' he raved, adding, 'How true that is!' Yes, how true, we thought. I wonder what it means? In the exciting world of John Prescott nobody ever makes a mere decision: on trains, 'We shall make a decisive decision!' he told us.

He got huge applause for his attacks on farmers, hauliers

179

and huntspersons. 'Did you see the Countryside Alliance outside, with their contorted faces?' he asked, his face contorted. He did refer to the fuel protests: 'That is no way to make decisions in a democratic country,' and added: 'They should make decisions the British way – by bunging a million quid to the Labour Party!'

No, silly, of course he didn't say the last bit.

26.09.00

One of the important issues at the conference was pensions, and the sense that old people were being denied a fair share in the country's new prosperity.

I sat in the front row for Tony Blair's speech. It was like the monsoon in a Somerset Maugham short story. Hot, steaming sweat flew all over the platform. His shirt was so damp you expected him to rip it off in mid-speech and call for horse blankets.

His eyebrows were on fire, blazing with commitment. At times he was excitedly hopping from side to side like a lonely line dancer. The Cabinet (remember them? They used to have a minor constitutional role in government) were herded into a set of seats below the leader and to his left, so that they were obliged to gaze adoringly up at him, with the exception of John Prescott, who took time out from beaming at his leader to glower at the sketch-writers.

The Prime Minister began with a ringing battle-cry. 'We're crap!' he told the delegates. 'Yes, we're crap all right, but we're not so crappy as the other lot!' He didn't quite put it like that, of course, but that was what he meant. It was that rarest of moments, an apology from a politician. The Dome, the fuel crisis, pensions, even Prime Minister's Question Time. But he was sorry, God he was sorry. He would never, ever do it again. Would a bunch of flowers help?

He was feeling our pain. 'There's the mortgage to pay... inflation may be lower, but the kids' trainers don't get any cheaper.' (How true that is. There's the riding trainer, the personal fitness trainer, the ski instructor – do you know what they charge these days?) He set a new record of 163 verb-free sentences, those phrases which, by omitting any doing words, appear to offer a promise without making a commitment.

Once he'd got the grovelling out of the way he was transformed. He leaped around as the sweat poured off him like a lawn sprinkler. Would he be the first party leader whose own perspiration made him slither off the stage and crash into the photographers?

Suddenly he departed from the text of the speech to put in what was meant to be a deeply felt, personal statement. 'If you ask me to put tax cuts before education spending – I can't do it …If you ask me to give two fingers to Europe, I can't do it' – except that he pronounced 'I' as 'ah', which is meant to indicate sincerity, as in, 'If you want me to reintroduce slavery, ah can't do it. If you want me to take little Leo's pet hamster and hurl him on the barbecue, ah can't do it.' Oddly enough, he didn't go on to say, 'If you want me to link pensions to the rise in incomes rather than inflation, ah can't do that…'

He has always had a love of clunky phrases, verbal Ladas. He banged on about his 'irreducible core' of beliefs. It sounded like something out of *The China Syndrome*. 'Bweep, bweep! The Prime Minister's irreducible core has gone critical! Put on this lead anorak!'

Moments later he told us that 'Before us lies a path strewn with the challenges of change.' That's the trouble with Blair speeches; they become pastiches of themselves. 'And it is littered with the beer cans of opportunity, knee-deep in the burger boxes and irreducible apple cores of hope,' you expected him to say.

At the end he told us we were on a journey, a journey worth making. But as well as a journey, it was a fight, 'a fight worth fighting'. So the Labour Party were to resemble British football hooligans, who also believe that no journey is complete without a fight. 'We shall hurl the bar stool of opportunity through the plate glass window of privilege,' he didn't say but presumably meant.

It was over. He stayed briefly for his standing ovation, then quickly marched off the platform, no doubt for an urgent swab-down and a bath in a tub full of Lynx.

27.09.00

The Tory conference that year was a strange affair. Ann Widdecombe, then shadow home secretary, called for police to have desks in local stores, or 'cops in shops' as she termed it, or 'the old Bill at the till' perhaps, or on car showroom forecourts you'd offer 'peelers 'n' dealers'. The Conservatives seemed especially pleased that the lovely Ffion Hague was accompanying her husband to various events. The announcer told us: 'Will you welcome William Hague – with Ffion!' which made him sound like a new floor cleaner: 'New lemony fresh Hague, with added Ffion!' It was an opportunity for us to learn about the new Michael Portillo who, at the time, seemed to be a rising star in the party. He had caused some excitement earlier in the year when he admitted having 'experimented with homosexuality' while up at university, at a time when most students spend their evenings experimenting with beer or drugs.

'Antes de ques te cases, mira lo que haces!' exclaimed Michael

Portillo. He had come out, at least as a Spaniard. It was the first Tory leadership bid to be conducted in a foreign tongue.

'I am half Spanish and proud of it!' he told the conference. Some of us can remember a time when few Tories would admit to having been to Spain, never mind having caballero blood coursing in their veins, still less addressing them in the language. It means, roughly, 'Look before you leap.'

But it was a dazzling show by Portillo Mark II. The Spanish half is clearly above the belt. Those thick, comfy, well-groomed lips, as lavish and plump as a leather sofa. (As Jeremy Hardy once said, 'You can tell those lips have seen a lot of Chapstick.') The fleshy hair, curled majestically in what was once a cruel quiff.

But no longer. This was the kindly, inclusive, humble, cuddly Portillo. 'We are a party for all Britons, black Britons, British Asians…We are for people whatever their sexual orientation!' Delegates near me stirred uneasily. To some of them, an inclusive Tory Party is like an inclusive Freemasons – it misses the point.

But he was so unrelentingly nice. He even thanked the electors for having thrown him out in 1997 and so allowed him to visit the real world, *terra incognita* for most politicians. Having memorized his speech, he could stroll around the stage making inclusive gestures. (A friend saw him rehearsing on Monday, when he was advised to stop making the cupping motion with both hands held upwards. 'It looks like, erm, you know…' he was told.)

But Portillo's was not the only unfamiliar proverb of the day. Speeches began to resemble that competition for runic rural sayings, such as 'He is a foolish man who wipes his bottom with a porcupine.' Mr Hague was asked what he would do for farmers. He blamed the problems of the countryside on the people in Islington wine bars. I must find out which bar he means, since all the nation's evil seems to be fomented in this spot. Perhaps it's called The Gay Gaucho. I do not know. 'Scrap the pound, ban hunting, blame the victim, and another bottle of your lightly oaked Rioja, Miguel…'

When he first became an MP, a farmer had told him, 'Mr Hague, if you ever see a satisfied farmer or a dead donkey, sit on it, because you'll never see another.' The conference roared with laughter, then fell strangely silent. What could it mean? Why are dead donkeys so rare? And why should you sit on them? After all, they are hardly likely to get up and walk away. And why sit on the satisfied farmer? What's he done to deserve being sat on? Was it his new battle-cry to the nation: 'Hague's clarion call: "Sit on dead donkeys"'?

Had he run it past his spin doctors?

'D'yer really think they'll understand a reference to moribund equine quadrupeds?'

'Oh, yes, William, whatever you do, don't drop the dead donkey.'

The grisliest moment of the day came when a host of 'celebrities' ran on stage for the culture debate. Mike Batt, Jan Leeming, Mitch Murray, Mike Yarwood, Ed 'Stewpot' Stewart – and they were the big names. The loudest cheer was for Antony Worrall-Thompson who has actually been on TV within the last decade. The rest were melted down by Madame Tussaud's years ago, possibly to make John Prescott.

04.10.00

Next day the weirdness continued. Tim Yeo, then the Tories' agriculture spokesman, decided to lead the entire conference down to the prom, where a 'country fair' was taking place.

When we arrived, William Hague was standing in front of a wagonload of hay. Mr Hague is the only party leader who has a set aside haircut. 'After the next election, we are going to have an agriculture minister who knows one end of a cow from a pig!' he said, bafflingly. A sign near him read: 'Never criticize a farmer with your mouth full.' On Tuesday Mr Hague had enjoined us to sit on dead donkeys. Is everyone baffled by this ancient folk wisdom, or is it just me?

With my opposite number from *The Times*, I approached a giant sausage, which was advertising British pork. Matthew tried to bribe the sausage to stand next to the rabbi. The rabbi? What on earth was a rabbi doing there? And why was there also a live pig, called Winnie? It sounded like the start of a joke. Or perhaps a typing error. 'This is a countryside demo. We'd better have a rabbit,' someone might have said, expecting an unemployed actor in floppy ears. Instead they got a Jewish holy man. The sausage declined the bribe. In any case, there was nowhere to put the money. Sausages don't have pockets.

'I'd want to be photographed next to William Hague because I look like him,' the sausage told us. It turned out to be a female sausage. ('I say, you're a saucy little chipolata, and no mistake,' goatish Tory MPs might murmur.)

I asked if she had always been a sausage, or if this was a recent career move.

'I'm not doing this for fun, you know,' she said crisply, 'the farming industry is in peril.'

Rebuked by a talking sausage! The sausage was on a roll, but I had pitifully failed to cut the mustard.

05.10.00

In October 2000 Michael Martin, a Glaswegian Labour MP, was elected Speaker in place of Betty Boothroyd. This was thought a controversial choice. After a long, exhaustive and puzzling electoral process lasting most of a day, most Labour MPs voted en bloc for Mr Martin, even though by recent convention it was the Tories' or Liberal Democrats' turn to have one of their own selected, and even though it was at times impossible to understand a word Mr Martin was saying. One of my fellow sketch-writers, Quentin Letts of the Daily Mail, *quickly named him 'Gorbals Mick' and the soubriquet stuck. Scottish newspaper writers, whose permanent grudge against the English keeps them warm on those long, cold, northern nights, were furious.*

Many Scottish people have written and e-mailed to complain about my comments on the new Speaker's Glaswegian accent. The Scottish press has also been deeply upset, but then the Scottish press thinks that everything in the London papers is anti-Scots, including the lottery numbers.

However, I have clearly caused much offence to our countrymen up in the North, who feel their culture has been unfairly traduced for the sake of a cheap joke. Therefore I am happy to say that, on reflection, it is time to redouble my efforts.

For example, yesterday Michael Martin held a press conference in the Speaker's house, which is a sort of impossibly grand maisonette built into the Palace of Westminster. He revealed that his wife did not feel comfortable there, and would rather stay in their flat in Pimlico.

This is a refreshing change from the Lord Chancellor, who also has a house built into the Palace. He caused much controversy by having hundreds of thousands spent to make the place look even more magnificent than it already was.

Perhaps Mr Martin will now spend a similar sum to do the opposite. He could have the ceilings lowered, the hot water pipes ripped out and a communal washing area with a stone sink put between his place and Derry Irvine's.

The Tories would go wild. 'How can the government justify the spending of £6.79 on a new outside privy for the Speaker's house? Not since the grotesque waste of public money on the Dome…'

Yesterday he faced a test worse than any offered by the hacks. The Tory awkward squad ganged up on him. They don't like him, they suspect he won the election on a rigged vote, they think he ought to be a Tory and they guess he's an easy target.

The hyper-aggressive Eric Forth, who must have been Flashman in an earlier life, toasting new bugs at the fire, produced a pompous rigmarole about how Betty Boothroyd had always tried to prevent ministers from making public statements before they came to the Commons. 'Yet, yesterday you gave a press conference outside the House before you'd been able to share your thoughts with members of the House!' Given that the normal mode of address to the Speaker is oleaginous toadying, this was remarkably rude and rather brave.

Mr Martin met the attack with dignity. He had done it to protect his family from the hordes of journalists. 'I will never stop you from speaking to whomever you want to speak to, and you will not stop me.'

As for Betty Boothroyd, 'I have the highest respect for her, but she is gone. Betty is no longer with us,' he said, making her sound like a much-loved family pet that they'd had to put down.

John Bercow tried to wrong-foot him with a long, convoluted question about John Prescott's absence from the recent debate on the fuel crisis, but Mr Martin stopped him dead with a trick answer: 'No.'

It's too early to say for sure, but the new man might just be settling in. Or will, once we can understand what he's saying. In the meantime, a final thought. The new Speaker is a Scot. So is the Chancellor of the Exchequer, the Foreign Secretary and, to give him his full title, the Lord Chancellor of England. The Prime Minister was educated in Scotland. So why do so many Scots imagine themselves to be members of a tiny, oppressed minority?

26.10.00

There were terrible, destructive floods in late October and early November 2000.

The Deputy Prime Minister made a statement about the storm havoc yesterday. This is the man who, at the Labour Party conference this year, took credit for the weather. 'No hosepipe bans!' he boasted.

Not yesterday. Only gentle summer rain, rain as warm and moist and welcome as the complimentary towelette handed out at the better Chinese restaurants, is brought to you by Labour governments. The disasters of this week are entirely due to Tory local authorities allowing houses to be built on flood plains. At last MPs have found a way of making the weather a party political issue. And they say the art of rhetoric is dead!

Once again, the House faced the terrifying Prescott wall of words, which sweeps down on a community of MPs, ripping out arguments, tearing down questions, hurling debris round members' knees. Often the hapless victims have no warning of what is on the way. For example, as the Lib Dems' Don Foster pointed out, the Prime Minister's press spokesman, Alastair Campbell, had said on Monday that he didn't expect there to be any statement on this topic today.

At this point, a freak surge burst over the riverbank. Pounding and foaming, the Deputy Prime Minister raged. 'Can I tell him that *I* make the statements when I make them to this House. Nobody else is responsible, *I* am responsible to this House, no parliamentary, no news spokesman, if I decide it is right to make a statement to this House, that's what I do, that's what I have done, and it didn't come from anybody else!'

A rant like that could carry a whole field full of livestock down the river. But suddenly there was one of those moments of calm, perhaps at the eye of the hurricane. After what seemed like an eternity – it was perhaps two seconds – he said, 'Oops, sorry, Alastair!' to delighted laughter.

But, as the weathermen always gloomily say, there's more to come. 'In regard to funding, of course we have increased in considerably during our own resources between the MAFF and ourselves, there has been an increase and what worries me most is we tend to plan for circumstances which are a lot less than we should readily expect now, what we assume to be extreme circumstances are being built into the structures we have,' he said, the water gushing out as if from a broken fire hydrant. Hansard writers, or the fourth emergency service as we think of them now, struggled valiantly to bring aid where it was most needed, but even they were helpless against the tide.

Statistics came crashing past. He was asked about the increased house building in the South-East. But the point about a maelstrom is that it always swirls where it is least expected. Suddenly, he was talking about failed water pumping structures on the east coast rail line. 'That was by alternative governments, so don't make that particular point, but we are now actually taking proper, putting the amount of resources and investment to move what we call extreme conditions which must now regard as normal...

'The Serplan [South-East regional plan] demand for housing was 33,000, I think when Professor Cope came along he suggested it was 55,000, we suggested that we would be 43,000 and the present building is about 39!'

This terrible torrent brought misery and despair to the peaceful folk of the Conservative Party, who can have had no idea of the devastation about to be visited upon them. Tragically they had only their environment spokesman, Archie Norman, to stem the deluge – the equivalent of trying to dam a swollen river with a whoopee cushion.

Mr Prescott suddenly abated, and as I left I could see blank-eyed Tories wandering dazedly around, trying to put back together the fragments of their shattered lives.

07.11.00

I went to the Conservative Women's national conference to catch Ann Widdecombe's speech. These gals make no concessions to the feminist *Zeitgeist*. Here were fund-raising books of recipes to tempt your hubby's jaded palate, all the chairwomen were addressed as 'chairman', and the only clothes stall sold cut-price neckties. You couldn't get near it for elderly women stocking up on presents for their menfolk, many of whom probably wear ties in bed.

There was not a dungaree to be seen; instead they were dressed in the kind of sensible clothes advertised near the back of the *Daily Mail*, the newspaper for old women of both sexes.

At the bookstall, where you could still buy jigsaws of John

Major, Miss Widdecombe had installed herself in front of a pile of her best-selling novel, *The Clematis Tree*. It has sold a remarkable 20,000 copies so far. 'Get your copies *of The Cannabis Tree*!' she shouted wittily. 'Sorry, I mean *The Clematis Tree*. Roll up, roll up, no sex or violence in *The Clematis Tree*!'

As a line of women formed, drawn by this unmissable offer, I reflected that, surprising as it might seem, Miss Widdecombe has become the Britney Spears of the Conservative Party.

Consider: she is not so much an object of desire for the opposite sex as a role model for her own. She has hordes of admirers who would love to dress like her, but don't quite dare. Like the American diva, she makes a great deal of her chastity.

Similarly, she is not blessed with a huge amount of talent, but makes up for it by giving everything she's got on stage. Indeed, the principal difference between her and Britney is that at the Ann Widdecombe show, it's the performer who does the screaming.

She appeared, and as always the ranting, the rage and the fury contain some ordinary common sense. 'Let young offenders out early, if they mend their ways,' was the gist of one section. 'We will wipe the slate clean and let them enter adult life without a criminal record!' was another. Just as Britney's fans would continue to cheer madly if she gave them one of the more difficult Mahler lieder, so the Tory ladies were unfazed by this proposal to flood our streets with newly released hoodlums.

Finally came her great encore, the fans' fave, the fabulous socks number. Apparently prisoners, instead of training for life outside the nick, spend much of their time knitting socks for other prisoners.

Last year they made 1.2 million pairs 'for a prison

population never more than 67,000! Where are these socks? What are they doing with these socks?'

The Joy of Socks is her show-stopper, like Britney's 'Whoops, I Did it Again'. They wouldn't have allowed her to leave without performing it.

At the end, they cheered and clapped, and those who were physically capable, around half, gave her a standing ovation.

08.11.00

All through Prime Minister's Questions yesterday, Caroline Flint, the Labour MP for Don Valley, had been bobbing up and down, desperate to catch the Speaker's eye and ask a question.

Even in the new Labour Party, Ms Flint is regarded as something of a hardline toady, an aardvark-tongued bootlicker, a member of an active service unit in the greasers' provisional wing. Colleagues mused idly about what form her question might take. 'Is he aware that my constituents are ecstatic about the new spending on health care? And that there have been several examples in the Doncaster area of the dead rising from their graves to praise my Rt. Hon. friend?' Or perhaps something about the Prime Minister walking on the floodwater to bring aid and comfort to the victims? Both would have been choice examples of the Flint oeuvre.

So there was a frisson in the air when the Speaker called her. Like experts in the work of Fabergé, we connoisseurs look to see just how many jewelled words she can cram into a single question, the way in which her craftspersonship lets the phrases sparkle and gleam from every angle, each reflecting back the glory of her leader.

Instead, she astounded us in a totally unexpected way. 'Mr

Speaker,' she said, 'my question has already been asked, so I will sit down.'

Sit down? *Sit down?* Without a single congratulation, felicitation or compliment to anyone? Just resume her seat, in silence? I saw members literally slack-jawed, their chins slumped onto their chests. Some raised the energy to flap an astonished arm in Ms Flint's direction. In an old H. M. Bateman 'The man who...' cartoon, the Tory front bench would have been depicted with great, bulging eyes and scarlet faces. Other MPs just looked very, very bewildered. And no wonder. Imagine the late Oliver Reed saying, 'No thank you, I've had more than enough,' or Tam Dalyell saying, 'Oh, sod the *Belgrano*. The Argies had it coming.' The stars seemed to shift in their courses and the solid earth trembled slightly beneath us.

26.11.00

John Prescott paid a welcome visit to the House of Commons yesterday to launch his department's new White Paper, 'Our Towns and Cities: The Future'. This is a classic New Labour document, being printed on glossy paper and illustrated with colour pictures of the Elysium that is the new Britain. Happy people, many from ethnic minorities, gaze productively at computer screens. Pensioners alight from a streamlined tram, which has just delivered them promptly and inexpensively to visit their grandchildren.

In New Labour's dreamland, canals are for strolling by, past bustling pavement cafés where laughing groups of people enjoy cappuccinos in the sun. And they're definitely not full of dead cats, condoms or rusted supermarket trolleys.

The prose has the same unreal quality. Nothing actually

happens, nothing tangible is planned. But, we are promised, there will be 'innovative developments', 'local strategic partnerships' and 'urban policy units'. Town councils will have 'new powers to promote well-being'. As members of society, people will need to be able 'to achieve full potential' while 'protecting the environment, both local and global'. To make sure this happens, the government's 'policies and programmes are the building blocks', and just in case we might have a niggling doubt that none of this means anything and that, even if it did, nothing would happen as a result, we are promised that 'visions of the future will be developed'.

There will be a 'key focus' here and a 'co-ordinated effort' there. The government, in its wisdom, has 'established a framework'. The whole thing resembles those fantastical architect's drawings in which slim, well-dressed figures stroll across tree-festooned piazzas, with no trace of empty burger boxes or gangs of glowering youths.

I was even more suspicious when I heard Mr Prescott's statement. The time to be wary of this government is when it breaks into capital letters. These always indicate not the real world, but some new initiative, programme or unnecessary quango. He is setting up Regional Centres of Excellence. He has established a Neighbourhood Renewal Fund. He is considering an Urban Policy Board and a Cabinet Committee is to hold an Urban Summit. Nor should we forget the Integrated Transport White Paper, the New Deal for Communities or the Social Exclusion Unit.

At one point he reminded us again that 'People make cities, but cities make citizens.' Tories giggled at this, crying, 'Wozzat mean?'

'Think about it!' he bellowed back, though I'm afraid it made me none the wiser. You could say, 'People make cars, but cars make drivers,' or 'People make alcohol but alcohol makes alcoholics.' This kind of talk spreads confusion among the very people who use it. Mr Prescott was asked about the technical description of a city. 'The city of York already is a city, as is my own city of Hull is a city, and that I think is the definition of city and town.'

Faced with this massive pile of abstractions, there was little that the Tory spokesman, Archie Norman, could say. 'The only time we see the Deputy Prime Minister,' he grumbled, 'is when he has a glossy brochure or a disaster to announce.'

Or both, I reflected yesterday, at the same time.

17.11.00

The environment always seems to bring out the worst jargon, closely followed by education. A month or so after the debate described above, Hilary Armstrong, the minister for local government, told the House: 'Local strategic partnerships will provide a single overarching local co-ordinated framework, which will enable local stakeholders to address issues that really matter to local people. They will prepare and implement local community strategies and local neighbourhood renewal strategies. They will allocate local neighbourhood renewal funds and rationalize local partnerships working to deliver better services... As cross-sector, cross-agency umbrella partnerships, LSPs offer real opportunities for streamlining existing partnership arrangements and to make them more effective by making better connections between individual initiatives.' What is frightening is that several backbenchers seem to understand this rubbish and echo it, banging on about effective targeting of stakeholder initiatives. So MP and minister become like two computers, hooked up via a modem, making noises – Squeak! Squeeeeek! Blip! – which only they can understand.

*Reform of the House of Lords continued to vex the government. Back in
2000, Downing Street had announced a new idea: anyone would be
allowed to apply for a peerage. Fifteen of them would be chosen by a
commission. The Downing Street spokesman gave them the felicitous
title of 'the People's Peers'.*

We gathered in a small room in Westminster to hear the names
of the first British peers to have nominated themselves. More
than 3,100 people had put their names forward, and the lucky
fifteen winners had been picked by the House of Lords
appointments commission. It was a public relations disaster.

I felt sorry for the commission and their chairman, a bouncy
fellow called Lord Stevenson. They clearly thought they had
done a spiffy job, and had selected fifteen supremely wise,
articulate, well-informed, thoughtful people. They seemed
hurt and bewildered by the hostility of our questions.

After all, it wasn't their fault that Number 10 had called for
a selection of 'the People's Peers', leading us to expect a cross-
section of society and a chance for ordinary folk to have their
voices heard in Parliament – and had also forgotten to tell them
that this was meant to be the general idea. In fact, later a
Downing Street spokesman detached himself from the debacle:
'They are the People's Peers in the sense that they are people
who put themselves forward for peerages.' Oh, right.

The fifteen names, far from being the kind of folk you might
bump into in the bus queue, were the traditional great and the
good who have been running this creaky old country for years.
But they are more than that: they are the grand and the
grandiloquent, the nobs and the nabobs, the posh and the
plutocratic – in short, they are the People's Panjandrums.

Most are plastered with honours already. Seven have
knighthoods. There are several MBEs and CBEs in there. They

are chairs of this commission or that, professors of the other, members of task forces, chief executives, diplomats, senior advisers, trustees of Glyndebourne, all inhabitants of that nether world of committees, boards, agencies, foundations, working parties and quangos.

Elspeth Howe, the wife of Sir Geoffrey Howe, is one. So overnight she stops being plain old plebeian Lady Howe, and emerges as the brand-new, ennobled – Lady Howe! In fact, she became Lady Howe for the second time when Sir Geoffrey was transmogrified into Lord Howe. As Lionel Richie so movingly put it, 'You're once, twice, three times a Lady…'

I'm afraid my colleagues took all this rather badly. Why are there no ordinary people? We asked.

'Um, an ordinary person is in the eye of the beholder,' Lord Stevenson said elliptically. Then he started digging his hole. 'It is entirely conceivable that a retired headmaster could be a person of great achievement,' he said airily.

Someone rather rudely asked why he of all people had been chosen to chair this commission. 'Aren't you a friend of Peter Mandelson?'

He admitted this. 'But there is nothing political in my relations with Peter Mandelson,' he said. As if. It's like saying there was nothing alcoholic in your relationship with George Best.

I asked if they had not found an application from a thoughtful, well-informed, articulate hairdresser or bus driver. Lord Stevenson resumed digging.

'That is too *simpliste*,' he said, using a language only rarely employed by hairdressers or bus drivers. 'There are a number of people who applied with, um, um, less obvious, um, high-falutin' achievements. But yes, no, you haven't got your hairdresser on the list.'

His spade was flying. Clods of earth landed all around us.

'One criterion is that the human being will be *comfortable* in the House of Lords. We have to feel comfortable taking part in debates. I'm not ruling out the thought that such a person might be chosen at a later date…'

So that was it. Put ordinary people in the House of Lords and they'd be *uncomfortable*. Give them a robing room and they'd probably keep coal in it. We filed out, avoiding eye contact, the commission members apparently unaware that they had said anything inappropriate.

27.04.01

Year Four

The election campaign was started with what most observers agreed was one of the most tasteless photo opportunities ever held. The Prime Minister went to a girls' school in South London where he addressed the pupils in the manner of a preacher.

Tony Blair took off his jacket and several hundred schoolgirls screamed. The election campaign had officially begun.

Even by the high standards of this lot, it made for a deeply cynical occasion. The Prime Minister had been to see the Queen. Now he had taken the prime ministerial limo to this Church school in a deprived area. To be fair, this particular school, St Saviour's and St Olave's, just off the Old Kent Road, has an important place in Labour history, being one of the establishments where Harriet Harman chose not to send her own children.

The Prime Minister had told us that he was going into the campaign 'humble and hungry'. Fat chance. He'd already had lunch, and as for humble, he doesn't do that. In fact he looked pretty pleased with himself. But you can't announce that you're going into a campaign 'plump and preening' or else 'vittled and vainglorious'.

He walked in, the photographers just missing a shot of him in front of an estate agent's board that read: 'Principles: For Rent'. The PM had a tight hold on David Blunkett, who in turn was holding his seeing-eye dog, Lucy, the parliamentary critic who once threw up on the Chamber floor. Lucy led the way into the school. At least someone knew which direction they were headed.

Inside the hall, light filtered through stained-glass windows. If you stood on the right-hand side of the hall, the lectern appeared to be just under a crucifix. The sound of hushed singing wafted up from the choir. Only New Labour would kick off an election campaign in the middle of a Madonna video.

A fat man with tattoos ordered the meeja to the back of the hall, in the manner of one reminding us that this was Mr Kray's mo'or and we'd berra keep clear, righ'? 'These seats,' he barked, 'are for the kids!'

What innocents some people are! The 'kids' existed only as a backdrop, as vital and yet as marginal to the overall effect as the extras in a Smarties ad, only unpaid. Some of them sang a song, 'We are the Children of the Future', another New Labour fib, since clearly they are the adults of the future and the children of the present. Can't anyone do their sums? Will the whole campaign be conducted through truisms that aren't even true?

Lo, he finally came, with clouds descending. We yearned for an embarrassing prank, a streaker perhaps, or a slow handclap. Nothing. There's something worryingly wrong with today's youth. He took off his jacket. It turned out to be the high spot of the day. Bathed in coloured light, the crucifix gleaming above him, he launched into statistics. A few years ago, the school registered '17 per cent five A–Cs, GCSE 5 per cent, now 50 per cent, so, well done, very good.' (This translates as 'A few years ago, 83 per cent of you, waste of space, now only half.')

Then he plunged into his election address for the voters, of whom there were very few in the hall. After a canter round the problems of negative equity, a 'Britain no longer marginalized in Europe', pensioners' heating allowances and other staples of playground conversation, he told them, 'Now, you the people will decide!'

'Or at least in the next election when a few of you might even have the vote,' he didn't add.

But by this time he had lost his audience, who were whispering to each other, staring at the floor, or else were fast asleep. It didn't matter. They were only the props. The whole event stank of spin doctors' sweat.

09.05.01

The big event of the election campaign occurred in mid-May, when John Prescott attacked a farmer in Rhyl who had just thrown an egg at him. Sadly I missed this event. Though heading north on the Tory battle bus, we were able to watch it (I counted) thirty-seven times on Sky News, which was showing on a screen above the driver.

The Tory campaign went to East Anglia. It was a big success. Everywhere Hague goes, people are happy and excited, craning to catch a glimpse of that beguiling, infectious smile.

They are less pleased to see her husband. Sometimes they even shout rude things at him. But everyone is thrilled to see Ffion. And she, who I assume is really bored out of her tree, looks overjoyed to see them.

Take the welcoming Tories at a hotel car park in Peterborough. There are some strange-looking people in this town. The local Labour MP is Helen Brinton, whom I like personally but whose wide mouth, always slathered with scarlet lipstick, makes me long to post a letter in it.

But she might be Helen of Troy compared to the people who turned up to greet the Hagues. Old men in battered straw hats. Oddly shaped women with angry faces. Two younger men with earrings, whose clothes could have come from Ronald

McDonald's skip. Yet when Ffion stepped off the bus and caught sight of them, instead of shuddering and scampering back on board she smiled as if they were her twenty oldest friends shouting 'Surprise!' at a birthday party.

When he speaks she sits in the audience beaming at him, laughing at his little jokes, applauding at the end as if she can't quite get over what a wonderful speech she has just heard for the hundreth time. She is the Tories' secret weapon. If they lose badly, they should make her promise to be the next leader's wife – if necessary, Ann Widdecombe's.

The Hagues arrived in a fleet of two helicopters. The first, the staff chopper, was marked 'Common Sense'. We wondered what the other would be called. 'Sheer Unbridled Lunacy' perhaps, or 'Political Correctness Gone Mad'. It turned out to be named 'Common Sense' too. The buses are all called 'Common Sense', and the phrase appeared several hundred times behind William Hague's head. As a slogan, 'Common Sense' sounds like simple common sense. But, as someone pointed out yesterday, common sense tells us that the moon is as big as it looks.

The Tory leader had planned a walkabout, but it had been mentioned in the local paper so people might have heard about it. In this election, anything that alerts ordinary people to the presence of a politician is like plain text wrested from an Enigma machine: it's a potentially lethal intelligence failure. The walkabout was cancelled in favour of a photo shoot.

He moved on to St Albans. There was to be a walkabout there instead. But it was raining, and common sense dictated that the walkabout should be held indoors, without any walking about. Common Sense, the bus, debouched the leader at the town hall door. No members of the public could even see him.

In all elections, the nominal contest conceals more complex and interesting battles. Now, in ascending order of bitterness, we have Labour v. Tory, Portillo v. Hague, Blair v. Brown and, what may be the most significant struggle of all, the people v. the politicians. The voters are rancorous, not against Tory or Labour, but against the lot of them.

So it was only a matter of time before the politicians started to retaliate. John Prescott was the first. 'I know where you live,' is particularly threatening from someone who has the electoral roll in his office.

18.05.01

Britain's most aggressive candidate stalked across the street in search of new voters to offend. According to the Voter ID sheet (the guide to every single elector provided by Millbank, listing name, address, phone number, political preference, star sign and favourite member of Hear'Say – well, most of those) we were visiting someone the computer had described as 'a firm Tory'. I asked Bob Marshall-Andrews why. 'Because I like to,' he replied grimly.

And he does make a scary sight. With his gimlet eyes, prop forward's build and lawn-strimmer haircut, the Labour candidate for Medway has been compared (by me, admittedly) to a cross between Dennis the Menace and his dog Gnasher.

The voter, a male pensioner, didn't stand a chance. As always, Mr Marshall-Andrews starts gently, to catch them off balance. 'Just came round to say hello,' he began. 'Things going all right here?' With any other politician, this would be small talk. With this one, it sounds like a demand for protection money.

'Not really,' said the man. 'Your lot ent done much for me. For a start they took away my mortgage relief.'

'But your mortgage is much lower now. How much is your mortgage? How much? It's not been lower for twenty years.'

The voter didn't recall. 'But they've done bugger all for me. Nah, leave it out.'

Even though it was now clear that he was like Alf Garnett without the ethereal charm, I wanted to shout out, 'Sir! You are tangling with the wrong man.' But he could not be stopped.

'I am definitely not voting Labour. All these bloody asylum seekers coming in, taking all, taking all – all our bits and bobs.'

'You don't want to send them home to be tortured, do you?' asked Mr Marshall-Andrews, his tone by now rather unpleasant.

The man looked as if he could live equably with that prospect, but forced himself to say 'no', before going on: 'What about the rest of them, then? Coming in by train, under the train on top of the train.'

'What,' demanded the candidate furiously, 'do you expect me to do? Do you want me to lie on the track, wait for the train and, if I see an asylum seeker, pull him off? Do you?'

The man hurriedly changed the subject. 'They took £5 off on housing, on mortgage relief, put it on the poll tax…'

'The poll tax?' roared the candidate, but as he gathered breath for the next onslaught, the man asked, 'Have you had a pension increase?'

'I. Am. Not. A. Pensioner!' Mr Marshall-Andrews said, as if explaining to a congenital idiot that he wasn't Liza Minnelli either.

'Well then,' said the man, with an air of triumph, 'you don't know what you're talking about!'

'I rebelled against my government, so don't you dare start talking to me!' Mr Marshall-Andrews bellowed. At some point the door slammed, and I wouldn't be surprised to learn that it was the candidate who did the slamming.

'Of course,' he said, as he stamped away, smiling the smile of one who has just enjoyed the fight he had picked, 'after Prescott you can't get inside anyone's house. Knock on the door and you hear them shout, "I give in."'

The Labour canvassers spoke with awe of their man's encounter with a send-the-lot-of-them-home voter the previous day. 'The difference between you and me,' said Mr Marshall-Andrews, 'is that you are a racist and I am not.'

'What did they do for us in the war, then?' asked the man, and was told about the Indian and West Indian regiments.

'While we're at it, what did you do?'

'I'm too young.'

'Well, you don't look it. And under no circumstances are you to vote for me. You will not vote for me!'

'I'll vote for who I please,' the man had ended lamely, making him, I suppose, a 'Don't Know' on the magical Millbank chart.

Mr Marshall-Andrews's majority is 5,326. At the present rate of attrition he should have it down to zero by polling day.

21.05.01

Keith Vaz, the minister for Europe, was accused of various kinds of unparliamentary behaviour. He responded firmly to the allegations by ignoring them and disappearing. I went to look for him in his constituency of Leicester East.

In the rest of Britain an election is taking place. But not, apparently, in Leicester East. Or this is Planet Vaz. Here we find no election, no campaign, no posters at all, except in Vaz's own window. The people of Planet Vaz have no need to be told why they should vote for their leader. For he is the Vaz of Vaz. His wisdom is unquestioned, for the simple reason that he is never there to be questioned. Why should he be? His people know of all his manifold virtues. If, unaccountably, they do not, the world's plenipotentiaries will tell them. In the latest publication hymning the praises of Vaz, Robin Cook, the Foreign Secretary, writes: 'He has been an astounding success as a minister…he has unparalleled knowledge…'

Other leaflets show pictures of the great one with his humblest citizens, visiting old people's homes, learning about their puny problems, such as traffic. How fortunate they are, for normally the Vaz meets only the wealthiest and most celebrated people. 'Keith Vaz met the world entertainer Michael Jackson and presented him with a gift…Keith told Michael he has quite a few of his records.' How fitting that two famous controversial recluses should have so much in common!

Some colleagues and I tried to meet him. (Keith Vaz, that is; it might have been easier to track down Michael Jackson.) We started at the Labour Party offices. This is Fortress Vaz. Normally during an election such places are full of bustle and jollity. This is locked, sealed and silent. I rang the entryphone and a suspicious voice asked my business and phone number. They promised to ring back. No young woman recently seduced by a philandering rake could have been more sceptical of getting the call than I was.

A Mr Keith Bennett, who turns out to be the agent of Vaz, came out. He told us that the Vaz whereabouts were 'a confidential matter'. He was not, strictly speaking, on the stump, 'But if he comes across a voter he might try to seek his support.' Since we didn't meet a single voter who had even set eyes on the great man, this seemed improbable.

We rang his previous agent, John Thomas, who lost the job a few days ago for no reason yet explained. He would not tell us why. No, he wasn't campaigning himself. 'I'm re-turfing my lawn.' Ah, the famous electoral re-turfing officer.

Out to the large home owned by the great one's mother. Four cars are parked in the drive, but evidently no one is in. Mrs Vaz is ill and disabled, but happily this has not prevented her from taking on the onerous burden of becoming secretary to her son's constituency party, giving her an important role behind the scenes.

Back at the Labour office, a couple of Tories, including the candidate John Mugglestone, had gathered to protest. No one left and no one came. Two policemen stopped to find out what was going on. 'We want to report a missing person,' the Tories told them. They smiled wanly.

The Vaz of Vaz has an 18,000 majority and will win next week. But as one of his enemies whispered, 'If Martin Bell was standing here, he'd walk in.'

22.05.01

Another candidate who went into hiding was Shaun Woodward, the former Tory MP who wangled the solid Labour seat of St Helens.

Shaun Woodward has not yet gone into hiding, like Keith Vaz. He's just elusive, like a yeti in smart casual wear. 'Lots of people want to meet him,' a party worker told me in an 'Oh, yeah, of course you'd like to win the lottery' sort of way. People in Labour's St Helens South campaign headquarters are guarded and suspicious, but compared to Fortress Vaz in Leicester they make you feel as welcome as a magnum of

Bollinger at a bottle party. 'He can't take time out to meet the press!' the man continued, as if I'd suggested that he might be off for a fortnight in the Seychelles.

But then why should he want to meet the press? The *Sun* has stalked him. The *Mail* pursued him with a mock butler – he's alleged to have once claimed that even his butler has a butler. He's defending a 24,000 majority. There's nothing in it for him. Instead he strides the streets, his trademark tweed jacket hooked over his shoulder, meeting the voters one by one, trying to persuade them – retail, so to speak – that he might be an arriviste millionaire turncoat, but he just happens to be the right arriviste millionaire turncoat for them.

I did my best to meet him. I told another young man at the campaign HQ that I knew Mr Woodward and he gave me an oh-yes-that's-what-they-all-say look. I said I had arrived to write the first ever favourable article about him, which was sort of true; more favourable anyway than the buckets of bile, spleen and toad vomit that have been poured over him so far. The young man said he would call and put my case. An hour later: no, Shaun was too busy. And I couldn't track him down. He kept his mobile turned off and used it only to say where he had just left. I felt as if I were asking the FBI where I might find their star witness, Luigi. 'My name is Gambino. Luigi and me, we go way back,' except that the Feds might give me the address.

The slur against Mr Woodward is that, as a millionaire turncoat carpetbagger, he knows nothing about St Helens. They're wrong. He knows everything, as I discovered when I finally tracked him down at the grand opening of Shopability, a scheme that loans nippy little four-wheel scooters for disabled people to go shopping. No candidate can afford to skip these events, and there he was with, I thought, a rather hunted look on his face. Goodness, he knows a lot about St Helens –

much more, I would guess, than most citizens of the town. The latest developments at Pilkington's Glass (self-cleaning windows), how many people lost their jobs at Ravenhead – he is stuffed with facts, figures, quotes and judgements.

He broke off for one of those weird Charles Addams photoshoots that candidates are obliged to attend. He was with various other candidates, the mayor, the TV comedian Johnny Vegas, and two jolly, young disabled women who loved the scooters because they go so fast. 'You get ten points for hitting a jogger,' one of them told me, 'but only if you keep his shoes.'

I went back with the Tory candidate, Lee Rotherham, a diffident young man who was actually born in St Helens and claimed to have met the Woodward butler. 'I met him at a party Shaun gave while he was still a Tory. He was in livery. He told me he was rushed off his feet, but he didn't look it. He had the elegance and poise of a very well-trained manservant. He gave me a glass of champagne.'

25.05.01

Foot-and-mouth disease was not yet eradicated, and during the election there was another outbreak in North Yorkshire. The hapless Nick Brown was sent to look into matters and, evidently, to spread the gloom around.

Mr Flabby, the minister of agriculture, arrived at the centre of the latest and horribly unexpected foot-and-mouth outbreak. It was a glorious day in the Dales, and if it hadn't been for the soldiers striding around Settle, the army vehicles packing the car park, and the lorries hauling mounds of dead animals away, you would have imagined you were in some Elysium, an

English Brigadoon, miraculously preserved from the other horrors of modern life.

We had been told that Nick Brown would do a short walkabout, presumably to glum-hand the voters. He did, if you count ten yards as a walkabout. He made his way from the ministerial car to the town hall door in around five seconds.

This was just enough time for the locals to tell him how they felt. 'Boo!' they remarked. Mr Brown scowled at them in his flabby fashion, and then flabbed his way up the town hall steps. Here the voters of Settle missed a trick, because right opposite was Sidwell's Bakery. A tempting tray of custard tarts was displayed in the window. Yet not one, not a single one of these, flew in Mr Brown's direction. Rightly are we Yorkshire folk celebrated for our dour forbearance.

Outside there was a gathering of farmers. One was in tears as he talked about having to kill his flock. Others were inchoate, barely capable of putting their feelings into words. With some, the tragedy has, perhaps, removed their powers of reason. Geoff Burrows, a farmer in Malhamdale, has had nearly 4,000 cattle and sheep shot. 'It's just a total excuse,' he said. 'They want to get rid of us. They've let it spread and spread and spread. They've been trying to get rid of us for four years now.'

Did he really think that Tony Blair wants to get rid of all farmers? 'Why else are they doing what they're doing? It's all these animal rights activists behind it...' This isn't so much an argument with holes as a colander, but then people here are desperate, capable of believing anything. One rumour says the disease was started on purpose. A woman was seen waving around a test tube full of the virus. Why? Nobody knows.

They take it very personally. 'On the day the Labour manifesto came out, Tony Blair was on TV, grinning and laughing and smirking and laughing at us, *at us*! He said that was the first day there were no new outbreaks, and twelve farms in our valley were taken out that day. That same day!'

Finally we were ushered into the Flabmeister's presence. He sounds a little more purposeful these days, less anguished, but still fairly flabby. 'We are bearing down on the disease,' he said, about twenty times. We were 'culling out cohorts' (neighbouring animals). Nationally we were 'on the home straight', he claimed a dozen times. Someone asked if he would still be in charge after the election. He replied – was he being wishful or just shell-shocked? – that he had enjoyed every minute of the job. 'It's been full of incident,' he said with flabby understatement.

Mr Brown is a protégé and ally of the more powerful Brown: Gordon. Whether he survives depends on the Great Post-Election settlement between the Prime Minister and his Chancellor. A culling out of cohorts is possible.

26.05.01

The film Return of the Mummy *has been playing in cinemas around the country during the election campaign. Margaret Thatcher, a woman more keenly aware than most of her own public image, awarded the title to herself shortly before she visited a marginal seat in the Midlands.*

It was *Return of the Mummy II*. Margaret Thatcher's Jaguar pulled up in Northampton market place. She was immediately surrounded by Tories, protesters, television crews, reporters, uniformed policemen, special branch officers, a man waving a four-foot cardboard cut-out of her, twin girls performing karaoke versions of Abba hits, a chap with an anti-Kenneth Clarke poster, a Scot with a rasping voice who accused her of hiding bribes from General Pinochet in a secret bank account – in short, a typical cross-section of modern British society.

She clambered out. A woman stepped forward and shyly handed her a banana skin, which she accepted as if it were a bouquet. So when the woman began to harangue her about Tory education policy she swerved smartly away.

'God bless Margaret Thatcher!' Conservatives shouted.

'Boo! Out, out, out!' others yelled.

'But she is out!' one of the Tories raged.

Somehow she made her way to a bald man and stroked his head. (I saw him half an hour later, but he was still bald.) The noise was like Omaha Beach. Mobile phones wheezed classical hits. Booing and jeering was answered by cheers. Photographers shouted: 'Here, Lady Thatcher!' A hundred shutters clacked. The Scotsman screeched: 'In a private account where no one has access!' The karaoke twins, Felicity and Jessica, performed to 'Money, Money, Money' at top volume.

A local TV reporter got close. 'Why are you afraid of the euro, Lady Thatcher?' Foolish fellow.

'Sterling is better!' she barked. 'If you're a broadcaster you should know that. Go on, out you go!' She poked him in the chest, hard, three times. He tried to flee into the crush, but she grabbed his microphone and held it aloft, like the spleen of a vanquished enemy.

'We wish you were still Prime Minister,' someone managed to yell above the din.

'Did you hear that?' she asked rhetorically. That's the merest common sense in her book. But things were getting dangerous. What Americans call a goat-fuck, an unstable, tottering, towering pile of photographers and TV crews, had appeared. Like a tornado, the GF requires the right extreme conditions, but once it has formed, it swirls across the land, menacing all life in its path.

Somehow we pushed along with her into the market. A little girl with panic in her eyes was shoved through to give her carnations. She handed them to someone I can only call a lady-in-waiting. The child fled from the GF.

'You're as good as the Queen!' a man shouted.

We neared the stalls. 'We must get away,' she said, 'we're *affecting their profits*!' This is the greatest offence in the Thatcher criminal code.

Much of the chat is surprisingly banal. 'How nice to see you!'

'Yes, haven't we been lucky with the weather!'

Then it all goes haywire. The face is deathly white these days, and her dark brocade outfit looked as if it had been run up from the curtains in a posh undertaker's. The effect is crepuscular, until the eyes blaze like a panther with a coke habit. A bold young woman asked her about Europe. She snorted, majestically. 'What if there were fifteen people who could decide what you did in your own house?' she demanded. The woman came back at her. It was madness. I couldn't hear what she said, but the Thatcher eyes spat fire. 'THAT would never allow any liberty to anyone! What a ROTTEN thing for any British person to say!'

We passed a stand advertising 'Any bag here, £2.99' but who needs any old bag for three quid when we had the greatest old bag in the land for free?

We were swirling now, faster and faster. Stalls were in danger of toppling as the GF heaved from side to side. Someone thrust a copy of her memoirs at her. 'Have you read this? It's a VERY good book,' she said as she signed it. More flowers appeared so that the lady-in-waiting looked like a Garden of Remembrance. Felicity and Jessica had reached 'Take a Chance on Me'. A brave man in a hat and a quite unnecessary green nylon-knit cardigan said we should join the euro. 'Just because Europe adopts the euro is no reason why we should! We have a *much older history!'*

What on earth did that mean? Who can say? And who cares?

She asks: 'Are we heading in the right direction? I don't know.' This is a remark she probably never made while in Downing Street.

'What would you say to Mr Blair if he came here?' a reporter asked, or rather bellowed across the abyss of noise.

'Not much!' she replied, to gales of laughter from the local sycophantic tendency.

The Scotsman kept shouting about Pinochet. 'And she's not even an MP,' he added.

'She's a baroness,' someone else said.

'No, she's a pain in the butt,' said a stallholder. The twins started, aptly enough, on 'Mamma Mia'.

'The NHS is a disgrace,' said an elderly woman, 'they should bring back Matron.'

'Things were run very well when we had Matron,' said the Mummy, before returning to her car. For that, I suppose, was precisely the point the whole visit was intended to make.

30.05.01

The election was won by the Labour Party, which lost a total of one seat to the Tories. I spent election night at the various party HQs.

No election night is boring, but this one came pretty close. At the ITN party, the glossiest bash in Westminster, hardly anyone even looked up from their champagne and nibbles when the conclusive exit polls were announced.

At Tory Central Office there was a mood of miserable, dull acquiescence. It was as if the entire party had been told that its dog had died. The only excitement came when Michael Portillo appeared on television and declared that, whatever happened, he truly hoped that William Hague would remain as leader.

My goodness, we thought, are things as bad as that? Portillo must be installing phone lines outside his house already.

Some took a different view. Over at the ITN bash, someone asked Norman Tebbit if Portillo's remarks meant that he had finally got cold feet. 'I wouldn't know,' Tebbit replied, 'I have never slept with him.'

Last time the Tories had looked stunned as if trampled by a herd of wild horses. Last night it was more as if an old and well-loved relative had finally died after a long and painful illness. Of course you were sad, of course you grieved, but you had had lots of time to adjust yourself.

One Tory official heard the exit poll at twenty seconds past 10 p.m. and said cheerfully that the BBC exit polls had been wrong for the European elections. We munched on little quarters of egg sandwich and decided not to tell him he was a total prat.

Later a more senior official arrived and told us that William Hague remained 'optimistic and upbeat'. Goodness, that man will stay optimistic and upbeat until the day they peg him out in the desert and hungry hyenas arrive to rummage around his intestines.

At Labour headquarters they had decided to exclude the writing press. Suspicious and surly-looking bouncers patrolled the pavements behind metal fencing. A kindly woman official explained that there was not enough space; the landlord wouldn't allow more people in, though another official whispered that 1,500 people had already been admitted. The odd soap star arrived.

I was reminded of the end of *Animal Farm*, when the lesser animals watch the pigs dressed as men, drinking with the humans in the farmhouse. 'The creatures outside looked from pig to man, and from man to pig...but already it was impossible to say which was which.'

Outside the HQ, we couldn't even do that, since workmen had spent two hours putting up silver sheeting over the windows. Now not even the passers-by could see their once and future rulers toasting their own triumph.

08.06.01

In spite of the many touching requests for him to stay in office (largely made by those who needed time to make their dispositions for the campaign to get his job) William Hague resigned the morning after the general election. Some leading Conservatives rapidly stood for the position of opposition leader. More decided not to. First out of the traps was Ann Widdecombe.

Lesser politicians have campaign launches. Only Ann Widdecombe would hold a campaign sinking. She called the media together in, appropriately, a sink estate in East London in order to scupper her political career, to send it to the bottom of the ocean. Last night, a backbencher once again, she slept with the fishes.

In years to come the underwater cameras that found the wreck of the *Titanic* will discern her superlative staterooms, the mighty engine housing, the allegedly watertight bilges, which failed at the critical moment.

It was magnificent. How we are going to miss that woman! She claims that she will be more effective from the backbenches, but that's meaningless – nobody is more effective speaking at 8.45 p.m. when all their colleagues are having dinner or getting drunk. We have lost her from the high seas; no more will we gaze at her billowing sails, admire the brasswork on the cannons, stir with pride as the ensign flutters proudly from the poop deck!

What made it perfect was that as she went down all the guns were blazing, specifically at Michael Portillo, a pocket battleship that had made the terrible mistake of approaching her broadside.

Crump! 'I don't believe that Michael Portillo is the right person to lead the Conservative Party!' Thump! 'This is nothing personal; all I can say is that this is what I sincerely believe.'

Nothing personal? She loathes him. 'I don't want today to turn into a personal denigration of Michael Portillo,' she added, to the sound of a twelve-inch gun firing shells into foot-thick steel. This means, in translation, 'I want you to take it personally.'

'I don't want to campaign negatively, but I don't have confidence in the way he wants to lead the party.' You could almost hear the screams of the trapped seamen, almost watch the ocean begin to churn as the great vessel shipped water and began its long journey to the sea floor.

Was she not sticking a knife into her colleague? someone asked. Perish the thought. 'If not supporting someone is sticking the knife in, then an awful lot of people will be doing that,' she said. Vendetta! Portillo! Armada! This was turning into a Mediterranean blood feud.

We had come to the Arden Estate in East London because she has been here a few times before and because she wants to make the point that Michael Portillo neither knows nor cares about the desolate lives led here. One woman, Vera Falk, aged fifty-nine, described how one local boy's hobby was setting his neighbours' cars on fire.

'Is your life really "a daily hell", like she says?' a reporter asked another elderly woman.

'Yes,' she replied quietly, as if agreeing that it looked like rain.

Ann Widdecombe was back on the attack. 'I have had quite enough of the people who surround him,' she said, meaning of course, Michael Portillo. We left the estate, perhaps imagining a few bubbles breaking the surface of the waves. All it needed was the band playing 'Nearer My God to Thee', and sparks as the seawater reached the ship's generator. By this time there were only a few survivors bobbing around on the swell, watching the ship's terrible yet eerily peaceful end.

10.06.01

The eventual winner soon announced his candidature, though few people at the time thought that he stood much chance.

Two more candidates stood for the Tory leadership yesterday. Neither seemed very exciting. Nevertheless, there is in the wings the statesman who can lead the party back to greatness. 'He is a man of outstanding determination, courage and principle,' said Iain Duncan Smith. 'He believes in the future of this country and our party with passion. He has enthusiasm and energy!' He sounds perfect. He should be the automatic choice. What are we doing listening to these pootling figures while a political Titan awaits the call, planning, brooding, pondering cruel fate, pausing only to toss Seb Coe over his shoulder? For Mr Duncan Smith was praising William Hague.

These are dark days for the Conservative Party when this latter-day Churchill is not even standing.

Mr Duncan Smith seems a decent and thoughtful man, but he is unlikely to inspire many people. 'I want to lead a crusade to put my party back into touch with the people,' he said, speaking as if he wanted to propose that we broke early for tea. To show us how sincere he is, he added that he would not be waving his wife and children in our faces. 'You will have no photos of any member of my family,' he pledged. (You'll know the race is getting tight when he changes his mind and his four children beg on television: 'Please vote for our daddy, because he is a kind man who tells us stories. And our cat Tiddles thinks so, too!')

Elsewhere Mr David Davis launched his campaign under a fashionable lower-case logo saying 'modern conservatives', the whole event themed in purple and yellow, like the blazers of an obscure but expensive prep school. Mr Davis is a witty and entertaining man in private, but in public suffers from thunderous dullness, though occasionally giggling to himself, as if enjoying a joke none of us would understand.

His nose has been broken in several places, possibly because he used to cartwheel out of planes for parachute jumps, possibly because he was in the Territorial Army version of the SAS, which means that he strangled the Queen's enemies with piano wire, but only at weekends, or as a colleague of his put it, 'He's so hard, he beats himself up if there's no one else around.'

In the end, though, both men produced a torrent of clichés. 'We must not break faith with our principles'; 'accept the need for change'; 'broaden our base and appeal'; 'time to close the book on divisions and talk about the issues that matter to people…a modern, bold, dynamic party'. I cannot recall which said which, though it hardly matters, since the same slogans could be mouthed by the Communists or the BNP these days.

The Tories have learned from Labour the power of resonant words, though like Labour they have yet to work out what, if anything, they mean.

20.06.01

Few of us guessed that it would be Iain Duncan Smith who emerged from this particular pack. At the time the favourite seemed to be Michael Portillo. His main challenger was in Vietnam on a mission for a tobacco company.

It was breakfast, launch and dinner, all in one. Michael Portillo had invited us to the Avenue, a chic London brasserie, in the hopes of thrusting his campaign into the stratosphere. Impossibly thin young men poured champagne and freshly squeezed orange juice. There were pastries as light as an angora rabbit's pubic hairs, and luscious tropical fruits, which we scoffed with Portillo supporters such as Nicholas Soames whose grandfather Winston Churchill so long ago described this very occasion: 'Pawpaw is better than war war'.

Then they brought on a sort of designer fry-up, with herbal sausage scones and tiny nouvelle bacon butties. The air was thick with former Kenneth Clarke supporters shafting their lost leader. 'Only Ken could go to Vietnam to flog fags to Asian teenagers and still be a man of the people,' one of them murmured to anyone who would listen. This campaign is beginning to get nasty, and about time too.

A wave of support entered the room. It was mounted on top of Michael Portillo. He looked superb. Everything about him is perfectly sculpted, especially the hair and lips. He already looks like his Madame Tussaud's model, which is more than most people there do. The caring caballero went round the room, introducing himself. 'Michael Portillo,' he would say modestly, so that one was tempted to reply, 'Yes, whatever happened to him?'

Francis Maude introduced him. 'We need changes,' he declared. 'We need big and serious changes. And a party that needs to make big and serious changes needs a big leader!' He was repeating himself, like the beginning of a Mozart concerto.

The big and serious leader (he is also, we were told, bold, generous and passionate, combining vision, resilience and unshakeable commitment) spoke without notes. He didn't need them. His speech could have been delivered by any of the other candidates. He wants to get back to values and principles. But he also demands relevance and passion. He insists upon a dynamic debate and a party that reconnects with the people.

I yearn for a candidate who has no truck with this nonsense about inclusiveness. 'This great party, which has served the British people for so long, must reconnect with its roots, its true values and its true beliefs. So I demand a return of the rope, the birch and teaching Johnny Foreigner a lesson, wherever he may be!' He'd sweep to power, in the Tory Party at least.

Mr Portillo accompanied his speech with an amazing range of hand movements. It was like watching an origami master. If he'd started with a sheet of A4 in his hands, he'd have ended with a paper model of the *Graf Spee*.

22.06.01

Mr Clarke finally returned from Vietnam, some time after the campaign had got under way.

Ken Clarke rolled up, literally. Everything about him is round. His face, his body, his belly, his eyes, even the movements described by his torso as he circles a room, are all spherical. If Lucian Freud had been there, he'd have grabbed his brushes, ripped Ken's clothes off and shouted: 'I want a crack at that!'

Mr Clarke was announcing his candidature for the Tory leadership. His platform – I hope readers will not mind if I use complex psephological jargon here – was 'Fuck the lot of you.'

To summarize his philosophy: 'I am the only candidate who can win the next general election, and if you don't agree you are even more stupid than I thought you were.'

It could just work. Tories love to be insulted, at least by the right people. He is the proles' version of the red-faced squire bellowing at the village idiot. Someone asked him, 'Surely you can't lead the party you so regularly insult?' and he replied that, so far as he could see, the Tory Party had no idea of how humiliating their defeat had been. In fact, the Tory Party had failed to realize anything much at all.

(The American comedian Henny Youngman had a joke: 'I said, "What's the matter with me, doc?" He said, "You're ugly."

'I said I wanted a second opinion. He said, "All right, you're stupid too."'

This is a perfect summary of the Clarke campaign, which is against the party as a whole, not just his rivals for the leadership.)

Boris Johnson, the new MP for Henley and a popular television performer, was at the back of the room. Boris, I hear, had a difficult session last week with Michael Portillo, who told him he had to decide whether he wanted to be a politician or a comedian. This is terribly unfair. Why is Boris the only MP out of 659 who had to make that choice?

Mr Clarke rumbled on. His oratorical style contains several different elements. Sometimes he chooses random words and barks them out in mid-sentence as if suffering from Tourette's syndrome. 'Can a pro-European like. MYSELF! Successfully lead the Conservative. PARTY?' This is based on Michael Foot's old style. It's as if the speech had fallen into a deep slumber in a comfy armchair, then suddenly woken up with a great harrumph.

Then there's the Winnie-the-Pooh, in which the words are dragged backwards down a staircase. 'AAAAS far as I can see the issue-of-the-sing' currency...' Bump, bump, bump goes the speech until it winds up in a heap on the landing.

He really doesn't mind whom he insults. Adam Boulton from Sky News pointed out that there was not much false modesty in his speech. 'Putting yourself forward for a job is not an occasion for false modesty,' mused Mr Clarke, 'unless perhaps on Sky television.' I'm sure Mr Boulton did not mind this jibe, but it takes a very confident politician to make it.

27.06.01

This column spotted Stephen Byers early.

The good news is that John Prescott is no longer in charge of transport. The bad news is that Stephen Byers is. Nothing he said in his first session of transport questions yesterday gave the slightest hint that he realized the size of the problem. Astoundingly he is thinking of handing over the east coast main line to Virgin Trains. To Virgin Trains, the greatest railway disaster since the collapse of the Tay Bridge!

He didn't even think that this was an odd thing to contemplate. No doubt if he had employed a builder who flooded the kitchen, demolished a retaining wall and made the master bedroom fall into the garden, he would hire the same man to build his conservatory.

The even worse news is that he is accompanied by a ministerial team of spectacular nonetities. I don't want to be rude to the teachers in our new universities, but this lot would easily fit into the geography department in an old polytechnic. There is a man with thinning hair who yesterday wore a grey suit with brown shoes. There was another man with a regrettable moustache. And a woman in a crumpled beige outfit.

Who are these people? It is hard to say. I assume they are Members of Parliament, though one cannot be sure, especially since so many constituencies these days have what are clearly fictitious names. (Think of Amber Valley, Wyre Forest, Mole Valley, Wansdyke, Weaver Vale, The Deepings and Anniesland – these are not real places but fairy glens.) They may have been told to wander in after the election and told to look as if they know where they are.

They have all, however, learned the New Labour jargon. The man with the moustache spoke of 'the area cost adjustment context of the White Paper'. He told us he was considering split bands and a fixed cycle for revaluations. He was looking not only at changes in banding, but also the ratio between bandings. So much for ignorant people who thought that a fixed cycle was just another word for an exercise bike.

The woman in beige replied to Gordon Marsden MP by talking about 'regeneration strategies due to a single regeneration budget'. Mr Marsden is too lively and interesting to be a minister himself, but even so he talked about his constituency (Blackpool)'s, 'special needs, due to its 180-degree periphery'. I suppose this means that half the place is next to the sea, so it has a special need for donkeys, roller coasters and kiss-me-quick hats. He too demanded a single regeneration strategy. It was all deeply gloomy.

04.07.01

Mr Gerald Kaufman, the man who would have been Neil Kinnock's Foreign Secretary if Labour had won the 1992 election, has an astonishing gift for keeping himself in the public prints. And if he has nothing much to say, he finds something else to do.

The House of Commons was rocked yesterday by one of those events that shock and thrill at the time, then echo resonantly in the mind for years to come. One thinks of the Norway debate, or Margaret Thatcher's farewell speech. Yesterday Gerald Kaufman walked in wearing a suit. Virtually all the other men in the Chamber were in suits, but none was clad in a garment remotely like this. No matador in his costume of lights ever possessed such a suit. Max Miller's wardrobe could have been owned by a down-at-heel accountant compared to this.

It was only one colour, but what a colour! Afterwards those of us who had seen the vision gathered together, like disciples who had seen the risen Christ, anxious to record each detail so that we could hold it in our memories and pass the knowledge down to generations yet unborn.

The hue was astounding. At first I thought I had never seen it in nature, then I recalled the weird, deep, luminescent pools of water that bubbled to the surface after Mount St Helens erupted, stained with livid chemicals from the earth's very core.

Terracotta would not do the colour justice, being too dull; ochre would be too yellow. Cinnamon came to mind, although the spice is too dark and woody. Someone compared it to murram, the orangey, clay-like surface of many African roads. All we could agree was that Mr Kaufman must be the only dandy who arrives at his tailor's with a Dulux chart.

And it wasn't just the colour. The suit was striped in broad, neat stripes, like a well-mown cricket pitch, one stripe glossy and the next matt, so that as light played upon the suit and Mr Kaufman moved, it shimmered sinuously.

The effect was completed by Mr Kaufman's nut-brown shoes and his nut-brown head, a tribute to the wonderful recent weather in Manchester Gorton. He looked, in short, as if Hannibal Lecter had taken up a job as a TV talent show host. It was a magnificent sight, eliciting gasps of mingled delight and horror from other MPs and from those of us in the gallery fortunate enough to see it. It quite took attention away from Iain Duncan Smith...

10.07.01

Granada Television wished to do an item on this suit, but sadly Mr Kaufman refused to wear it for the cameras. And, I suspect, scared by the coverage it had received, he never wore it again, at least not in my sight. Meanwhile, the first round of the Tory leadership contest achieved nothing, since the bottom two candidates tied, and the whole thing had to be run again. Nor was the second round any more decisive.

Another inconclusive result! Ecstasy and bliss! I've never seen the Tories look so happy. All the cares of last month have rolled away as they joyfully face days of more cajoling, bribery, lying, insults, plotting and voting! This truly is why they were put on this earth. If I were an undecided MP, or a supporter of either Michael Ancram or David Davis, both of whom have been finally ejected from the contest, I would go home this weekend, send the butler out for pizza, take a bottle of something cold plus a portable phone out to the garden, and sit in a deckchair waiting for dozens of pleading, plucking, importunate calls. They should settle for nothing less than a peerage and the governorship of somewhere warm.

Ann Widdecombe was among the first to appear in the committee corridor where the voting took place. 'I voted for Ancram and I got someone to witness it!' she barked, as if any of us would dare to doubt her word.

Various others spoke as if the national press was actually a line of particularly ragged national servicemen. 'Vair good, vair good!' one said.

'Carry on!' said another, as if to half a dozen spud-bashers sitting on upturned buckets.

Keith Simpson, an MP who looks like a provincial solicitor with a subscription to *Health & Efficiency*, but who has one of the sharpest minds in the place, declared he had voted for 'the Führer!' which we assumed to be Michael Portillo. This is not quite the image the compassionate caballero is trying to project this year.

'All the ballot papers have numbers on "for administrative purposes"!' snorted Mr Simpson. 'It takes me back to my days in the whips' office, when we'd have known the result by now!' ('Or last week,' a voice said sibilantly at his side.)

Someone asked if Nicholas Soames had already voted. Mr Simpson replied, clearly having the time of his life, 'Humphh. He'll come in here after lunch, looking like an old labrador, scratching himself and farting.'

Iain Duncan Smith emerged. 'I've switched my vote – to Iain Duncan Smith!' he said.

'And they say he hasn't got a sense of humour!' boomed Mr Simpson, whose insouciance about whom he insults is rather engaging and reminiscent of Denis Healey.

'I voted for the Spaniard,' said John Wilkinson, as if he couldn't quite remember his name, but didn't like to let a dago by.

Kenneth Clarke came along. 'Urghhh, wurgh, urr,' was his opening remark. It takes him a long time to clear his throat; there's been so much down there.

I popped along to hear Michael Portillo speak at a lunch. 'We have been a party that is against things,' he said, 'and we need to be a party that is for things.' Hmm, make what you will of that.

'If I am leader of this party, everything we do will be consistent with who we are and what we are'. You could spend a long time picking the bones out of that.

Back at the committee room Tories were still voting. Nicholas Soames came by and didn't fart once. Anthony Steen said gravely that he could not possibly tell us how he had voted, but that his views were 'very well known'. This is a man whose great fame is off the record.

Cheryl Gillan told us that the whole thing had excited her so much that her weight had gone down by six and a half pounds. Now young women face another peril: anorexia, bulimia and Tory leadership contests.

Finally the result was announced. Almost nothing had changed. Hooray! Cheers and rejoicing all round! Any Tory MP who had been dreading that the contest might produce a clear result could relax, sit back and look forward to the best weekend of their lives.

13.07.01

The battle for the Tory leadership was surprisingly bitter. When Ken Clarke turned out to lead the field, the grandest of all grandees, Sir Peter Tapsell, marched up to Boris Johnson MP, who had voted for Clarke, and bellowed in his face: 'You. Have. Personally. Destwoyed. The Conservative Party!' (Sir Peter has a slight lisp.) The final result, the choice of Tory Party members around the country, was due to be announced on 12 September. Events in New York and Washington the previous day having superseded it, the declaration was made on the thirteenth.

You had to feel sorry for Iain Duncan Smith. He has just pulled off the most astonishing coup: a man who was hated and reviled by members of the last Tory government and who remains almost unknown outside the House of Commons is now the leader of what is still the second-largest party in British politics and the longest-surviving party in the Western world. Three months ago his elevation would have seemed inconceivable. Yet his coronation yesterday had all the excitement of a village fête forced indoors by the rain.

Outside there was a single media tent, perched like a bivouac on the blustery side of Smith Square, and a pair of satellite vans – indicating rather less media interest than when Margaret Thatcher blows her nose. At the climax of previous leadership elections we have heard whoops of joy and cheers of exultant delight. Yesterday there was just a torpid silence, a sense that we – politicians, officials and journalists – were irrelevancies on the fringe of a real and suddenly more terrible world. Politicians adore pomp and furbelows and the sound of trumpets. Yesterday there was nothing.

Sir Michael Spicer, the returning officer, stepped onto the stage and said drily, 'Here is the result of the ballot for the leadership of the Conservative Party. The total number of valid votes was…' Mr Duncan Smith had won with a remarkable 61 per cent of the vote, yet the room hardly stirred, except for one Tory columnist who would have cheered the election of Michael Fabricant as leader.

Mr Clarke came forward and managed a pleased and congratulatory grin as he shook his rival's hand. How do politicians do this? Are there training schools at which they teach the rictus grin, the smile of delight that seems to say, 'Thank heavens it's you! I could never have coped with the job myself.'

The speech was, perhaps, ever so slightly barbed. 'The party desperately wants to be put back in a winning position,' he said, and since his whole campaign had been based on the notion that IDS could do no such thing, it was perhaps a faint lip-curl of contempt. Then he disappeared, like, as ever, a man who has just recalled that he has left a half-finished pint and a bag of crisps on the bar.

Mr Duncan Smith came forward and thanked everyone: the returning officer, the people who counted the votes, the vicar for the use of the hall – not the last, of course, but it would have felt appropriate. Then he was gone, leaving us only with a brief flap of the hand.

Over at Downing Street you could almost see the sneery grin on the face of Alastair Campbell. They probably think it's the best result they could have had. They might be right, but the last Tory leader who created such smug delight in the hearts of the Labour Party was a harsh, middle-class, right-wing, plainly unelectable woman called Margaret Thatcher.

14.09.01

In 2001 the party conferences were held as usual, but shortened. The normal screeching noise as the party faithful tore strips off one another seemed for once quiet and muted. Newspapers meanwhile were full of terrifying scare stories: 'Bin Laden: I'll Nuke Britain' was fairly typical. Everyone had only half a mind on what they were doing.

There's been a lot of glum silence in Brighton this week. Gordon Brown launched a ferocious attack on past governments that had almost brought the British economy to its knees. He turned out to mean Labour governments. He had no harsh words for the Tories, but then he had no harsh words for the Ovalteenies either. In New Labour demonology the Conservatives are marginal, barely worthy of notice. The enemy is within. 'We have not made the mistakes of the last two Labour governments…' said Mr Brown. The delegates, many of whom had passionately supported those Labour governments, sat in glum silence.

Tony Blair was nowhere to be seen. This is highly unusual at a party conference, but the Prime Minister is fully occupied now, straining every muscle, stretching every sinew, in a life and death struggle, the outcome of which is still uncertain and which could bring a horrifying disaster.

Yes, the battle against Gordon Brown will take years and not months. There is no easy solution. The perils of action are terrible; the dangers of inaction even greater. He must succeed in building a great anti-Brown coalition, which will take every ounce of diplomatic skill he possesses.

The scale of the menace was made clear by the Chancellor's speech. It was a bid for world leadership. Downing Street will not be big enough for him. 'Not just nationally, but internationally, justice for all!' he raved. Like his greatest rival, he has started to extirpate verbs. 'World-class public services! Security and stability – yes!'

He himself was a small figure at the end of the vast hall. But his image was broadcast live on giant screens above his head. The camera was somewhere below him, so that every time he made a gesture, his hands filled the screen in front of his face. There was the karate chop. The pointing finger, the double flat palm, the exultant waving arm as if he'd just scored a winning goal, and the hand that swooped across his face like a panicky pigeon. As he became more excited, his hands bunched aggressively.

Fists of fire! He knocked out imaginary enemies, smashed his way through people who are neither prudent or cautious and who abandon tight fiscal disciplines for irresponsible quick fixes. Crump! Biff! Wallop! He was Marlon Brando on the waterfront. 'I coudda been a contender! In fact I am, and don't ever forget it!'

Slowly and churlishly they gave him a standing ovation, before returning to their usual morose silence.

01.10.01

The government cunningly interrupted the Tory conference by calling an emergency debate on the world situation.

For the first time yesterday the Prime Minister began to sound tired. His voice was hoarse; now and again he would grope for the right word. He had the air of a man in that fog that comes from too little sleep for too long.

The brain continues to function, but more slowly. It needs to be kickstarted – rebooted – at frequent intervals. Churchill achieved this with brandy, though President Blair doesn't have that resource. In this weary state you must remind yourself over and over what your priorities are and what is truly urgent; everything else seems to melt into the white and misty distance, half glimpsed, necessarily ignored.

Does he, I wondered, after each short sleep have just one second of peace and contentment before he remembers what is happening, and the old horde of problems, cares and anxieties springs up like an army inside his head? Does he recall with longing a time before 11 September, when the world seemed an almost manageable place and the worst problems he faced were hospital waiting lists and Gordon Brown?

The Tories had crammed into the Chamber and squeezed onto their benches. There is almost nothing the average Conservative MP will not do to escape his own party conference. Perhaps the evening start of the debate was cunningly timed to provide an excuse for missing two whole days.

The House was in full agreement with itself, which is usually a bad sign. The Prime Minister was heard in silence. His voice often dropped to a hush. He began to sound like one of those reporters on the videophone from Afghanistan, as if there was a delay between his thought-processes and what we were hearing. Several Tories went out of their way to praise him; they can hardly believe how much he resembles their fantasy idea of what a Tory leader should be like.

But even Labour's traditional fundamentalists bound themselves in moderation. Tam Dalyell, a man who believes that wars should be fought on pacifist principles, asked whether the government's law officers had advised the Prime Minister that the bombing was in line with the UN Charter.

What did Tam expect? That the Prime Minister would reply: 'Of course they didn't, you fool! Do you think I would ask that bunch of tossers whether they wanted one lump or two, never mind consult them about something important?' Instead he said quietly, 'Yes.'

Then he returned to Downing Street for the long haul. One wonders how much longer he can carry on hauling. It must be hell.

09.10.01

The Tory conference finally got under way and Mr Duncan Smith made his first leader's speech.

At the end of the speech by Quentin Davies, the Tories' new spokesman on Northern Ireland, a member of the audience threw up on the conference floor. 'God,' said another member of the shadow cabinet, desperate to look on the bright side, 'I wish we had more speakers who could get that raw emotional reaction.'

Well, Iain Duncan Smith is not one of those, at least not yet. He didn't give a terrible speech. It was just not remotely exciting. He spoke with feeling but without passion, with common sense but without urgency. He addressed the conference as if he were the colonel of the regiment, warning the men about the dangers of sexually transmitted diseases. It was something that had to be done. But he could hardly pretend he was enjoying it, or that he did not find the whole process deeply embarrassing. 'Now, chaps,' you expected him to say, 'you open this little foil packet and, um, you, then you ...Anyway, carry on.'

He arrived on stage looked somewhat bemused. Whereas William Hague was an 'out' baldie, proud to let his dome shine like a beacon of hope to other slapheads, IDS is in denial. He had what looked like an inch of make-up on his scalp. As they say in the States, if you dug it up you'd find Jimmy Hoffa in there somewhere.

His expression seemed to be saying, 'What am I doing here?' The expression on the delegates' faces asked the same question. Well, they should know. Time and again they have been presented with strange new leaders whom they were instructed to admire: Ted Heath, Margaret Thatcher, John Major and William Hague. Some, after time, they learned to love. Others still make them shudder. IDS is the first one for whom they are wholly to blame.

The only burst of enthusiasm came when he attacked the euro. Even his encomium of the Tories as the nice party – 'Find out who's volunteering for the local charity; as likely as not you'll find a Conservative' – failed to thrill them. A man just in front of me began to snore gently, then suddenly jerked awake, remembered where he was and fell asleep again.

But perhaps there is hope. The greatest speakers often have a speech impediment or verbal mannerism, which helps us focus on their words. There was Churchill's growl, Enoch Powell's Black Country accent, Nye Bevan's high-pitched whine and so forth. Mr Duncan Smith has a frog in his throat, a great big green frog, one would guess, if the noise it makes is anything to go by.

'Stan – gurgh – dards will rise faster…It would be wrong to assume that the tide al – wooghh – ways rises…As a Con – kek kek kek – servative, I am proud!'

It was hypnotic. And there was nothing he could do. It kept returning. I feared that when he reached his peroration, the frog would suddenly leap from his throat and a massive green IDS gob would fly though the air, possibly landing on my sleeping neighbour. But he did not say anything exciting and, after a slightly delayed standing ovation, went backstage for a long drink and a box of man-sized Kleenex.

11.10.01

The foot-and-mouth crisis rumbled on for most of 2001. In October it turned out that an important research programme had gone catastrophically wrong. The new agriculture minister had to account for this to the House.

Margaret Beckett came out fighting. Her aim was to disgust the opposition into silence, and she very nearly succeeded. When she announced that 'the pooled brains came in the form of a paste', I almost ran gagging from the Chamber; what it must have been like on the abattoir floor I hardly dare to think. (Actually I was reminded of those dysentery-inducing dishes whizzed up by Hugh Fearnley-Whittingstall on Channel 4. 'I mashed the pooled brains with a little garlic and red wine before spreading it on crispy melba toast. Unusual, but delicious!')

The Environment Secretary was under terrific pressure over her decision to bury the bad news about lab tests on sheep brains. The brains were being testing for traces of BSE. However, it turns out that the researchers hadn't been given sheep but cattle brains to test. This would be as pointless, scientifically speaking, as spending four years trying to make weapons-grade uranium out of navel lint.

When this appalling fact emerged, Mrs Beckett put a brief announcement on her department's website at 10.30 p.m. to say that the research programme might have been flawed. It didn't mention cow brains, sheep brains, or, come to that, Spam. Mrs Beckett claims that she got the news out as quickly as possible, without waiting to give a press conference the next day.

Now it turns out that there might have been a double disaster. There's no reason to be sure, we were told, that the sample of sheep brains (which turned out to be cattle brains) was actually representative of all the brains that were being tested, some of which might in the end turn out to have been sheep brains all along. In which case, if the tests turn out to be positive, we may be looking at a *sheeperdämmerung* in which 40 million sheep, rams and ewes will have to be slaughtered.

Who needs Osama Bin Laden when we have our department for environment, food and rural affairs to cause havoc and misery on its own? Or, as the minister said, as if in a scene from the Hollywood horror flick *Pooled Brains IV*, 'To put it brutally, would the sample that should have been sent be discovered at the back of the fridge in some dark corner of the Institute of Animal Health?' (Beginning to pulse, no doubt, with a strange green light, as it opens the fridge from inside and slithers silently towards the young female lab assistant.)

Meanwhile Mrs Beckett began raging at her tormentors, as if any attempt to question her judgement was an assault on the whole of British farming, or what's left of it. She demanded furiously: 'What is it? For which? I am supposed? To apologize?'

And she produced the favourite New Labour stunt. Unable, after more than four years, to continue blaming the Tories for all their multitudinous crimes against humanity, they now blame them for daring to question Labour ministers over what they have done. 'They are trying to exploit the issue and blow it out of all proportion in a dangerously irresponsible way!' she said. It's a pretty good rule of thumb that when ministers start accusing the other side of dangerous irresponsibility, they know they have no case.

23.10.01

As well as having a great big frog in his throat, quickly named Freddie the Frog by some elements of the tabloid press, Mr Iain Duncan Smith turned out to be a less than hypnotizing speaker.

The received wisdom about William Hague was that he was brilliant at Prime Minister's Question Time, but hopeless in front of the public. In that case his successor must dazzle the electorate, because at PMQs so far he is a wash-out. He is a bore, a terrible, thumping, ground-shuddering T. Rex of a bore.

Things may change. He is on what the Americans call a steep learning curve. But at present, if there were giant tree sloths in the Chamber they would greet his arrival by dropping from their branches and dashing away. Doctors would use his interventions as a breakthrough for research into insomnia, except that they would need to work in teams, since few could stay awake for more than a minute at a time, like those scientists who collect the poisonous fumes that belch from the mouths of active volcanoes, and yet manage to stay alive by always getting out in time.

I myself propped my chin up on a ballpoint pen and just managed to stay awake, though I kept drifting off close to unconsciousness and had to rely in the end on a tape recording.

It is hard to convey on the page the sheer numbing quality of his boringness. How can you express it in mere words? In *Howards End*, E. M. Forster brilliantly described the sensation of listening to a Beethoven concert. Some wine writers risk making themselves look idiotic by using words to describe taste. (As with the Riesling that I once saw described as having 'topnotes of cinnamon and vanilla, with a hint of Nivea cream'.) I must follow their brave example. But first, allow me to quote an IDS question in its entirety:

'The, er, what I say to the Prime Minister, it isn't going from one extreme to the other, because he has taken, he has given a valuable lead, which I applauded him for, in building this coalition, for example, with the Arab states, so, will perhaps he be aware of this condition, that as I am, their dismay as they look at convicted terrorists using our legal system to avoid their natural judicial process. And when we were asking, this is the point, when we're really asking our allies to make huge efforts in part of their war against terrorism, isn't it time to ensure here that we can make, make sure that they cannot shelter behind our laws? And I so say in that same spirit to the Prime Minister, we stand absolutely ready to work with him to tackle the problems that there are now being caused by the Convention on Human Rights. Surely, this is the point, when the law is wrong, the law must be changed!'

At the end, his voice rose to an angry shout, but of course this is the bore's fall-back; if you can't rouse emotion in other people, you pretend to create it in yourself.

What makes an IDS speech so very narcoleptic is, I suspect, the way that the voice rises and falls very slowly. This movement is, however, never synchronized with what he is saying. Like the tide on the rocks, it is both rhythmical and arbitrary at the same time. When we listen to someone in a conversation, we expect the tone of their voice to tell us the important part – saying, 'Surely this is the point,' doesn't have that effect.

He is also harmed by small but deadly verbal infelicities. 'So, will perhaps he be aware of this condition, that as I am, their dismay...' is the kind of convoluted phrase we might all use now and again. In a public speaker it is lethal. The listeners' brains, unable to cope easily, switch off and resemble a frozen computer screen, apparently ready for action, but in fact dead to all input from any source.

I am not saying IDS's condition is terminal. But it requires a lot of work, soon.

25.10.01

The IDS question quoted above was 171 words long. The following day's Hansard kindly cut out all the repetition, the clunky circumlocutions and the unnecessary additions, bunged in some punctuation, and got it down to 129 words.

Tony Blair was in the Middle East, so John Prescott was in charge of Prime Minister's Questions. He was magnificent. Like a tanned if somewhat overweight Australian lifesaver, he stood on the shore, took an enormous breath, dived into the waves, and I swear did not breathe again until the whole half-hour was up.

On and on he plunged through the thundering breakers. Trick questions swept and spumed over his head. Rip tides tugged from below, dragging him towards the jagged rocks. But nothing could stop him as he stormed onwards through the brine.

We watchers on the beach peered into the foam, desperate to catch a glimpse to show us he was still afloat. For whole minutes we would think he had gone under, but then we could see an arm or a strand of hair and we knew that hope was not lost. It was an exhibition of superb courage and resilience.

The terrifying ordeal began with a question from Michael Ancram, who was standing in for IDS. Would Mr Prescott confirm that the first objective of the war was the removal of the Taliban regime?

Here was his reply (and I apologize for quoting it at length, but nothing else will convey the full excitement of his bravura performance): 'First, objectively, can I welcome the Rt. Hon. member to his new position as Leader, Deputy Leader, of the House. [Laughter, since this is not actually Mr Ancram's job, but that hardly matters.] He has indeed held that job for two different Prime Ministers [eh?] which it shows he has got some pretty shifty footwork.

'Our objectives are clear, indeed in reading the Hansard of yesterday, the Rt. Hon. member did ask about these objectives, they were confirmed by my Rt. Hon. friend the Foreign Secretary, the objectives remain the same and indeed it has been made clear by the Prime Minister in his speech yesterday that the objectives are clear, and the one about the removal of the Taliban is not something we have as a clear objective, it is, but is, but is possibly a consequence that as the Taliban clearly giving protection to Bin Laden and the UN resolution made it absolutely clear that anyone who finds them in that position declares themselves as an enemy and that clearly is a matter for these objectives!'

Labour members cheered as his head bobbed up above the waves. He was still alive, still swimming!

There was a moment's respite when a Tory, Richard Spring, asked about the bed-blocking crisis in the NHS. Big mistake! Back in 1995, Mr Spring was caught by the newspapers in what they call a steamy threesome romp – bed-blocking indeed – and his promising ministerial career ended.

'The bed situation, it's something he's pursued considerably in the past,' Mr Prescott said, getting some laughter, but using up precious breath.

A Labour loyalist asked about abandoned cars.

'Many of us are receiving complaints about many empty cars!' he exclaimed. This from Two-Jags himself, who always has one empty car, and often two. Tories fell about in mock ecstasy. David Davis held his face in his hands. Eric Forth looked as if he might explode.

But still he flailed onwards, our unsinkable Deputy Prime Minister. He had checked the figures for Lewisham: 6,000 abandoned cars, and not one of them a Jaguar! The sharks were circling, but he breasted the waves without even noticing their fins. Labour MPs cheered him on for his pluck, his resolve, his sheer guts.

Moments later he had confused heroin with marijuana, claiming that 90 per cent of the world's pot came from Afghanistan. But now we were all cheering him on. At 3.30, he had reached the safety of the shore, a hot towel and a huge gulp of oxygen. Not since Captain Webb first crossed the Channel in 1875 had we witnessed such a British swimming triumph.

01.11.01

The 2002 edition of the Conservative diary has dropped onto my desk. As the frontispiece they have a weird, spooky, truly scary picture of Iain Duncan Smith. He is eerily lit, so that part of his face is unnaturally bright, whereas the other half is in a Stygian shadow. His skin appears to have a waxen sheen, and there is a curious gleam in his left eye.

I can imagine the dialogue: 'Perhaps you would care for a drink?'

'Gosh, thanks, Mr Duncan Smith. A glass of red wine would certainly hit the spot!'

'Ah, sadly I cannot offer you red wine. However, you will find that this decanter contains something very similar, yet strangely different...'

But then the whole Conservative Party presently resembles

a graveyard on the outskirts of an old city. It would be a bright and cheery night, but the moon is hidden by clouds. Now and again they part and reveal – what? Is that a stooped human form, creeping between the tombstones? Or a predatory animal about its nocturnal purposes? Or just a branch of the ancient yew tree, rattling against the door of the mausoleum?

There are curious noises in this graveyard, which might be the cry of birds, but which could be of a more sinister origin. The wailing of a lost soul, perhaps, grieving for its past, trembling for its future.

Then the lowering clouds part again and we see the doors of the sepulchre slowly open. Out into the eerie half-silence comes – the leader of a boy band!

Yes, it was the new front-bencher Tim Collins, young, alive, alert, and possibly the only member of the shadow cabinet without chains rattling round his ankles or moss growing in his hair.

Mr Collins made a speech that was funny, aggressive, sarcastic, biting and very loud indeed. It was not the greatest speech we have ever heard but, by goodness, it was vigorous. He seemed to be dancing round the miserable, groaning, clanking cadavers who surrounded him.

His topic was the government hiding bad news, and specifically the way in which Stephen Byers seems to have bungled the Railtrack imbroglio. Mr Collins was helped hugely by the fact that Mr Byers had decided to stay away from the Commons (he was engaged on a vitally important minibus tour to a bridge, somewhere in the North-East, followed by – well, that wasn't quite clear, but definitely followed by something. Anyway, he was absent.)

'In all the annals of arrogance,' Mr Collins said, 'this utter contempt for Parliament bulks large.' (I would love to read a book called *The Annals of Arrogance*. One entry could be the time Lord Longford insisted that his book *Humility* should be displayed in Hatchards' window.) Why, Mr Collins said, on *The World at One* no less an authority than the BBC's Andrew Marr had stated that his absence had caused 'irritation in Downing Street'.

A Labour backbencher, Chris Pond, leaped to his feet to say that that had not been said on the programme.

'Not only did I hear *The World at One*,' retorted Mr Collins with airy insouciance, 'but I appeared on it!'

And so on. All right, it wasn't fantastic, but it was amazing to see a Tory with what seems to be real, liquid blood running through his veins instead of embalming fluid. He finished with a fine, grotesque image. 'He has moved at a snail's pace to answer questions, to improve transport and to raise standards on the railways. And as long as the Prime Minister continues to ignore all considerations of honesty and honour and keeps this man in office, he will leave a trail of slime right up to the door of Number 10!'

At which the Speaker asked him to withdraw his remark.

'Naturally I withdraw!' said Mr Collins with a merry smile, before falling back into his seat and joining the undead all around him.

04.12.01

For the first time ever, the Commons held a session of questions to the minister for women. This followed questions to the minister for trade and industry, who turned out to be one and the same person.

The Tories tend to be scornful of Patricia Hewitt. Her shadow, John Whittingdale, said that her 'much-vaunted manufacturing summit' – Ms Hewitt is keener on talking shops than workshops – had produced £20 million for a partnership with Pizza Express, while the climate change levy will cost an extra £100 million. Disgraceful. Ministers should be topping themselves if they can't deliver.

Then they got on to wind power, and I'm delighted that Bob Blizzard MP had plenty to say, though there was nothing from Roger Gale. Viscount Thurso, the only genuine lord ever to sit in the Commons, who calls himself rather coyly 'John' Thurso, declared that 'In Scotland, we have some of the best wind, wave and tidal resources in the world.' Are we now going to get angry Nats going round shouting, 'They're our tides!' and 'Hands off Scotland's wind'?

Ms Hewitt, as ever, sounded like one of the old Blue Peter presenters before people on children's TV learned to say things like 'wicked' and 'check this out, kids!'

'I'm sorry,' she fluted, 'that my hon. friend does not like modern windmills. I think they're rather beautiful.'

I longed for her to go on: 'To make one, you'll need the cardboard centres from six toilet rolls, and the rotor arm from an ordinary family car. But don't forget to ask Dad first!'

Then suddenly the Speaker changed the subject. Ms Hewitt left the harsh world of commerce and industry, or such of it as remains, and became the concerned, sharing, compassionate minister for women.

Caroline Flint MP had the honour of being the first woman to ask the minister for women about a women's issue. She wanted more provision for childcare. Ms Hewitt nodded encouragingly, as if to a somewhat backward child who doesn't know which side is which on the sticky-backed plastic.

'The Women and Equality Unit has raised this issue with the chairs of the Regional Development Agencies,' she trilled.

We were off and running. Talking shops were everywhere, liaising closely over key issues on an ongoing basis. We heard of the 'Social Enterprise Unit and Early Child Care Partnership', the 'gender Pay Audit' set up in the Welsh Assembly, plus 'co-ordinating best practice' and 'comprehensive guidance for carrying out reviews'.

Nobody actually said anything like, 'There should be more places where children can be cared for while their parents work' – where would be the jargon in that?

Sandra Gidley for the Lib Dems said that the Equal Opportunity Task Force had called for a legal liability to audit and to highlight gender discrepancies. Ms Hewitt replied by praising Fair Play Champions, whoever they may be.

Throughout this torrent of talk, this Sargasso Sea of quangos, committees, task forces, helplines, tribunals, partnership groups and regional boards, the Tories sat silent, terrified of giving even the slightest hint that they might be unreformed male chauvinist porkers.

But as the end of the ten-minute session loomed, when Ms Hewitt told us that, in her own department, she had set up a 'partnership group between management and workforce' to examine gender discrepancies, and went on to say, 'I look forward to the day when we have the first parent job-sharing ministers,' they could stand it no longer, and a deep communal groan rose from the opposition benches.

Had they finally cracked? Would one of the last few remaining knights of the shires demand that women MPs be paid less, on the grounds that they spend much of their time looking after their children?

No, the ten minutes were up. But there are plans to extend the session. Good.

18.01.02

They say that the quickest remedy for feeling affectionate about the House of Lords is to go there and hear a debate. But I always enjoy my visits. And their lordships still have a lot of influence. Everything that matters has to go through the Upper House: terrorism, justice, education, health. Its continuing role is vital and its membership is of the first importance. So it was vital to hear what they had to say about the glue on Christmas card envelopes.

As I arrived, Lord Tordoff was on his feet. A Lib Dem, Geoff Tordoff is chairman of the greeting card standards committee, or some such. He was replying to Lord St John of Fawsley, a majestic figure from our imperial past, who should himself appear on a greetings card in scarlet robes with a robin on his mitre.

Norman St John Stevas, for it was he, wanted to know about last year's arrangements for the Lords' Christmas card. Lord Tordoff said that they had been just fine and dandy.

Wrong answer. Norm rose in his full pomp. Did the noble lord realize that he was, like Bognor, his last resort? He had been quite unable to obtain satisfaction from anyone about what seems to have been the Christmas card from hell. The card had followed the 'barbarous' custom of standing on its side (I would point out that, if it were not for the House of Lords, few of us would realize just how barbarous side-standing cards are). And this card wasn't even barbarous in the correct fashion. 'It fell down, and having fallen down, it refused to get up!'

(People as superb as our Norman expect to be obeyed. Only a modern, yobbish, doesn't-know-it's-born type of Christmas card would refuse to rise at his command.)

It got worse. 'The envelopes were too small. When I put the card in them, they burst. And the glue had long ago lost any adhesive quality. I had to send out my secretary' – a word that he carefully pronounced 'se-CRETE-ary' – 'to buy a glue stick, at her own expense!' Peers shuddered at this revelation, not least that Norman's poor se-CRETE-aries have to buy their own office supplies. But they had not yet drained the cup of horrors.

'While the exterior had a beautiful picture of Westminster Abbey, the interior said that it was Westminster Cathedral, which must be the greatest anachronism of the millennium!'

Many of us had thought that this epithet applied to Lord St John himself. Astonishingly, Lord Tordoff seemed less than appalled at all these monstrosities. He referred to George V's views on the last resort ('bugger Bognor') – perhaps a mistake, given their lordships' close interest in buggery. He said that he himself had had no problem licking the envelopes. 'My spit must be more adhesive than the noble lord's,' he mused.

That, we reflected, must be why Norman pronounced the name of his assistant in such a curious way. She was not a shorthand typist at all, but a supplier of secretions, since his own are not up to the job.

Lady Hilton, who is in charge of the arts committee, apologized for the labelling mistake. Peers rallied round her. Lord Tordoff spoke of her 'infinite trouble'; Lady Trumpington paid tribute to her 'extremely hard work and leadership'. You'd think she was Shackleton, leading her men to safety across the frozen wastes, not someone who'd chosen a Christmas card.

Lady Walmsley wanted a card devoted to the Parliamentary Choir. Surprisingly loud cries of 'No! No!' greeted this idea. Lord Tordoff looked pained. He had seen all those calendars 'produced by Women's Institutes, and so on'. He clearly wanted the Parliamentary Choir on a card, but only if its members were naked.

Next to speak was Lady Gardner of Parkes, who as Trixie Gardner the dentist came over from Australia to earn money from the NHS, or 'bash the Nash' as they say, and stayed here to play a crucial role in legislating for modern greetings card technology.

I can't remember what she said, as I was too busy pondering how she might look in a nude calendar, and what a terrible effect this might have on Lord St John's production of saliva. But at least she could advise him to rinse and spit.

And they want to reform the House of Lords. Why?

23.01.02

I love questions to the new agriculture ministry, or DEFRA, as it's known. It sends me off into morose daydreams. For a department that's supposed to celebrate nature's bounty, it's surprisingly full of gloomy news. In the midst of life, we are in DEFRA. It also handles fisheries. Ann Winterton, who is a Tory spokesperson, was worried yesterday about stocks of white fish in the North Sea. She asked, 'Does the proposed cod and hake recovery programme override the current West Waters Effort Limitation Scheme as set out in EU paper 650/9?'

Oh, the romance of the sea! The salt spray smacking against our cheeks! Names such as Patrick O'Brien, C. S. Forester and Ernest Hemingway sprang to my mind and crowded into my thoughts.

'He is there,' said the old man, and he scraped a squid off his leg as he said it. 'Yes, he is there.'

'Where is he, old man?'

'Out there,' he said, and he pointed out to the sea with his leg of good Galician oak.

'But where out there is he, old man?'

'In the water, of course. He's a fish. Where else would he be, you idiot son of a Mexican whoremonger?'

'But if I find him, old man, and I hook him, and if I land him and I bring him back to port, I may have contravened the West Waters Effort Limitation Scheme as outlined in EU directive 650/9.'

'Well, tough cheddar.'

I snapped out of my reverie. Alun Michael was talking about the regeneration of rural areas following the end of the foot-and-mouth outbreak. He was praising the new slogan that his department has come up with to get people out into the fields: 'Your countryside! You're welcome.' He seemed pleased with it.

I thought it sounded rather ambiguous. 'You're welcome' can be a sarky thing to say. It's like the new tourism slogan they have invented for the whole country: 'UK, OK.' That could mean anything. For example there's an American licence plate that reads: 'Oklahoma is OK.' But as well as meaning 'terrific', 'OK' can also mean, 'Not bad, I suppose.'

Why don't they go for a more practical slogan: 'Visit the countryside. But don't track sheep doings into the house!'

01.02.02

New Labour is a daisy chain of hatred. Start by plucking one flower at random. Jack Straw hates David Blunkett, who he thinks is trashing everything he, Straw, did at the Home Office. Blunkett is disliked and mistrusted by Gordon Brown, because Number 10 has been trying to build up the Home Secretary as Blair's replacement, as and when Blair chooses to go.

Gordon Brown and Robin Cook hate each other for some obscure, distant reason, already lost in the Caledonian mists.

Cook also hates Peter Mandelson, but then so does everyone else.

You may wonder where the Chancellor and the Prime Minister come into this. They deeply resent and mistrust each other, but like conjoined twins (they share a heart of stone), who know that one can survive only at the expense of the other's life. In this case, of course, there are no parents around to take the terrible decision, so it's going to be nasty. It already is.

Mr Blunkett, who yesterday introduced a White Paper on immigration, asylum and nationality, must have been delighted to be cheered and applauded by so many MPs. His speech was a huge success. Admittedly, his fans were nearly all Tory MPs, but when you live in a snake-pit sometimes you have to make friends with the mongoose, an old Parsee proverb that I have just invented.

The Home Secretary came to the Despatch Box without his dog Lucy, but with a vast yellow braille printout of his statement. You could tell he was sincere; he felt every word. There must be laws, he said, which would mean that new immigrants understood English and had a basic knowledge of our society.

'Hear, hear,' the Tories yelled.

'We will modernize the oath of allegiance, to make clear the fundamental rights and duties of citizenship,' he went on.

'That's very good!' a Tory shouted.

'Secure removal centres will enable us to protect the integrity of the system,' Mr Blunkett continued.

'Excellent!'

'Yah, yah.'

'That's bloody good, well done!' The opposition was loving every moment. Labour MPs were eerily quiet.

The gist of Mr Blunkett's talk was that he had inherited a

terrible mess and was finally doing something about it. Normally you would expect him to have blamed eighteen years of Tory misrule for this situation, but not yesterday. It was left hanging in the air, but we were clearly meant to allow the word 'Straw' to crawl into our consciousness.

Oliver Letwin, the Tory spokesman, seems to agree with Mr Blunkett on almost everything, though he may think that the Home Secretary is even more perfect than the Home Secretary does himself. He has only tiny, tiny little criticisms. He reminds me slightly of those old-fashioned motoring correspondents who would praise a new car wildly, then in a desperate attempt to find something bad to say would add: 'If there is one thing wrong with this magnificent British roadster, the ashtray is slightly too small.'

Mr Letwin congratulated the Home Secretary on tackling the causes of the shambles that he gallantly admitted he has inherited from his predecessor.

Mr Blunkett, who had admitted no such thing but merely implied it, feebly tried to blame the Tories. But you could tell his heart wasn't in it.

'You will have the backing of the whole House in bringing order to your predecessor's chaos!' Mr Letwin merrily continued.

Dennis Skinner looked ill. He called Mr Letwin 'the Home Secretary's puppet', which provided us with a new daisy chain: Straw v. Blunkett v. Skinner v. Letwin. These are cross-party floral tributes, which garland the whole House.

08.02.02

Stephen Byers, the transport minister, seemed to lead a charmed life. Everything he touched turned to disaster. Yet he walked away unscratched from every one of these catastrophes.

Stephen Byers arrived in the Commons yesterday with all the carefree sangfroid of a man who has just heard that his plea for clemency has been rejected, and that the prison canteen has run out of everything for his last meal except liver. He left to the loud cheers of his colleagues, walking past half the Cabinet, who reached out to slap him, pat him, stroke him and generally praise his miraculous return from the political dead.

The reason was, as it always is, the amazing, transcendental uselessness of the Tory opposition. Some suspect this is deliberate. The last thing the opposition wants is for Byers to go. They might get someone competent in his place.

There is another more depressing explanation. They really are this bad. They, or at least their spokeswoman, Theresa May, even let him get away with admitting that he had stretched the truth till it snapped when he spoke on the Dimbleby programme last weekend. 'That is obviously something I regret, and I welcome this opportunity to clarify matters,' he said.

It's a useful line. 'When I said I had no further territorial demands in Europe, I may have inadvertently given the impression that I would not invade Poland. I welcome this opportunity to clarify matters.'

'Father, I welcome this opportunity to clarify my position. I did chop down that tree.'

It's Labour's new message: 'Trust us! We admit we're liars!'

The Tories began by treating everything he said as a huge joke. When he talked about the *Mirror*, they hissed comically. When he blamed civil servants for his problems, they roared with laughter. When he said that the impartiality of the civil service was one of our greatest assets, they chanted, 'Was, was!' and chortled merrily.

Then Ms May stood up. She wasn't awful, just nowhere near good enough. Her reply had clearly been written long before she heard the statement, so she didn't even pick up on Byers's admission that he had been producing porky-pies as fast as the Saxby factory.

Clichés dribbled down like ketchup from a plastic bottle. 'A day of humiliation…a despised secretary of state…' Mr Byers for the first time began to smile.

Two backbenchers, Richard Shepherd and Brian Mawhinney, did land punches. Tam Dalyell broke Labour ranks by quoting the department's permanent secretary, Richard Mottram, who had famously remarked: 'We're all fucked, I'm fucked, it's the biggest cock-up ever and we're all completely fucked.' Except that Tam was too fastidious to use such language. Instead he asked what had caused Sir Richard to 'say that the department would be – well, I'll use the word "stymied".' As in, 'I suppose a quick stymie is out of the question?'

In the end Mr Byers walked free. He is not yet terminally stymied.

27.02.02

It turned out that Labour MPs had been encouraged to offer Mr Byers their enthusiastic support partly because they had been promised some action on fox-hunting, against which they had always voted by huge majorities while the government appeared unwilling to do anything to turn a ban into law.

Once again the Tories failed to dent the armour-plated

complacency of Tony Blair and the government. It was like using toy swords to deflect an SAS squad – brave but pointless.

We had a curious moment at the start of question time. A Labour member, Tony McWalter, began by seeming to make the usual obsequious 'enquiry'. If they ever invent fat-free lard, it will resemble a New Labour MP.

The Prime Minister, said Mr McWalter sombrely, had been subjected to 'unflattering and even malevolent descriptions of his motivation'. So far, so greasy.

But he went on. Would the Prime Minister give 'a brief characterization of the political philosophy that he espouses and which underlies his policies'?

The place collapsed in mirth. Tony Blair with a philosophy? A political philosophy? And a philosophy that underlay anything at all? You might as well ask Ludwig Wittgenstein whether he'd voted for Gareth or Will on *Pop Idol*. Or enquire of Vinnie Jones whether dualism was an apt response to pre-Cartesian thought. Philosophy is not what Tony Blair is about.

But it is what Mr McWalter is about. A former university lecturer, he is an expert on the work of Immanuel Kant. Possibly he hoped that Mr Blair would say something on these lines: 'Yes, I always keep a copy of *Critique of Pure Reason* on my bedside table. It helps me to work out what John Prescott is saying.'

But he didn't. Instead he looked amazed. Baffled. Gobsmacked. He flannelled while MPs continued to laugh and hoot. In the end he stumbled into saying: 'I think the best example we can give is the rebuilding of the NHS, for example the appointment of Sir Magdi Yacoub as…'

Getting brilliant foreign surgeons to do your work may be a good idea, but it hardly amounts to a philosophy. Never mind. I expect that even now, kindly whips are tending to Mr

McWalter in a soundproof cell and introducing him to the philosophy of Vlad the Impaler.

28.02.02

Two masters of our mother tongue appeared in front of select committees yesterday. I popped along to pick up some tips. First up was Sir Richard Mottram, permanent secretary at transport, and the man who famously said at one stage in the Byers debacle, 'We're fucked, I'm fucked, it's the biggest cock-up ever and we're all completely fucked.'

This makes him certain winner of the Plain English campaign award for 2002, and we had hoped for more of the same yesterday. However, Sir Richard was in a more relaxed frame of mind. This was probably because he was to be grilled about the failure of the Teeside Development Corporation, an event that occurred before he joined the department. Thus he was technically responsible, but not to blame. This is precisely the opposite position from his boss, Stephen Byers.

Anyhow, his geniality made it unlikely that he would repeat his celebrated remark, so I cut along the corridor to hear another maestro, John Prescott. He was not in a good mood. Seeing my colleagues, he said, 'More crappy reports on Parliament today,' and of course he was right. He gabbled through his opening statement, scowled at the committee and dangled his arm over the next chair, like the baddest boy in school staying cool while being told off for smoking.

Then he started talking. Heavens, he was fast. Words tumbled over each other, one after the other, in no evident order, sometimes unconnected to the words that went immediately before.

A Prescott answer resembles a cattle stampede. There are hundreds of words penned up in his brain. Then one sees a break in the fence and runs for it. The others rush through in, terrified of being left behind. Soon the words are scattered over the prairie and no one can round them up.

The poor stenographer tried. She hunched over her shorthand machine, fixed and determined not to lose a single word. Now and again a face muscle would twitch. Paper poured out of the back of the machine like tickertape in an old Hollywood movie. I swear I smelled smoke.

On he rushed. 'Prime Minister has shown importance of the sustaining conference, Rio 10, I think Kyoto rather dominated Rio 10 and we tried to put our views and the importance of the sustainable conference…'

I roped a phrase and dragged it back. 'The sustainable conference'! That's where Mr Prescott spends his time – all at this one, single, mobile yet permanent, sustainable conference. 'About which we discussed from Doha to Monterey and on to Johannesburg, and this is a global framework, we need to bring it back together in a complete frame as indeed it was in Rio…'

The stenographer's fingers whirled across her machine. It was like watching Alfred Brendel forced by Nazis to play 'The Flight of the Bumblebee' on an electronic keyboard. 'And I met the Nigerian leader, er, the Nigerian leader, and he said that when he pulls the levers, nothing happens, so we need a better form of governess, a governess is something we ought to be talking about…'

What? Mary Poppins? Or did he mean governance? Who can say?

'My position is that I want to make our position clear…the example in Germany is just one example, for example.'

The stenographer left. She was not replaced. No doubt she had gone to lie down in a darkened room while her line manager refused to send anyone else. 'This is madness. I'm losing all my best people. You'll have to call him off...'

05.03.02

Hunting came back to the Commons yesterday. MPs spoke with anger, scorn and passion. Especially passion. Ann Winterton, the Tory spokeswoman, started a Mills and Boon novel for us. Hunting had helped her to become an MP, she said, since 'it was through my membership of the South Staffordshire Pony Club that I first met my hon. friend...'

Heavens, she was galloping back down memory lane to that blissful time when she first set eyes on Nicholas Winterton, now her husband and a fellow Tory MP.

MPs craned forward, eagerly listening. Would she describe his steaming fetlocks as his hot breath scorched her cheek? ('Do you like riding?' he murmured, his blue eyes boring into her like a mechanical dibber. 'I love to put one foot in the stirrup and then swing the other across my horse. Do you like getting your leg over?')

But our romantic reverie was interrupted by the Deputy Speaker, who pointed out that this was only the brief debate on the business motion, not the motion itself, and so Nick Winterton whinnying and pawing the ground was out of order in every sense.

When Ann Winterton popped up later, she had forgotten all that and merely pointed out that she had been, at seventeen, the youngest ever joint master of foxhounds.

At seventeen! I was a Teenage MFH! It wasn't surprising though. With her scarlet jacket, and a voice that could summon an errant hound from over a mile of moorland, she cast terror into the other side.

Poor Lorna Fitzsimons, for instance, tried to intervene. Farmers in her constituency were concerned about education, housing and health. Tories cheered wildly. This was their point! The government was using hunting to make people forget its innumerable failings. 'You have shot your fox!' said Mrs Winterton, and she should know.

Gerald Kaufman promised huge trouble if the government didn't bring in a full anti-hunting bill, pronto. 'The whole point,' he said, in that quiet yet sinister fashion that makes Hannibal Lecter sound like Graham Norton, 'about being as sickeningly loyal as I am, is that when you do rebel, you rebel with a vengeance!' He then slipped out of the Chamber, presumably for a nice piece of liver washed down with Chianti.

William Hague was sarcastic. He said shooting foxes was pointless, and described how a farmer had failed to kill one with four rounds. 'They don't line up to be shot by firing squad,' he said. 'We don't have laser-guided shotguns!'

Gerald Kaufman had returned. He wiped a morsel of fava bean from his mouth and said: 'That farmer doing the shooting must have drunk fourteen pints…'

Then Ann Widdecombe. Welcome back! She was magnificent, her voice piping and peaking so piercingly that it could make the millennium bridge wobble once more. Mr Hague – 'my Rt. Hon. friend, my Rt. Hon. and wonderful friend, my Rt. Hon. and *fantastic* friend' – had said that the anti-hunt people were toffs.

'Toffs? Anti-toffs? I was one of the people who voted to keep hereditary peers!' she reprised. As for the argument that banning fox-hunting would destroy jobs, 'You might as well claim that if you abolish crime the police will be out of work, abolish ill-health and doctors will be out of work!'

Yes, foxes were hunters themselves. But, she asked, wobbling with fury, 'Do MPs take their standards from the animal kingdom?' Well, yes, they do, but that's not the point. She sat down as Labour cheers drowned out the ringing she had created in our ears.

19.03.02

Gordon Brown introduced his sixth Budget in April 2002, late because of the tragic death of his baby daughter. Because it increased National Insurance contributions by a penny in the pound on all income in order to pay for an improved NHS ('Robbing the rich to help the poorly,' as the FT *put it), it was described as a reassertion of Old Labour values and a challenge to the Prime Minister himself.*

To sum up its contents: this was a Budget for a typical bingo-playing small businessman with several children, who has just inherited £249,999 and decides to celebrate by going out in his low-emission van for a few pints at a pub where they brew their own ale. On the way back, pissed, he drives into a tree and is whisked to hospital where, after a ten-minute wait, his hip is replaced. There's no pressure on beds, so he stays as long as he needs, but it doesn't matter, because the Chancellor has made VAT optional, or at least told businessmen to think of a number and pay that.

So his night out will have cost him nothing. Or a lot less than before. For the rest of us, with 1p in effect going on income tax, it will be rather a crock, not least because Mr Brown invariably leaves the bad news out of his budget speeches. As Iain Duncan Smith said, 'He has turned small print into fine art.'

All Brown budgets are much the same. There is the tight, taut, anal-retentive language of the boy who probably had his piggy bank bolted to the floor of his bedroom. He used 'stable' or 'stability' thirteen times, and we had a welcome return of 'Prudence', who was dropped after he got engaged, but who came back yesterday with five heart-tugging mentions.

In between these there were many uses of 'sustained', 'steady', 'strong', 'cautious' and 'disciplined'. Indeed, he used 'disciplined' so much that the speech began to sound as if it ought to have been blu-tacked up in a West End phone booth. Take this: 'In the interests of fiscal discipline, I will maintain our cautious rules and lock in the tight fiscal stance…hotel visits arranged discreetly.'

I made up the last four words, but you get it. Moments later he was again promising 'a small tightening of the fiscal stance'.

'I don't know, Doris, I have this one client, Scottish gentleman he is, wants me to get into me Madame Bondage kit and tighten his fiscal stance, and all the time I'm thinking, "Blimey, I could murder a cup of tea."'

The important part of the speech is the bit rarely mentioned in the papers next day: the opening twenty minutes or so in which the Chancellor describes the miracles he has wrought for our economy.

This is a tour round what I think of as Gordonland, a happy, smiling, prosperous country in which unemployment is disappearing, debt is dwindling, growth continues at a frantic rate, and all is sunshine compared to the grovelling misery of those condemned to live in the rest of Europe, the USA, and worst of all Japan, where, cast far from Gordonland, impoverished workers have to eat the Toshiba boxes they are too poor to live in.

This is all meant to contrast, I assume, with Blairland, the poor, grimy, crime-ridden country in which we are actually obliged to live.

Gordonland by contrast is isolated and oblivious to all this. It resembles that ship made up of apartments, which cruises the world with its cargo of rich people, now and again reaching port, occasionally glimpsing real life through binoculars from the bridge, seeing but never dwelling among the wretched folk who cannot afford to live aboard.

One day, he is saying, your nightmare will be over, I will be Prime Minister, and we will all live cocooned from any financial problems, in the great floating Elysium that is Gordonland.

18.04.02

'We are consulting on the sheep envelope in remote rural areas,' said Elliot Morley, who's minister for stuff in the ministry of rural stuff, or whatever it is called this week.

The sheep envelope? What in heaven's name is that? Is it a gigantic Jiffy bag? Does the ministry send them out to farmers with instructions? 'If you think your sheep might have foot-and-mouth, just pop them in this pre-paid envelope and mail it to us, if you can find a postbox big enough.'

Whenever I go to see questions on rural affairs they have yet more of this jargon. And it's all different. They do their turn once a month, and every four weeks they come up with language that nobody has ever heard before, anywhere.

It must be like a script conference on a comedy show. 'I know, why don't we have a question on "the economic appraisal of the effect on UK agriculture of modulation proposals"?'

'Yeah, love it, love it! And then we could have Tory backbencher Michael Jack ask, "Who are the winners and who are the losers in the modulation stakes?" Stakes, steaks, geddit"?'

'Yeah, then we can get someone to tell the minister "not to go the whole hog down this route". We can give it to Richard Bacon MP if he's available!'

Then you have Elliot 'Bring Me Sunshine' Morley back to talk about the problems of 'rural-proofing'. This seems to have something to do with 'grazing regimes'. Nobody knows what these are. Perhaps they are military juntas whose members eat a lot of snacks.

'Generalissimo! The traitor Ainsworth has been discovered in the act of stuffing a dead goat into a sheep envelope. Permission to have him tortured!'

'Mmmf, shorry, my mowfs full a' the mumment...'

I nodded off briefly, then woke to hear my friend Anne McIntosh ask a question about the European Wee directive. Is this yet more jargon, or are the Tories claiming that the EU is now instructing us how to micturate?

No, apparently she meant the directive on Waste Electronic Equipment. This now has to be disposed of at huge expense. Already people are bringing the squalor of our great cities to the countryside, by dumping old microwaves and stereos on farmland, so that farmers have to pay to have them taken away.

And fridges! Parliament is now obsessed with fridges, which have to have ozone-depleting chemicals stripped out of them before they can be sold on to Third World countries. This means they will have to be dumped, also flouting the WEE directive.

Back in January Michael Meacher, the environment minister, blamed the EU for the fact that we in Britain had done nothing to prepare for these new rules. It now turns out that it was all the fault of his department.

His boss, Margaret Beckett, explained why he had, hmmm, misled the House, or as she put it, 'He did withdraw from the more, er, um, *high-flown* language he had used.'

Or as we said when we were young, 'Liar, liar, pants on fire!'

19.04.02

The Queen, shimmering in electric blue, came to Westminster all to address both Houses of Parliament. It was the first important event of her jubilee celebrations, though you might think they had been going on for several years already. Don't worry, there's lots more to come!

She is one of the few reigning monarchs to have left the hall without receiving a death sentence. The old place, 905 years old and still standing, looked superb. A few weeks ago the Queen Mum lay in state there while queues several hours' long formed to get a look at the box.

The Tory MPs also looked superb. They had been encouraged to wear morning dress in order to show up the slovenly slobs and slatterns of the Labour Party. Thousands of furry little spongebags must have been slaughtered to make their trousers alone. Some of the women wore hats the size of cartwheels.

It was an astute political move. In tomorrow's local elections there will be many voters who will say, 'Well, the economy is doing well, and they're putting more money into the NHS. On the other hand, those Tories do know how to dress properly.'

It was the Queen's fifth appearance at a similar event. I spotted Shaun Woodward. He comes to Parliament rather less often. There should have been a fanfare of trumpets just to welcome him back. And Keith Vaz, the Great Vaz of Vaz, was also making an equally rare appearance. Truly we were privileged!

The Speaker arrived on the dot with his eight followers. It was a moving moment. How many people raised in the Gorbals have their own personal procession, or 'posse' as the rock stars call it?

Then the Lord Chancellor, Derry Irvine, with his procession, including his trainbearer, Mrs Nora Dobinson. Say what you like, but New Labour does make the trainbearers run on time.

Next came the Honourable Corps of Gentlemen, wearing enough egret feathers to stuff a sofa. And, even more magnificent, the Yeomen of the Guard. They marched up towards Lord Irvine, a riot of scarlet and gold. You could almost see him thinking, 'Hmmm, Beefeaters. Soon be time for a G&T.'

The band of the Grenadier Guards at last stopped playing elderly, mimsy, wispy British tunes, elevator music written presciently before we even had elevators, and switched to Handel. Our blood began to course at last.

The state trumpeters, all in embroidered primrose tabards, filed in along a balcony and stood under the great stained-glass window. For them it works as camouflage. The scene was perfect: rich, grandiose, deep-dyed, sodden with history, ceremony and flummery. It only needed the ghost of Charles I, with his neck bared, to make it look complete.

The moment had come. She was a minute late, then two, then three. Surely Byers wasn't in charge?

She finally appeared and processed down the aisle, looking frightfully happy, towards the dais at the end, where there were two big gilded armchairs, sort of Ikea thrones.

Then we hear from two contrasting Scots. The Lord Chancellor, his voice plummy, orotund and essentially English, heaped praises on her. She hadn't actually conquered Everest, won the Derby or run the first four-minute mile, though you sensed from his speech that it was thanks to her that other people had.

Next another, less privileged Scot, Michael Martin, talking about the diversity of races, cultures and faiths that make this country a 'vibrant' place to live, sharing power with our European neighbours – all straight out of a New Labour manifesto.

Then he solemnly handed his speech over to her – no, not so that she could work out what he'd said! He had spoken slowly and carefully. We understood almost every word. At this moment some wretch's mobile phone rang out.

Finally we heard Her Majesty herself, her speech also tinged with Blairspeak: 'Change has become a constant; managing it has become an expanding discipline' – the kind of stuff you might find on tonytalk.com.

And at the end, an echo of Mrs Thatcher, with her promise to carry on, and on, and on. Prince Charles was not present. But did we hear a deep, racking groan, carried on the wind from Highgrove?

01.05.02

I went to the Guildhall Art Gallery in the City of London to watch Lady Thatcher unveil a statue of: Lady Thatcher. Iron Lady meets Woman of Marble! The effigy is made of stone, it's around seven feet high, and it's so white and pristine you want to spray it with graffiti. It could not be more perfect for the time or the place.

The sculptor is Neil Simmonds. Michelangelo said that he

didn't create statues; all he did was chip away the surplus stone to discover the image within. Imagine cutting away all those tons of rock and finding…Margaret Thatcher! What a terrifying surprise!

(It turns out that the sculptor's studio, in Dartford, Kent, is next door to a depot which provides clothes for Bosnian refugees. I'm told she kept breaking off from her sittings to give them lectures on the British way of life.)

The Guildhall was full of those chaps wearing neck ruffs that resemble antimacassars in a very posh boarding house. The statue itself was covered in a black velvet shroud, so that she looked rather like an Afghan woman just before the fall of the Taliban. She and Denis arrived. She was wearing a sort of purple housecoat, as if about to do the vacuuming with a gold-plated Dyson. She had her famous swept-back hair, as if it had just been tested in a wind-tunnel.

Tony Banks, the famously plebby Labour MP who is chairman of the Commons art committee, introduced the statue to us. 'She is almost as famous, dare I say it, for her handbag, which you will see when it is unveiled.' There were dark mutterings of 'but it's on the wrong arm'. Would she be obliged to hit her stone handbag with her real one?

Mr Banks explained how there were rules that forbid the statue from appearing in the Commons lobby just yet, since she is insufficiently dead. However, he said, these might be changed before too long. She might even make it, while still alive, by 2004. At present there is nowhere to put the statue. But, as he didn't quite say, someday her plinth would come.

The cost of the statue had been met by an anonymous donor. It was between £40,000 and £50,000. 'I don't know who he is, and I think it's better that I do not know,' Mr Banks said. At this point Norman Tebbit could be heard going round the room predicting that it would turn out to be Richard

Desmond, Labour donor and publisher of top-shelf magazines such as *Monetarist Babes* and *Intransigent Chicks*. 'You are as controversial in marble,' Mr Banks said, 'as you are in real life.'

Controversial in marble! She looked thrilled. She would like to be controversial in marble, in bronze, in granite, in stainless steel, in platinum or pink blancmange. She was loving every moment. Adulation, and more of it! That's what makes her come outdoors, even when the moon isn't full!

And Mr Banks, desperate to find things to say that would meet the occasion without enraging what's left of the Labour Party, hadn't finished. 'When policies are forgotten, if I may say so, the fact that you were the first woman Prime Minister will not be forgotten.'

She looked puzzled. Forgotten? How could she be forgotten? Was he mad? Were we all mad?

Finally she got to whisk the shroud away. 'It's marvellous,' she said, 'but it's a little larger than I expected. Though as the first woman Prime Minister, I am a little larger than life!'

(Murmurs of approval came at this piece of literal self-aggrandizement.)

'I was fortunate to be there rather longer than some of my colleagues, and so that is the way to portray me!'

(I would have expected some quiet retching at this stage, but heard yet louder grunts of approval from the chaps in the antimacassars.)

'I am very grateful to the sculptor for portraying me in a way that pleases me very much. Do remember! We had staunch Conservative principles!'

I looked up at the oeuvre. It has no eye sockets. I don't quite know why, but perhaps I could guess.

21.05.02

Index